PSYCHOTHERAPY WITH FAMILIES

An analytic approach

Sally Box,
Beta Copley, Jeanne Magagna and
Errica Moustaki

ROUTLEDGE & KEGAN PAUL
London, Boston and Henley

First published in 1981
by Routledge & Kegan Paul Ltd
39 Store Street, London WC1E 7DD,
9 Park Street, Boston, Mass. 02108, USA and
Broadway House, Newtown Road,
Henley-on-Thames, Oxon RG9 1EN
Printed in Great Britain by
St. Edmundsbury Press
Bury St Edmunds, Suffolk

Library of Congress Cataloging in Publication Data

Psychotherapy with families.

1. Family psychotherapy.   2. Psychoanalysis.
I. Box, Sally.
RC488.5.P79   616.89'156   81-7320

ISBN 0-7100-0854-6

To our patients without whom this book could not have been written

CONTENTS

Acknowledgments ix

Contributors x

Introduction: Space for thinking in families
Sally Box 1

1 The family and its dynamics
 Margot Waddell 9

2 An outline of the history and current status of
 family therapy
 Susan Zawada 25

3 Introducing families to family work
 Beta Copley 35

4 Re-enactment as an unwitting professional
 response to family dynamics
 Ronald Britton 48

5 Working with the dynamics of the session
 Sally Box 59

6 Making space for parents
 Anna Halton and Jeanne Magagna 75

7 Psychic pain and psychic damage
 Gianna Henry 93

8 The micro-environment
 Arthur Hyatt Williams 105

9 The aftermath of murder
 Roger Kennedy and Jeanne Magagna 120

10   Use of an ending to work with a family's difficulty
     about differentiation   136
     Nonie Insall

11   Change in families: some concluding thoughts   153
     Sally Box

     Glossary: A discussion and application of terms   160
     Errica Moustaki

     Bibliography   173

     Index   177

ACKNOWLEDGMENTS

We would like to thank our colleagues, in the Workshop and elsewhere, who have helped with the development of this approach
and given us their encouragement and support to write the chapters for the book. We would like to thank especially our secretary,
Mrs Anita Cotten, for all the interest, patience and unstinting
work she has put into the book. In relation to the glossary,
Errica Moustaki would like to acknowledge the contributions, and
help of Gianna Henry, Jonathan Smilansky, John Steiner and, in
particular, Sally Box, Beta Copley and Jeanne Magagna.

We also want to acknowledge all those of our friends and families
who may have had to put up with various sorts of discomfort arising from our preoccupation with this book.

For reasons of confidentiality, it has of course been necessary
to disguise the circumstances of the families discussed so that they
will be generally unrecognizable, to all except possibly themselves.

It may be that even so some families think they recognize themselves and if so we hope they do not mind.

CONTRIBUTORS

Sally J Box is Principal Social Worker in the Adolescent Department, Tavistock Clinic. She practises and teaches psychotherapy and its application in relation to individuals, families and other institutions. She has worked in residential and therapeutic community settings in England and the USA; and became engaged in family therapy during the 1960s in California.

Since joining the Tavistock Clinic in 1969 she has integrated this interest with her developing psychoanalytic understanding of individual and group dynamics; and as Chairman of the Young People and Their Families Workshop sought to foster a psychoanalytic approach to work with families.

Ronald S Britton works as a consultant psychiatrist in the Department for Children & Parents, Tavistock Clinic, and as a psychoanalyst in private practice. He has also acted as consultant to a number of community institutions and social service departments in the last decade; in particular, in the development of 'Young Family Centres' as a form of 'Day Care' for vulnerable families with young children as an alternative to Day Nurseries. A particular interest of his at the Tavistock Clinic has been developing an approach to families who are unable, or unlikely, to make use of Clinic treatment, but who remain a source of anxiety to social agencies involved with them.

Beta Copley trained as a Child Psychotherapist and engaged in the practice and teaching of individual psychoanalytical psychotherapy with children, adolescents and adults. She is interested in the application of learning derived from psychoanalysis to a wider field such as Youth Counselling, Family & Group Relations Work. Currently Child Psychotherapy Tutor, Chairman of the Adolescent Department Family Workshop at the Tavistock Clinic and tutor to the one-year course on a Psychodynamic Approach to Child and Adolescent Psychotherapy, Centre for Postgraduate Psychiatry, Uffculme and Charles Burns Clinic, Birmingham.

Anna Halton originally trained as a nurse at St George's Hospital, London, worked as a sister at the Cassel Hospital, then, via a university course in Social Administration, moved into social work.

x

Worked as a social worker in a child guidance clinic in Liverpool and in London for Family Service Unit in Camden. Trained as a psychotherapist at the Tavistock Clinic, where she is employed as a senior social worker in the Adolescent Department.

Gianna Henry is a Principal Psychotherapist in the Adolescent Department of the Tavistock Clinic where she is engaged in individual and family therapy and is Chairman of the Individual Psychotherapy Workshop. She is co-organizing tutor of the Observation Course (first two years of the four-year Child Psychotherapy Course) and is responsible for the organization of Psychoanalytic Theory Seminars for the above-mentioned four-year course.
    She is organizing tutor of a course at Rome University, accredited by the Tavistock Clinic, identical in content to the Observation Course.

Nonie Insall after leaving university, worked as a child-care officer and later as a generic social worker. Preferring to specialize in work with children and their families, she joined the Child and Adolescent Psychiatry Unit in Guy's Hospital and, after four years there, moved to the Adolescent Department of the Tavistock Clinic in order to further her interest in psychodynamic work.

Roger Kennedy is now at the Department of Child and Adolescent Psychiatry, Guy's Hospital; formerly Child Guidance Training Centre, Tavistock Centre. Child Psychiatrist in the NHS, Trainee Psychoanalyst, Institute of Psychoanalysis. Publications on groups with psychotic patients, language and psychosis; co-author of Fontana Modern Master on Lacan, to be published. He is also a playwright.

Jeanne Magagna is currently working as a psychotherapist with individual children and adults and engaged in family and marital therapy both in private practice and in the Royal Free Hospital. Engaged in teaching courses on observation of 'normal' families from the time the first infant is born and in consultation with child-care establishments. Has worked in America as a Headstart (pre-school nursery) Teacher, a Special Educator in an Adolescent Unit. Subsequently moved to London and worked as School Counsellor and a Social Work Tutor.

Errica Moustaki trained as a clinical psychologist at the Hebrew University in Jerusalem. She worked in an adolescent in-patient unit which stimulated interest in research with families. For the last four years has worked with adolescents and their families in this country, and engaged in research focusing on the way family relationships are expressed in spatial terms, for instance, in the way that a family organizes the home environment. Currently she works as a Senior Psychologist and Psychotherapist in the Adult Department of the Tavistock Clinic.

Margot Waddell trained at the Tavistock Clinic as a child psychotherapist. Working latterly with adolescents and families in particular, she is currently working in individual psychoanalytic psychotherapy, mainly in community settings, with a special interest in
the treatment of women. She is engaged at the Tavistock in teaching
and lecturing on psychoanalytic concepts.

Susan Zawada graduated as a clinical psychologist from Birmingham
University, then worked in the Children's Department of the
Maudsley Hospital for three years which is where she first became
interested in family therapy. For the past four years she has been
Senior Clinical Psychologist in the Adolescent Department, Tavi-
stock Clinic.

Arthur Hyatt Williams was born in Birkenhead, and his childhood
was spent on the Wirral. Intending to be a biologist, he won a
medical scholarship. He studied medicine at Liverpool, and became
a psychiatrist in the Army. Thereafter he worked at the Cassel
Hospital. He was regional psychiatrist for SE Met RHB, Consultant
Psychiatrist at the Tavistock Clinic from 1962 until retirement in 1979.

INTRODUCTION:

Space for thinking in Families

Sally Box

This book is about experiences of work with families and about
some of the ideas that have grown out of these experiences in the
light of a particular background of psychoanalytic theory and
practice.

The emphasis on thinking in the content highlights the importance we attach to the essential relationship between thinking
processes and states of feeling. It stems from the notion that the
available 'space for thinking' in any one family, as in any individual, bears a crucial relationship to patterns developed for coping
with mental pain and ways of responding to life experience; that
it serves both as an indicator of the quality of mental life and also
as the most necessary condition for its development.

It is probably true to say that there is an increasingly wide-
spread interest today in how people learn and how they think. For
instance, what are the conditions for thought, of an independent
and creative kind, in contrast to reactions that are impulsive and
without thought, on the one hand, or determined in a stereotyped
way by unrelieved custom or unquestioned authority, on the other?
More specifically, from the point of view of this book, what prevents
family members from developing their own identity and becoming
independent individuals, able to separate themselves from the
others – both internally and externally – so that they are not
further perpetuating a pattern of life 'in the shadow of the
ancestors' (Scott and Ashworth 1969). These are some of the questions that arise from our work with families in the light of the
psychoanalytic principles on which it draws.

While our focus is clearly not upon directly influencing specific
ways of thinking and behaving, we are interested in providing
opportunities for family members to shift old patterns and unblock
pathways to new ones, so that their capacities for 'learning from
their own experience' may develop and their scope for living be
correspondingly enriched.

The book is the outcome of a clinical workshop whose members
share a tradition and interest in applying these principles to the
understanding of groups and institutions, and who believe in the
crucial relevance of them in application to work with the institution
of the family.

The approach is based on two particular developments, (a) that

of object-relations and psychoanalytic practice derived especially
from the work of Freud, Melanie Klein and others who have
elaborated her ideas, especially W.R. Bion; (b) the application of
this to the understanding of group relations following the work of
Bion and others such as A.K. Rice, P.M. Turquet and Elliott
Jaques. The common feature in these is the significance attached
to the part played by unconscious phantasy in the elaboration and
development of human relationships; all of them emphasize the use
of immediate spontaneous feelings for elucidating these 'inner
worlds of relationships' or 'shared phantasies' as they emerge
within the boundaries of the session.

To a large extent, therefore, the approach represents a number
of shared views and questions about the nature of human functioning, which relate directly to the body of knowledge and the concepts that we draw upon for understanding and interpreting the
behaviour of our patient families.

For instance, the value placed on trying to discover the truth,
in psychological terms, is based on the view that (apart from its
scientific implications) this is actually important for mental growth
and development. 'Falling back on analytic experience for a clue',
Bion writes in 'Transformations', 'I am reminded that healthy
mental growth seems to depend on truth as the living organism
depends on food. If it is lacking or deficient, the personality
deteriorates' (1965, p.38). By this I am not suggesting, of course,
that we are attempting to discover the truth of ultimate reality,
but that there is a psychic reality which can become more known
and that efforts to evade it may be seen as the basis of much
malfunctioning in the family. Hence the importance attached here to
providing a chance for the family members to get in touch with what
their feelings and reactions actually are; and to be able to think
about them. In 'Learning from Experience' Bion discusses the
relationship between the experience of frustration and the capacity
to face reality, and reminds us how Freud recognized thought as
being stimulated initially in response to the experience of frustration - 'An infant capable of tolerating frustration can permit itself
to have a sense of reality, to be dominated by the reality principle.' Continuing, Bion then draws the distinction between
'procedures designed to evade frustration and those designed to
modify it' (1962a, p.29). It is a crucial distinction in helping us
to understand what is happening in the families we see. Our concern about what conflictual or otherwise painful issues are having
to be avoided is related to the realization that it is by their
avoidance rather than their existence that such issues are more
likely to block or sabotage growth and creativity. That is, we are
not in the business of attempting to remove conflict and frustration so much as providing space for their recognition and integration as an inevitable part of life and, within manageable limits,
as possible bases for new thought.

Hence the work we are describing is about making space for
unacknowledged and disowned parts of the family and for the
behaviour that masks them. We suggest it is through active

engagement with these aspects of all the individuals in the family, as they emerge in their relationship to ourselves, that the possibility for their acceptance and integration can occur. Only so, in this view, may the foundations be laid which make for the kind of modification and growth that must spring naturally and from the inside (not just in response to pressure from outside) if they are to spring at all!

The family can be seen as a particular sort of institution with its own culture and specific modes of dealing with life. It is made up of individuals whose behaviour and experience we know to be affected by the system of interlinking relationships of which they are a part. At the same time the individuals also contain deeply embedded characteristics - or internal relationships - which we believe do not lend themselves to change simply through an alteration in the structure of the family system, but require to be understood in action, as it were, and to have their unconscious meaning interpreted. It is these dual aspects of working with the family as a unit which constitute both the difficulties and fascination of the task.

I am aware that many workers, including former analysts, have in their work concentrated exclusively on seeing families. We cannot but be impressed by the devotion and thought that some of them have given to finding ways of meeting the kind of intractable problems that these families present.

All of us who work with families for any length of time are bound to be exercised by the qualities of extreme negativism, acting out and other sorts of intransigence that we meet in many of them. Indeed many families are referred as families because none of the individuals in them is willing or able to use individual therapy and until recently it is doubtful whether any analyst or therapist would hope to succeed in treating them individually even if they wanted it. It does not seem at all surprising, therefore, that people have sought totally new ways of approaching these problems.

The work of Minuchin or Palazzoli, for example, with the families of anorexics is particularly challenging in terms of the means and nature of the changes that are described. It is always difficult to know what each of us actually does when we are with families. There is a notorious gap between what people say they do and what they actually do! Moreover, one often finds oneself closer in style to some who profess a very different approach. For this reason alone, there is no substitute for description of what is said and done in the therapy sessions. We appreciate this principle in other books and have attempted to support it with the inclusion of direct clinical material throughout this one. Clearly evidence is important, however difficult to establish, but one cannot for ever dodge the wider implications involved in different approaches and these seem much more complicated. For instance, while I think we would find ourselves quite in tune with the way the dynamics of a family are described and understood in some of the clinical examples cited by Palazzoli, for instance, and even with some of the interpretive interventions she mentions, most of us part

company with her on 'epistemological' grounds - to use her own
word - and in relation to the 'ploys' and strategies which she
advocates as an integral part of her approach (1978). At the same
time we think there is a valuable heritage of literature and
experience in which analytic principles have been applied to groups
and institutions which has only just begun to be tapped. There is
a long way to go, in terms of the development of appropriate skills
in applying these principles to families before we can be more
clear about their limitations. At the moment we are more conscious
of our own.

Some current preoccupations within the field of psychoanalysis -
in relation to narcissism, narcissistic states and perverse relationships - are especially relevant for understanding and handling
these phenomena and a number of relatively recent developments
seem particularly helpful in bridging the gap between the understanding of individual and group dynamics and between intrapersonal and interpersonal functioning. The concept of transference is a core one both in our work and in the book and has
been central to psychoanalysis since Freud first introduced it in
1900, but ideas about the nature of what is being transferred,
particularly in terms of the significance of phantasy, and of the
effect it has on the receiver are constantly changing and developing. So we have inherited, for instance, elaborate notions of
identification, important modifications on the original idea of
countertransference and developments about notions of projection
culminating in the specific concept of projective identification with
its rich offspring in Bion's model of container-contained (1967,
pp.67-70). The latter, developed as it was, through work with
borderline psychotic patients, is of particular value to us in our
work with families.

In the opening chapter, Margot Waddell discusses these concepts in relation to specific clinical examples. After putting the
family in its social context and touching on some of the issues
involved in the change from couple to family, she concentrates
especially on the implications of the processes fundamental to
family functioning that come under the heading of projective
identification - in terms, first of the way they operate in the
family, then of the way they are lived out in the transference
relationship to the therapist in the sessions.

The importance attributed to the part played by phantasy in
the mental elaboration of events occurring in external reality
clearly influences the significance attached technically to the work
done with the transference as distinct from the actual external
relationship between the family members. In fact this may be one
of the major features that differentiates one type of approach
from another and accounts for some of the contrasting views described by Susan Zawada in her chapter. Here she reviews the
development of family therapy from its beginning to the present.
She describes different approaches and highlights the problem of
evaluating outcome. (Indeed, with families, perhaps a more
accurate picture might be gained over more than one generation -

in terms, for instance, of the kind of mating and parenting
experience the children are able to offer when they become adults.)
The survey reminds us, I think, of our difficulty in getting to
grips with the different values involved in different approaches
and in the different views about human nature and human growth.

One of the issues about family work that we have not attempted
to resolve is that of appropriate criteria for deciding between
individual and family treatment. Unless the work is in a setting
which does not provide for both, there are in practice liable to be
a number of different variables which enter into the decision and
we feel we simply do not know enough to make any definitive
statements about it. There are some indicators which are suggested
in the book and some families who clearly could not accept any
other way of being seen, if only because no one individual owns a
wish for help on their own behalf. In general, I think these
indicators would not differ markedly from those suggested by
Frieda Martin (1975) although her actual way of working and her
idea of an analytic approach differs from the one described here.
Apart from these broad indicators, more specific attention is given
in the book to drawing a distinction between a way of working
during an initial exploratory stage and the way one would work
with families in long-term analytic type treatment.

In her chapter, Beta Copley compares three families in which
she saw some or all of the members for exploration and worked
with them about what kind of psychotherapeutic help they wanted
and could use. She describes their functioning, as it emerges in
the relationship to the setting and herself, and discusses her
thoughts about the criteria it suggests for determining the next
step.

Sometimes, the logical or only realistic next step is for parents
to be worked with on their own - with or without a child in individual treatment. Sometimes one or more children are already in
individual treatment and this may operate as something of a
contraindication for family treatment. But work with the parents
raises particular issues of its own - many of which are familiar to
those who work in traditional Child Guidance Clinics. In the first
part of their paper, Anna Halton and Jeanne Magagna consider
some of the problems of management involved in setting up treatment for a parental couple. They go on to describe, in the second
part, the process of treatment in one case, elaborating on some
of the relevant concepts, such as that of shared phantasy. They
address specifically the issues of co-therapy with this couple and
the use of the therapist's countertransference in relation to each
other for understanding different aspects of the couple in therapy.

The theme of co-therapy is explored further in relation to work
with the whole family in Arthur Hyatt Williams' paper, where he
describes the long-term treatment of a family in which the adolescence of the two children heralded disruption of the tenuous
balance in the family dynamics and was accompanied by violent
outbursts that could be seen to shift from one member to another.
The boundary between the family as 'sanctuary' and as 'prison' is

discussed in relation to the problems for these adolescents to grow up and leave home.

Roger Kennedy and Jeanne Magagna describe the particular dynamics and reactions in a family where a murder had taken place and suggest from their work with this family how the process of getting in touch with the regret and remorse involved can, first, be defended against by characteristics of perverse sexuality, and then can bring with it the attendant dangers of a 'life-risking' psychomatic symptom which symbolizes an identification with the attacked murdered person.'

In many cases referrals come to us with a long history of contacts with other agencies. In his chapter Ronald Britton relates the dynamics of such contacts and the enactment that is often evoked in the workers concerned to the dynamics of the families with whom they are dealing. He discusses the phenomena of the 'repetition compulsion' in these terms, goes on to compare this view of the system to that of family therapists who base their approach on General Systems Theory, and considers some of the implications of the principle of 'dynamic equilibrium' in terms of Freud's concept of the 'constancy principle'.

In my own chapter, I have discussed, in relation to clinical material, some of the technical issues involved in providing a method that is suited to our overall stance of trying to offer people a chance to develop the use of their own experience and to draw upon it as a basis for thinking and choosing new possibilities or reviewing old ones. I have attempted to compare work with two different families in terms of each one's characteristic approach to containing anxiety in the family and to suggest that the differences are reflected in the differential experience for the therapists in their effort to provide containment in the treatment.

In one way and another all these ideas represent a growing interest in what becomes of unbearably painful, conflictual or otherwise unmanageable feelings which arise in an individual and threaten to overwhelm him. Whether the individual is himself able to digest, metabolize and use the feelings as food for thought, or whether he must find some other way of managing is what determines the crucial outcome in every day to day crisis of this sort. Those familiar with the work of Mrs Klein may appropriately be reminded of the distinction between what she has called the paranoid-schizoid position associated with processes of splitting and idealization on the one hand, and that of the depressive position associated with the capacity for concern, to symbolize and to tolerate pain on the other. In a paper entitled 'Development of Schizophrenic Thought' (1956) Bion draws on these earlier analytic concepts to show the link between the individual's difficulty in tolerating frustration, the hatred of reality (internal and external) that is a function of that difficulty, and the consequent detrimental effect on perceptual processes. He shows in turn how the mechanisms of splitting and projective identification described by Mrs Klein, while a necessary part of development, can be used to defend against awareness of painful reality and at the same time to prevent such reality from providing the possible basis for the development of relevant thought.

Gianna Henry's chapter describes how one family began to shift from the paranoid/schizoid to the depressive end of the spectrum in the course of their therapy. She introduces the term 'psychic damage' to discuss the kind of impoverishment and distortions that may be a function of the family members' efforts, individually and collectively, to defend against 'psychic pain'. This and Nonie Insall's chapter both portray how the related difficulties of mourning are worked with in the context of the sessions and the ending of treatment. But in the family described by Mrs Insall the defences are of a more primitive kind. The use of mechanisms of projective identification are more pervasive, and the way that members use each other to express aspects of themselves is reflected in their difficulty in appreciating the significance of the therapists as separate individuals. The process of the treatment described suggests how, from being somewhat chronically attached to each other within the family and to institutions outside it, the family used the limited time available to begin differentiating and working on the implications of being separate.

Finally, all the key concepts are defined in the glossary and Moustaki has added a section on each, describing their development in terms of analytic theory and discussing their relevance in terms of application to our work with families. In view of the importance attached to direct experiences with the family on the basis of the worker's understanding and interpretation of them, we have attempted throughout to provide sufficient clinical material for the reader to think for himself. But it may well seem too much and certainly if read all at once would prove quite indigestible! Probably each chapter represents something of a meal in itself and about all that can be comfortably digested at one sitting.

In sum, while sharing some ideas in common with other family therapists, I think there are a number of features which differentiate this approach from most others found in the literature on family therapy, including other 'object relations' approaches, both in terms of philosophy and technique. That is, like others, we have been interested in understanding the dynamics of the family as a group, but unlike most, our interest is on actively interpreting the family's use of projection in the ways that its members perceive and engage the therapists. In this sense the way the family experiences the therapist and the way the therapists experience the family represents the crucial evidence and material worked on in the session, and the attention throughout to the underlying meaning of behaviour and to the processes of transference and countertransference in the sessions seems to be in contrast to other approaches, especially those which are informed by a more behaviourist model.

These ideas form the background of the approach which constitutes the theme of this book. The rationale for such an approach is a matter for discussion throughout but clearly relates to our particular view of therapeutic processes. The attempt to create a space for the family to relive conflicts as they emerge in the context of the therapeutic setting is related to the value we see in this as a basis for successful internalization. Such internalization is in turn seen as the key to the modification of internal structures or internal object relationships and it is this which constitutes the process of change with which we are concerned.

1 THE FAMILY AND ITS DYNAMICS

Margot Waddell

WHAT IS MEANT BY 'THE FAMILY'?

When we speak of 'the family' we are referring in a very general
way to a group of people whose relationship to one another is
determined by ties of kinship. Yet the assumptions behind any
particular reference are bound to be highly specific within a given
historical and cultural context. In our society, for example, the
family might normatively be described as a socio-economic unit
organized around a heterosexual pair. Even more specifically, the
meaning of the word 'family' for any single individual will be
inseparable from his or her experience of their own family. So that
when we examine individual families and their modes of relating we
find ourselves far from the normative definitions of the historian,
sociologist or anthropologist (in relation to whom any one family
will seem as often the exception as the rule). We find ourselves
nearer to a much more personal situation, relating to a group
which may be characterized by the nature of the interactions
between individual members; by the dynamic processes which
underlie the more evident structural bonds, processes which can
be seen to be so common, so specific, so recognizable as to be
given a label - 'family dynamics'.

While it is the case, on the one hand, that in Britain by the age
of sixteen only about 60 per cent of children are living with both
their biological parents, it is also true, on the other, that 90 per
cent of children are born to couples, whether married or not,
within a so-called conventional family situation. Thus the family
therapists will often be working with single parent families, second
families, re-formations of families and other kinds of grouping.
Yet the nature and development of the dynamic processes which
prevail in such situations will usually be found to be functions of
nuclear family interactions, early in origin (with important cross-
generational links) and largely unconscious, but which may become
conscious in the course of therapy.

The purpose of the present chapter is to provide an overview
of a number of such family dynamics seen within a psychoanalytic
framework, and to convey some sense of relevant aspects of the
theoretical background to the therapeutic work with families that
is being done in the Workshop. The detailed ways in which specific

family dynamics, normally unknown or unnoticed, may be
uncovered and explored; how we and the family try to understand
them in the process of therapy, will be the subject of later chapters. The immediate intention is to review what it means to speak
of 'family dynamics' by bringing together different kinds of
examples of family functioning. It seems appropriate, in the light
of the theoretical framework for the work described, to view these
processes to some extent historically, starting, that is, from the
couple's 'shared object' – the baby – and tracing the roots and
development of familial processes from that point.

PROCESSES OF FORMATION

People enter the 'institution' of the family by birth. It is at this
point that what had previously been the dynamic of a couple
relationship (itself influenced by internal parental figures)
becomes part of an external reality. The 'institution', then, is
already the composite of two others – the mother and her family,
the father and his family. This is a simple, self-evident statement,
yet in terms of the forming and maturing of a family, the birth of
the baby has to be seen as a particular kind of event, for it marks
the beginning of dynamics which may establish continuing and
quite specific patterns of relationships in the future of that family.
With the birth (or perhaps, even with conception) a triangle comes
into being in the external world which may already be part of an
internal triangle, or shared phantasy, between the couple. It is,
in other words, now an observable triangle, as opposed to one of
which the reality is largely internal. Problems relating to triangles
now become focused in problems of relating between people: the
possibility of exclusion, of shifts in pairing, of victimization,
jealousy, competition, as well as the more positive, newly shared
and intensely experienced bonds of parenthood.

The change from couple to family is likely to bring into play
aspects of relating between the parents which they had not
experienced with each other in the same way before. Their baby's
birth may evoke in each not only caring, devoted, protective,
deeply loving feelings, but also quite infantile and dependent ones,
such that the apparent asymmetries between physically strong
adult and helplessly weak baby will not be the only, or even the
most important, formative differences.

For together with the infant's actual helplessness is his phan-
tasied omnipotence. Together with the mother's mature physical
and emotional competence are other feelings of inadequacy and
dependence mobilized by the mother/infant interaction – the stir-
rings of early feelings in relation to her own mother. Such emotions may be experienced with an intensity which causes her to
feel at times like a powerless infant herself.

Melanie Klein's theories of early infantile development provide
essential insight into what may be happening in the family at this
stage. The nature of the infant's earliest internalizations and

projections has a lasting effect not only on his or her own psychic development but on the basic meaning of mothering, fathering, and parenting, that operates within that individual family. This is, of course, a two-way process, in that the child is also liable to be an object for the parents' projections. The infant's earliest environment is largely determined by what his parents, usually primarily the mother, bring to the situation; and their capacities to separate out infantile and adult feelings. The feelings of the baby may make the mother feel competitive. Or the father may be undergoing his own quite specific struggles and changes: earlier anxieties, for example, are often re-evoked by exclusion, sensed or actual, from what has become the primary couple, mother and child. (The high incidence of extra-marital relationships at this time may not be simply a function of sexual unavailability.) In a therapy session, the therapist's contribution may be to try to sort out some of these things: where the feelings come from, how they are being expressed, what significance they have, the nature of their impact on the family group and on the 'therapy' group.

CONTAINMENT

In this very emotive situation one particular action or interchange may have a multiplicity of meanings. Cases of baby-battering, for example, often stem, at least in part, from the mother's despera-tion at her own inability to meet what seem like tyrannical demands from her child. In the large number of cases involving potential or actual battering, either parent may be temporarily overwhelmed with infantile rage by the experience of inadequacy. The parent's feelings may become mixed up with the baby's in such a way that the adult restraints are lost and physical violence is resorted to as an expression of impotence, fear, anger and primitive anxiety. Yet one of the dynamics we have become better able to understand is the normal capacity to bear some kind of anxiety. This is des-cribed by W.R. Bion (1962a). If the mother feels temporarily incapacitated, father, hopefully, will in turn be able to help bear the mother/infant couple's relationship. A typical situation might arise over feeding: mother has become tense and exhausted to the point where the baby is unable to suck. Noticing mother's distress the father in apparently quite simple ways may be able to provide crucial emotional and physical support. Holding the baby, reassuring mother and child, making a cup of tea or whatever, can express the way he is 'taking in' the experience and thereby holding the couple until the mother's renewed strength and calm enables the baby to feed again. This illustrates one aspect of what is meant by 'containing' - the capacity on the part of a parent or therapist to take in another's feelings for a time, thereby bringing relief and support, and to use this experience to help them appreciate more accurately what the other is feeling. An understanding of the importance and efficacy of this process has had a considerable influence on the way we work with families.

Sensitivity to the feeling in the group may enable the therapist, temporarily, to take over, to 'hold' or 'contain' some of the painful or unbearable aspects, whether of the individual or group, until they can be understood, worked through and perhaps integrated again. A family's capacity to do this may vary from day to day and week to week. None the less, over time, the general psychological impact of the baby's feelings on the parental couple is likely to be very powerful. The extremities of satisfaction and frustration experienced by the infant, the gratification of blissful fulfilment on the one hand, and the enraged, destructive impulses on the other are the states of mind described in Klein's paranoid-schizoid position. It is this stage of object formation which is dominated by processes such as splitting, omnipotence, idealization and denial.

Particular areas of interaction may acquire special significance. The degree of anxiety, for example, which such behaviour generates will vary from parent to parent. So will the mother's ability to contain certain feelings and to be aware of the areas of identification and separation between her own needs and the baby's. Likewise the father's capacity to support the intensities of this interaction, to be a sustaining emotional presence, will be being tested for the first time. These are all on a continuum of past dynamics in the parents' families, present ones being set in train, and others to come, the roots of which are being established in these early days of family life. Whether over time these dynamics are dealt with as problems within a functioning family system, or whether they take on a disturbed or pathological quality is, of course, very much related to environment in the more usual sense of the word. The kinds of life stresses which the group as a whole, or individual members within it, undergo: the general family circumstances; questions of finance, housing, jobs, friends, schools, community, health, all have crucial roles to play in the family's capacity to maintain some kind of equilibrium in their complex interrelationships.

THE FAMILY AND THERAPY

The therapist's relationship with a family will usually begin at the point where problems have been acknowledged - though this acknowledgement is often focused on one or two individuals, rather than being experienced as a problem of the family group as such. The task is then to uncover what underlies the more obvious manifestations of family stress or group disintegration; to recognize the less easily distinguishable dynamics which may originate in the parents' own experience and be mobilized in the family group at a very early stage. It is important to emphasize what kind of 'uncovering' is meant here. It does not signify the mere 'exposure' of aspects of family life which have been kept hidden perhaps from consciousness as well as from observation - a process which may be experienced as very persecuting by the family members. A rather different process is involved; one in which the therapist draws on his/her own feelings and reactions in the situation to illuminate and share some of the difficulties, as they are felt in the session, in a less persecutory way. The therapist's role is to bring together insight into what is, and has been, happening within the individual psyche on the one hand - the intra-psychic mechanisms - and a sense of the nature and functioning of group phenomena on the other - the inter-psychic mechanisms.

In this way the immediate therapy situation may be drawn on to illustrate family dynamics which have been going on over time. The vertex is that of the here and now rather than the historical. Two brief examples will illustrate the process. The first demonstrates how the therapists, by observing and interpreting the way they were themselves being related to, were able to make explicit family dynamics which originated in each parent's previous history but became focused in relation to the couple's 'shared object' - their newly born baby. With the birth the case shifted from 'marital' to family therapy. It had been noticed by the co-therapists in early sessions that both the husband and wife, but particularly husband, would constantly try to engage one or other therapist in a kind of pairing, to the exclusion of the other partner. The continuous attempts later by the baby (who would be brought to the sessions by the parents) to involve one or other parent or therapist in an insistent eye contact had the effect of distracting from what was going on with the parents. The baby was not only, in effect, doing the same as the parents - trying to establish a pairing relationship at the expense of the others present, but was also expressing in the session a way of dealing with a constantly fended-off fear of being left out, rejected, excessively jealous or alone. It was not until the baby's behaviour was pointed out and its relevance to the family group interpreted that the father was able to recall how intensively he had tried as a child to monopolize *his* father by holding his attention, how he would insist on pairing to the exclusion of sharing, and how this way of being had extended into his subsequent intimate relationships, particularly with his wife.

The behaviour of the six-month-old baby in this setting seemed to point to the importance, felt by each member of the family, of getting into a single pair relationship - the expressed need to hold one another's attention. In this kind of process lies a strengthening of the bases for development of the classic triangle already in the making, as we have seen, in the internal experience of the parents, and often the source, later, of overt jealousy, competition, withdrawal, rivalry, exhibitionism. As I have suggested, it is frequently the manifest behaviour in such situations that is considered the 'problem'. The underlying meaning is harder to recognize.

The second case also relates to the 'uncovering' of processes which had been set in train very early in the family's history. This time attention was drawn to the family's difficulties by violent 'acting out' on the part of the only child when he became adolescent. The child, a fifteen-year-old boy, was initially referred on the grounds of his excessively aggressive behaviour towards his mother, and because of the conflict stirred up in the marital relationship by the disparity between that hostility and the strikingly close and affectionate bonds between father and son.

In the course of therapy it was discovered that, at the time of the pregnancy and birth of her child, the mother's image and sense of esteem was extremely low. Her feelings were reinforced by two major factors: her sexual relationship with her husband had been physically painful to her over a long period of time and, second, shortly before she became pregnant she had had a dermoid cyst removed, the nature of which, containing as it did bits of hair, glands and nail, she found monstrous and repulsive. When the baby was born she experienced him as a mixture of the horrible and the perfect. The 'good baby' she wished to give to her husband – indeed to a large extent handed him over to the father's care – for contact between the baby and herself was composed, in phantasy, of badness and disgust. The extent to which the monster/saint split, which originated in the mother's feelings, was later expressed in the boy's actual personality and behaviour was very striking and became the focus for the therapeutic work. The course that the boy's development was taking was closely in tune with, and contributing to, the family splits, particularly his mother's phantasies.

I have taken this rather dramatic example as an extreme representation of a dynamic which is easily recognizable in family interactions – the way in which family members enact certain roles or develop certain character traits which have been in some sense unconsciously assigned, fixed and colluded with from very early on.

The family themselves are often well aware of some of these characteristics and on one level may be quite conscious of the nature of the relations between them. Indeed, with families seen in treatment, these manifest roles often constitute, in one form or another, the 'presenting symptoms'. In other words, the family may experience them as the problem which has been brought to therapy to be 'removed' or 'cured' – for example, the under-achieving child, the phobic adolescent, the over-anxious mother, the impotent father. Statements such as 'she's the quiet one', 'he's a noisy rascal', 'he's doing brilliantly', 'she won't lift a finger', are as common as sibling rivalry, cross-generational competition, jealousy and similar easily recognizable phenomena. They are part of normal family functioning. Their precise nature may never be particularly noticeable or so significant as to constitute family pathology as opposed to the normal ups and downs of family life. For an early established family dynamic may operate quite normally and only later become problematic, pos ibly precipitated by some crisis or a developmental stage in one of the children's lives which apparently has no relation to the problem.

THE FAMILY AS A 'GROUP'

The difficulty is to determine what lies behind the disturbance;
what certain psychological traits and modes of behaviour in the
individual may mean to the group; what is implied for the individual by the group's functioning; what, in a phrase commonly used
by family therapists, is the family's 'hidden agenda'.
  Individual and group functioning are not, of course, separable
in any simple sense. One of the most important factors which has
become clarified by psychoanalytic work with families is the way
in which the mechanisms of the individual psyche find expression
in family group terms, and how, by treating the family itself as
a kind of psychic entity or unity, the unconscious processes may
be revealed. The individual, for example, may as a mechanism of
defence against anxiety, in an attempt to preserve the integrity of
the ego, make a split between good and bad objects. Sometimes,
in the infant's behaviour such a process is referred specifically to
the breast as a kind of prototype of this splitting - the baby
tending to see one breast as idealized and the other as bad. In the
same way in the family, unity, either of the marriage or of the
group, may be preserved by splitting good qualities into one family
member and bad into another. In object-relational terms, the
group splits off its own angry, bad, irresponsible parts into one
member who then becomes designated as a bad object. In such
cases a lot of the blaming, however unpleasant and potentially
damaging, may be quite explicit and conscious. But slight shifts
in the balance of relationships may precipitate a pathological
situation which requires therapeutic help to resolve. In the families
of disturbed children it is often the case that the child has become
the embodiment of certain family conflicts which have not been
overtly expressed, only covertly, and often unconsciously,
through the child. The ultimate example of this process is explored
in Edward Albee's play 'Who's Afraid of Virginia Woolf?', in which
all the couple's conflicts, hatreds, bitterness, inadequacy are split
off into a child who, as it emerges, does not even exist. If, by
looking at such splits in the therapy situation, the underlying
anxiety - be it separation, fragmentation, madness, sexual
deviance or whatever - can be stated and understood in comparative safety, the starkness of the splits may be greatly reduced
and the 'victim' of them be enabled to get better.
  An example, which in the light of these processes suggests that
family therapy might have been more appropriate than the individual therapy that was actually offered, is provided by a family
of two small girls. The elder daughter, Sally, came into therapy
when she was six, highly disturbed and anti-social. In the course
of her four year treatment she improved considerably. During
that time, however, it was possible to observe a familiar phenomenon - as Sally got better her younger sibling, Jane, became

increasingly violent, fearful and out of contact. It was as if the
family disturbance was being located in the most vulnerable member, so that first one child then the other functioned as a 'scapegoat' for the family disharmony. It seems that, upsetting as it
was to contemplate each child as a case for treatment, it was in
some sense easier to do so than to confront the extent of the
disturbance in the parental relationship. As so often when the
defensive stakes are high, this family was too threatened to consider being seen as a group, but could tolerate the idea of therapy
for an individual child. Zinner and Shapiro (1972) put the issue
very succinctly: 'a variety of parental coercions interact with the
child's own requirements to fix him as a collusive participant in
the family's "hidden agenda"' (1972, p.523).

PROJECTIVE IDENTIFICATION

In the foregoing example the family dynamic takes the form of the
group's conflicts (primarily marital) being located in the individual,
who, for reasons of her own pathology acquiesced in the assigned
role. Recent thinking in family dynamics and psychoanalytic work
in an object relations mode has, however, shown that in many
disturbed families the reverse process also occurs. That is, what
appears to be a group problem or an interpersonal conflict within
the family may be the consequence of one member's intrapersonal
conflict becoming a group concern. The psychological mechanism
determining both processes is the Kleinian notion of projective
identification. This concept can be perceived as emanating from
individual analysis, but it has become central to our work with
families both in terms of the unconscious processes in operation
between family members, and in such a way as to enable understanding of the family dynamics through the therapists' experience
of the family and the family's of the therapists.
    Klein herself gives an account of the mechanism in her paper
'On Identification' (1955) in which she states that not only destructive and bad parts are projected into others, but good parts as
well, for instance, for purposes of communication, or for safe
keeping. She describes projective identification as bound up with
developmental processes arising during the first three or four
months of life, both, as I said, as a mechanism for defending
against anxiety - by splitting off destructive or bad parts of the
self - and as a fundamental influence on object relations. Inter-
preters of Klein take up the term 'projective identification' to
describe how the object may be perceived with characteristics of
the self, and the self be identified with the object of its projection
(e.g. see Segal 1964).
    The mechanism provides an explanation for feelings and inter-
actions which are familiar as part of normal functioning. One may,
for example, feel one is like somebody as a result of attributing
one's feelings to them. In this case the motive might be one of
communication, feelings may be being transferred for the purpose

of being understood. But the same process with a different motive
might function as a means of control: in attempting to make another
person experience what one is feeling, one might be trying to take
possession of them. It may be used, as we have seen, as a way of
expelling or disowning bad thoughts and feelings - by getting
other people to think and feel and take responsibility for them -
defensively in other words, perhaps with the purpose of avoiding
excessive conflict within the individual ego, or between the partners of a fragile relationship. In any such case it is clearly
important to establish what the motive is, but at the same time to
recognize that there could be more than one - that the projective
identification may be serving a multiple function.

In family therapy we have found that awareness of the role and
function of projective identification both in the family setting and
in relation to treatment itself is crucial. One kind of family, for
example, might use it as a means of expelling and disowning
unwanted parts of the self. It might be found, as in one family,
for instance, that the mother has an intensely close and loving
relationship with a son, whose frequently surly and unco-operative
behaviour is a source of constant battles with his father. While
consciously disapproving of, and upset by, the tensions between
the boy and his father, the mother is, perhaps, at the same time
gratifying, through her rebellious son, her own frustrated desires
to revolt against her father. Indeed in her choice of husband she
has found a man in many ways similar to her father, to neither of
whom is she able to express any aggression.

Alternatively, we can see the mechanism operating in a different
situation - the kind of family in which one child is attractive,
successful, popular, kind, and the other difficult, socially isolated,
bad-tempered, average to mediocre in work, occasionally delinquent. (See, for example, the Smith family referred to in Chapter
3.) Over time, the split may get reinforced - all good qualities are
invested through a process of 'idealization' in the girl, all bad
through 'denigration' in the boy to the detriment, in different
ways, of each. A third kind of example may be given in slightly
more detail, this time of the pattern operating the other way
round - from the child to the parent figure. This family had
separated, re-grouped and separated again. Dan, the oldest of
the three siblings, was eleven when his parents parted. His mother
began living with an older man of whom the children, especially
Dan, became very fond. At the same time, being the oldest, Dan
was in some sense expected to be the strongest of the three children and a support to the other two - losing in the process a reli-
able support for himself, in that both his parents were preoccupied
with forming their new relationships. After four years or so his
mother's second relationship also broke up and she set up home
with a third man and became pregnant soon afterwards. At this
point, Dan, unlike the other two children, opted to stay not with
his father (with whom close contact had been maintained), nor
with his mother (with whom he was also on very good terms), but
with the man of his mother's second relationship. On examination

it became clear that a strong element in this choice was that Dan's
frustrated need for protection from his own parents meant that he
was projecting his own protectiveness, previously felt towards
the younger children, into this surrogate parent. With these feelings somehow lodged in the adult, they then elicited for the boy
the very kind of protectiveness which he himself had lacked. The
object of his dependence was, in fact, a person who was himself
usually very dependent and unreliable and who, unlike the other
adults in the situation, never became a biological parent.

In the first two instances problems occurred when the mechanisms, adopted to maintain a kind of uneasy family equilibrium,
themselves failed. Not only destructive feelings and impulses, but
also more positive, indeed idealized, abilities and talents were
respectively parcelled off into individual members of the family in
such a way that a particular mental structure became over-
represented in a single individual. In these cases the function of
the projective identification was clearly primarily defensive and
concealed unworked-through anxieties, needs and repressed feelings on the part of the parents. It may often be the case that
over time the child's experience of himself will, in fact, be affected
by the ways in which the parents have treated, and indeed perceived him – in turn a function of their own internal processes,
needs and anxieties. The third example relates to a much more
constructive use of projective identification in the family group.
By attributing part of himself to an adult man, the boy in this
complex family situation was finally able to enjoy the protectiveness thus elicited.

PROJECTIVE IDENTIFICATION AND FAMILY FUNCTIONING: A
CASE HISTORY

A more extended example will provide a clearer sense of how these
kinds of unconscious identifications develop in a family over long
periods of time, resulting in deep disturbances which may, as in
this case, manifest themselves in quite serious individual pathology. As we have seen, the disturbance of one family member
may often be evidence of the family's need to maintain unity as a
group, or as a couple, with the kinds of consequences we have
been looking at. Such was the situation in the Lang family. John
was referred by the school counsellor because of his fear of looking like a homosexual. The counsellor knew that there were long-
standing marital problems in the family and felt that they might
be willing to come all together to discuss their son. This working-
class family consisted of mother, father and John, aged seventeen,
and two younger brothers. In the sessions father and mother did
almost all the talking and John remained the largely silent but firmly
designated, index patient. It was his problems that were the parents'
repeated complaint: he was totally preoccupied with his uncertainty
about whether or not he looked like a 'pouf'. Everywhere he went he
heard people calling him a pouf or a queer. He could hear people

saying these words from car windows or as he roared by,
helmeted, on his motorbike. He had become unable to go to school
or, at times, even out of the house except wearing his helmet. He
was slovenly, dirty, rude, unhelpful, provocative to his younger
brothers, obsessed with his bike and obsessed too with his
inability to turn off appliances (lights, cookers, taps, etc) or to
lock up properly. Sometimes it would take him five minutes to
leave the house – he would have to check and re-check, or get
one of his friends to do it for him.

Early in the treatment it became clear that there were many
other problems in the family besides John's. His were simply the
most dramatic and most immobilizing. Yet whenever the co-
therapists attempted to make this explicit the parents would resort
to what became a familiar smokescreen of bitter marital rows. The
rows usually focused on sexual anxieties and mutual accusations
and recriminations, particularly by father against mother. The
most recurrent charges were over the close friendship she had
had with another woman when the children were young, to the
exclusion of father (as he maintained), and over the extreme
proprietary feeling (which he stoutly defended) towards his former wife, from whom he had separated two years earlier. Mrs
Lang defended herself, asserting that the closeness of her friendship with her woman neighbour was the consequence of neglect
by her husband, and the charges of her having other relationships were figments of his imagination. The one good relationship
in the family – repeatedly stressed by Mr Lang – was that between
father and John.

Towards the end of the family sessions, the emphasis began to
shift slightly from John to father, and in particular father's own
sexuality. For instance, an occasion was described in which father
and John went out together to see if father could actually hear
John being called a pouf. Crossing the road, John said he heard
someone say 'pouf' to the pair. One of the therapists enquired how
was it possible in a situation like that to know to whom the word
referred. This comment introduced a new dimension to the therapy
– a more generalized awareness of problems of sexual identity
pervading the group. The nature of sexual roles and identities
in the family began to come up in other quite specific ways. For
example, in one session mother gave an unusually distressed
account of an occasion when she had asked her husband to make a
rabbit hutch for the children. He had not done so but when he
found his wife finally doing it herself he accused her of trying to
be a man. The apparent simplicity of the anecdote belied the
family's intense anxiety which lay quite close to the surface but
could not be expressed directly.

John later came for individual therapy and poured out his dis-
like and contempt for his father – feelings which had not been
expressed in the family sessions. A major element in this hostility
seemed to lie in his feelings that his father looked effeminate.
The word he repeatedly used to describe his father – 'a joker' –
could, to all intents and purposes, have been 'pouf'. He felt that

he physically resembled his father, had similar speech patterns
and mannerisms, and had indeed been close to him throughout
childhood, sharing interests and identifying strongly until two
years previously. It was then that his problems had begun. This
seemed to coincide, in terms of material from the family sessions,
with a trip by mother and children to Spain, during which John
had seen his mother flirting with a hotel waiter. It also emerged
that it was at this time that mother, having discovered that father
had been having a number of affairs, insisted on living apart. She
had accepted him back once in the intervening period but separated when he again started having sexual relationships. John's
expressions of contempt and disgust for his father's behaviour
were extreme, and sessions were spent venting his anger and
scorn. Meanwhile, however, his original symptoms began rapidly
to disappear.

Such phenomena are clearly multidetermined and not subject to
simple explanation, yet the processes of projective identification
are strongly in evidence. It seems that the largely unconscious,
or at least preconscious, fear of the father about his own sexual
identity may have been split off into his closely identifying son.
The only remaining manifest glimpses of the pathology in the
father were the obsessional preoccupations with his wife's potential
infidelities, his exaggerated characterization of her friendship with
another woman as homosexual, and his own promiscuity.

An aspect of this case which should have been given more emphasis at this point is the extent to which John may have been a
ready receptacle for his father's projections. It has been indicated
that projective identification is an unconscious process which takes
place between two people (in either internal or external reality).
This can, in some cases, actually involve collusion, but it may not
necessarily go as far as that. Some differentiation has to be made
between 'receiving' and 'colluding with' the projections. It is
important not to see the object of the projections as necessarily
passive. The point is that the object, the second person as it
were, may be involved to a varied extent, according to the readiness or vulnerability with which he receives the projections. In
John's case it may be that unconsciously he felt that he had to
replace his father at the point of marital breakdown, and that in
the process his oedipal feelings were re-evoked. As eldest son he
could identify with father as seducer, perhaps the waiter in Spain
trying to put his hand on his mother's bottom (for so the story
went). If, then, John identified with one aspect of his father's
sexuality - the sexual relationship with his mother - it may unconsciously have seemed necessary to him to defend against the
danger of closeness with mother, lest he experience the relationship as incestuous. It was thus, perhaps, less frightening to him
to hear from others accusations of his homosexuality, for, however painful, this protected him from the far worse oedipal anxiety
over his relationship with his mother. If some version of these
hypotheses were right it would be easy to see how readily John
might receive his father's projection. Possibly his obsessive rituals

were also rooted in this area of unconscious sexual guilt - the necessity of checking and re-checking turned off cookers, lights, etc., being an unconscious need to verify that the feared seduction of mother by son had not in fact occurred.

In these descriptions the focus has been on the role of projective identification within families. To have discussed the issue in this way is to suggest, misleadingly, that there is a separation between the two functions of projective identification mentioned earlier - in relation to the family situation and in relation to the transference in the treatment. In the family work we have been developing together, the two are in fact hardly separable. For it tends to be through the therapists' awareness of how the family are experiencing them, as well as what they are themselves being made to feel, and their ability to interpret that, that insight is gained into the dynamics going on in the family itself. For it is through a sense of the ways in which the family are engaging and relating to the therapist that it becomes possible to uncover the underlying meaning of the disturbances.

As will be seen, in analytic work with families countertransference has a central role. In a direct sense the countertransference may consist not only of the therapists' reactions to the family and their problems but also of feelings that belong in the individual or the group as a whole but have been projected into the therapist by means of the process just described. Less directly, the mechanism may also play a part, in terms of the therapists' feelings about each other, evoked especially by the family's perception of the sort of couple they are. These feelings may change significantly according to the kinds of projections that are being made: the nature and meaning of 'coupleness', or the lack of it, within the family.

The ways in which these changes may occur in a single session and how the therapists in that session work with the mechanism of projective identification are illustrated in detail in other chapters. However, a more general example of the way these processes are worked with over time may be provided by an exploration of the notion of containment in a family therapy setting. It often becomes clear when a crisis of some kind is taking place in a family - in terms of marital tensions, children's problems, illness or even death - that the family's ability to cope, to 'contain' the anxieties evoked by these situations, is importantly related to the parents' own experience of containment of the kind discussed earlier in the chapter, both in childhood and in their current adult relations. The degree to which adult intimate relationships may bring into play powerful feelings of dependency, frustration, anger or whatever - especially in the context of the birth of a child - has already been suggested. Such feelings are derived in large part from earlier bonds in infancy and childhood, and are re-evoked in particular situations.

The following example of specific therapeutic interaction, drawn from a paper by Sally Box (1977), demonstrates especially clearly how family disturbances may be uncovered through close attention

to the dynamics between the family and the therapist involved in
the case. The example shows how the problems of containment,
reflected in the experience of the therapist, may offer a key to the
central dynamic of the family situation. It is an interesting case
in that it provides a study of a frequently unrecognized issue –
the masking of emotional disturbance by, for example, physical
illness, retardation and mongolism in a family.

The paper describes a young woman, Jenny, who came for
treatment in a crisis, culminating in fears about suicidal impulses.
In the initial exploration with her, it gradually became clear that
she was struggling with a number of conflicting feelings around
the fact that she had a mentally retarded sister, Mary, about whom
she felt both a strong sense of duty and enormous resentment.
She had tried unconsciously to deal with those feelings by becoming the main caretaker of a physically crippled young college
friend. But in the face of her friend's dependency she became
afflicted with the same guilt-ridden and, on some level, murderous
feelings which she had long experienced in relation to her sister.
Her response was to want to regress to being helpless and cared
for, like her sister. A decision was made to include Jenny's
parents for a few sessions and the therapist immediately felt
intensely affected by a present, but as yet unspoken, weight of
emotion. She drew upon this to recognize aloud the enormous
burden being passed from one to another in relation to Jenny's
sister. It then became possible for the family to share, for the
first time, their previously unexpressed concerns and anxieties on
each other's behalf, and also the different sorts of pressure each
had been under over the years. It emerged, for example, that
when, during a year when her mother had been unwell, Jenny was
virtually in charge of the house and particularly of her sister,
she had come under increasing pressure from an aunt to hospit-
alize Mary. In the event of Mary actually being sent away, Jenny
had suffered acute feelings of responsibility of which her parents
had hitherto been ignorant. It also slowly and painfully emerged
that mother too had powerful feelings of guilt and responsibility
about Mary, stemming from her sense of having been unready to
have a baby and her inadequacies over nurturing her in the early
stages. Mary's institutionalization had presented a crisis for her
as well as Jenny and, as it turned out, for father. All three had
difficulties visiting Mary and had never been to see her together,
or had her home for a visit. What was discovered in the course of
the sessions, and in the talking that went on between Mary's
parents, meanwhile, was that her father did not hold his wife
responsible, as she had feared, for her reluctance to bring Mary
home for a visit. On the contrary, he shared it. They went on a
joint visit to see Mary and found that they could even enjoy it
when shared in that way.

As may happen in some cases [the paper concludes] this couple
seemed able to make considerable use of the few sessions they
had. What had evidently been a taboo area, now became a matter
of mutual interest and concern to be explored together. They

felt they had work to do but already experienced great relief. Also, and almost immediately, Jenny was able to function again comparatively normally. Although she continued treatment for herself, there is little doubt that the weight of the burden she carried was lessened when her parents could open themselves with each other to entertain their part of it.

It is possible in this case to draw a parellel between aspects of the therapist's function in work with parents and of that of the parents themselves in providing a modicum of containment for the painful emotions of their children. The example is intended to show how, in the course of the family's development, this function had gone awry; how the therapist attempted to provide a containing space and to offer an experience of helping the family face and bear something of the violence, guilt and despair that they brought to sessions. It is clearly not a matter of therapists soaking up all the pain themselves and being left with it, but rather of working on it inside themselves in order then to give it back verbally so that their clients have a better chance of integrating and managing it for themselves.

CONCLUSION

Since the time when therapists are likely to have contact with a family is at the point of crisis or breakdown, it is with the material behind the family 'myths' that they will be primarily concerned – with the analysis, that is, of the different kinds of defensive behaviour adopted by the group, and with the anxieties and unconscious processes which underlie them. The most relevant concepts in thinking about these processes, and in actually working with families, turn out to be strikingly similar to those prevailing in early infancy such as splitting, denial, idealization, denigration and projective identification. This suggests that dynamics of family functioning may significantly conform to some of those more primitive mechanisms.

Through examining at length the nature and functioning of what may be taken to be the centrally useful concept in this work – that of projective identification, along with concomitant concepts of containment, transference and countertransference – an attempt has been made to elucidate the ways in which it is possible to get in touch with the more fundamental, obscure, unconscious dynamics within a family. Kleinian theory originally developed out of clinical experience with individual children who were at an even earlier stage of development than Freud had considered. In applying these notions to group functioning, Bion (1961) has emphasized that similar primitive processes are at work. Both these areas draw on fundamental family dynamics, but in individual and group therapy the family itself is not actually present as a unit in the therapeutic work. In the psychoanalytic approach which is now being developed in the Workshop, insights learned from the study of the child and of the group come together in the family which is after all the locus of the dynamics on which psychoanalysis is based.

2 AN OUTLINE OF THE HISTORY AND CURRENT STATUS OF FAMILY THERAPY

Susan Zawada

Unlike psychoanalysis, with its one seminal originator, family therapy and theory did not grow clearly from the work of one or two major figures. Instead the ever growing movement of workers interested in working with families has as its ancestors a great variety of pioneers of different disciplines, backgrounds and orientation. With such diversity of influences in the past it is not surprising that there is currently considerable heterogeneity in contemporary theory about, and treatment of, normal and disturbed families.

Certain psychoanalytic writings can lend credence to the notion that the family movement has its roots back at the beginning of the century. Thus, in 1909, Freud reported the treatment of 'Little Hans', in which the father was introduced as the active therapeutic agent in the treatment of a phobia in a five-year-old boy. Indeed, here Freud worked solely with the father to affect change in the son. In 1921, Flugel published 'The Psychoanalytic Study of the Family' and, in the 1920s the Child Guidance Movement began, where it was the standard practice for a worker to work with a parent, in addition to the primary psychotherapy being undertaken with the child. Several years later, in 1936, the ninth Psychoanalytic Congress discussed 'Family Neurosis', and both Grotjhan (1929) and Laforgue (1936) wrote comprehensively on the notion that individual neuroses in a given family complement and condition one another. However, while it is clear that before the Second World War there was some evidence of theoretical and clinical awareness of the importance of the family, essentially both psychoanalytic theory and practice remained almost exclusively orientated towards the individual, a 'one-body psychology' (Rickman, in Bion 1961).

The idea of trying to understand and change a family appeared at mid-century, at the same time as many other changes in both the culture and social sciences of post-war North America and Europe. One particular cultural phenomenon of immediate relevance to the present discussion was a re-emphasis on the family, and especially on the importance of the nuclear family, following the upheavals of the war. Simultaneously, group therapy was developing (e.g. Bion 1961), social psychiatry was concerned with the effect of total institutions and the efficacy of therapeutic

communities (e.g. Goffman 1961; Maxwell Jones 1952), and man
and other animals were being regarded by behavioural scientists
as inseparable from their environment (e.g. Skinner 1953).
Psychoanalysis too was developing and changing. Having gained
general acceptance as a treatment method during the 1930s, and
having provided useful concepts and procedures for the mass
need during the war, psychoanalysis became established, and was
being taught in universities, informing therapists, educators and
parents.

Psychoanalytic thought also began to diversify, and here it is
essential to pay attention to the divergence between developments
in psychoanalysis on either side of the Atlantic. In some senses
the British movements mirrored these other changes adumbrated
above with the emergence of the stress laid on object relationships,
the organism (in this context the individual) being seen, not in
isolation but rather in interaction with its surroundings, as part
of a unit (mother-child dyad, family, marriage, institution,
group). Thus we see in the contemporary British School of
Psychoanalysis a fundamental emphasis laid on object relationships
and developments from object relationship theory, including the
concepts of projective identification, transference and countertransference and containment, as described by, among others,
Klein, Winnicott, Bion, and now, as applied to family work, in
this book. However, these advances in theoretical understanding
and conceptualization are frequently ignored or misunderstood in
the current family therapy literature, where the terms 'psychoanalysis' or 'psychoanalytic' are most often used to refer to a
topographical model of psychoanalysis, with an emphasis on instinct
theory, linear causality, and the discovery and working through
of early repressed traumata. So, for example, a British writer,
Walrond-Skinner will still write: 'in some treatment intervention,
such as psychoanalysis, healing and change spring from insight
gained with the early traumata of certain childhood events'
(1976, p.21) and goes on to refer to 'the remote (Freud) or
extremely remote (Klein) roots of traumata' (op.cit., p.26). Such
a proposition appears to be echoed by the majority of North
American family therapists and theorists although it is, in fact, a
misdefinition of the term 'psychoanalytic' as currently applied.
This paper would like to propose that this misconception accounts
for a good deal of polarization and conflict which may well be
redundant.

While psychoanalysis has been diversifying, it has also been
being questioned and challenged. Thus, as psychoanalysis was
developing and becoming powerful and prestigious in the late
1940s, so various workers were becoming aware of some of its
clinical limitations. An essential notion in the traditional medical
model of psychiatry that carried over into the psychoanalytic
world was that a disturbed individual could be plucked from his
environment, have his intrapsychic problems resolved by providing insight and relieving repression., and then return to his
natural social situation transformed, and able to cope. However,

therapists began to notice that individual change sometimes brought with it consequent changes in the family or social situation, and conversely, that family resistance could produce resistance to change in the individual. Often this was an accidental discovery, but workers began to try to grapple with the idea that family factors could be related to individual pathology and change. Simultaneously, various frustrations with the traditional psychoanalytic approach began to emerge, particularly in relation to the treatment of schizophrenia, and to the treatment of behavioural difficulties and delinquency in children, coupled with the problem of working conventionally with impoverished and deprived patient groups. All these factors led workers to consider the family as the particular focus of attention.

It is generally acknowledged that Ackerman, a child psychiatrist and analyst, was one of the first therapists to take the revolutionary step of bringing whole families under direct observation in interviews. During the 1940s he had become interested in the family as the focus of attention and wrote 'we must see the family as a social and emotional unit', emphasizing explicitly the interrelatedness of family members, and describing work with the family as a treatment modality in its own right, rather than one of many choices of technique to treat an individual. However, throughout North America and Great Britain it appeared that gradually various workers and institutions were making similar discoveries and having similar thoughts while essentially working independently of one another. Thus, for example, in 1949 in London, Bowlby published his short but extremely influential paper 'The Study and Reduction of Group Tensions in the Family'. In this paper Bowlby described several occasional 'conferences' with the whole family, as part of his ongoing work with the individual at the Tavistock Clinic.

Concurrently, in California, Gregory Bateson and his colleagues were conducting a research project which was formulating and testing a broad systematic view of the nature, etiology and therapy of schizophrenia. The theory of schizophrenia they presented is based on communications analysis, and more specifically on that part of communication theory based on Russell's Theory of Logical Types. From this theory, and from observations of schizophrenic patients, they derived a description of a situation called the 'double bind', a situation where it is hypothesized that 'no matter what a person does, he cannot win' (Bateson, Jackson, Haley and Weakland 1956). Bateson et al. suggest that a person caught in the double bind may develop schizophrenic symptoms and they discussed how and why the double bind may arise in the family situation. This research, and the work it stimulated, was to have a fundamental impact on the whole field of family therapy and theory. It laid emphasis on the family as being the unit of dysfunction but also introduced the models and language of cybernetics and communication theory to the behavioural sciences and the therapeutic arena. The approach suggested that the interchange of messages between people defined relationships, and that these

relationships were stabilized by homeostatic processes in the form
of actions of family members within the family. The therapy that
developed out of this view emphasized changing a family system by
arranging that family members behave, or communicate differently
with one another. It was a therapy based not upon psychodynamic
principles nor upon a theory on conditioning. The central issue
was about how people were communicating at the moment that was
the focus of attention.

By the 1960s the family therapy and theory movement had begun
to surface and become institutionalized. Various landmarks emerged
at that time. In the United States, for example, the Ackerman
Institute in New York was founded in 1960, the journal, 'Family
Process' published for the first time in 1962, and in 1964, the
Philadelphia Institute was founded. In Great Britain R.D. Laing
published 'The Divided Self' in 1959, 'Self and Others' in 1961,
and 'Sanity, Madness and the Family' in 1964. In the preface to
the last book Laing acknowledges his debt to, among others,
Bateson, Jackson, Shapiro and Wynne, with whom he discussed
his research into the families of schizophrenics in 1962. As
Bartlett (1976) has shown, Laing 'rarely includes the reciprocal
action of the designated patient, much less the totality of the
reciprocal actions of the family members as a system', ideas Dicks
was beginning to attempt to elucidate in relation to marriages
(Dicks 1963). None the less, as Walrond-Skinner writes: 'Laing
and his associates have been extraordinarily influential in developing an intellectual climate conducive to viewing psychological
disorders from within a framework of dysfunctional interpersonal
relationships' (1979, p.4).

Since the early 1960s the family therapy and theory movement
has expanded considerably, and it continues to do so. Various
writers have attempted to differentiate the schools of family
therapy that now exist. The first published attempt at such a
classification is the paper by Beels and Ferber (1969) which merits
some detailed attention by virtue of its now being regarded as a
'classic' paper in the family therapy literature. For the purposes
of the present paper the discussion of the Beels and Ferber paper
will also serve as a vehicle to introduce, and briefly describe,
several key schools of family therapy.

Beels and Ferber state that the therapeutic 'relationship (in
family therapy) has for its definite and agreed upon purpose
changes in the family system of interaction, not changes in the
behaviour of individuals. Individual change occurs as a by-
product of system change'. Further, they state that all the family
therapists they reviewed would agree that 'the first purpose of
working with a family group is to improve its function as a family
.... to promote its growth and differentiation' (ibid., p.285).

Beels and Ferber propose classifying family therapists in terms
of how they individually present themselves to the family they are
treating, that is, essentially in terms of how they intervene in a
family. Thus they divide 'conductors' from 'reactors', the
'reactors' being further divided into 'analysts' and 'system

purists'. Beels and Ferber state that the 'conductors' (who are
described as usually being powerful, charismatic therapists, and
who include Ackerman, Satir and Minuchin) 'conduct a meeting
with a very definite end in view. They arrange with the family a
new experience in the possibilities of relating to one another, and
they are quite direct about setting that experience up' (ibid.,
p.293). The 'very definite end in view' is decided upon by the
family therapist and is coloured by his or her own value judgments
and notions about appropriate family functioning, and the majority
of 'conductors' appear quite unabashed about making clear their
own belief systems.

The 'reactor/analyst group' in which Beels and Ferber include
Wynne, Boszormenyi-Nagy and Framo, is described as being distinguished by a terminology and interest which is said to be more
or less similar to that of a psychoanalytic tradition:

> they believe that the individual carries within him a non-rational
> and unconscious truth which when encountered meaningfully in
> the therapy, will help to set him free.... For Boszormenyi-Nagy
> and Framo the heart of the therapeutic undertaking... is the
> uncovering of the distorted internal part objects of the family
> members, especially the internalizations and projections of the
> parents within the current family.

Beels and Ferber attempt to show how Wynne's concept of 'Trading
of Dissociation' relates to the Kleinian concept of projective
identification. 'Wynne writes "here I refer to a system or organization of deeply unconscious processes, an organization which provides a means for each individual to cope with otherwise intolerable
ideas and feelings"' (ibid., p.305). They discuss how Boszormenyi-
Nagy locates the prototypes of many defensively split-off and
projected part objects in the parents' experience of their own
parents and how he completes the three generational picture of this
phenomenon which, it is suggested, often results in psychological
disturbance in the third generation. Boszormenyi-Nagy describes
his version of the therapeutic working through of the parent's
attachment to (or denial of) the grandparent objects, as essential
to the therapy. Thus the 'reactor/analyst' group do indeed appear
to use certain current psychoanalytic concepts and values in their
clinical work, although it is clear that no solid psychoanalytic
model underpins their theorizing.

The third group Beels and Ferber describe are called 'reactor/
system purists'. They, including Zuk, Haley and Jackson among
others, take as a general basis for their theories communication
theory as first developed by Bateson et al. The therapist inter-
venes in the family's communications system, actively gaining
control of it by various deliberate techniques, to affect change in
the whole family system. Although grouped as 'reactors', Beels
and Ferber make it clear that this group are also activists of a
certain kind. These workers do not think that 'the truth of the
unconscious shall make the family free. The curative agent is the
paradoxical manipulation of power, so that the therapist lets the
family seem to define the situation but in the end it follows his

covert lead' (ibid., p.296). Beels and Ferber maintain that all reactors do have an end in view for the therapy, but that they gain control of the family in a way that is more indirect and complex than the conductors who 'make no bones about the matter'.

Beels and Ferber's paper is over a decade old now. Where it is still useful, it is proposed, is in the way it draws attention to therapists' differences in styles and value systems. It also highlights how even these therapists who would maintain they do not control the therapy, do in some senses exercise power over the joint work through their control of the setting and the communications attended to. However, the categories proposed quite clearly have had limited usefulness in providing a taxonomy of family therapy and theory, particularly since over the past decade the 'systems view' has moved from being a minority point of view to a position of central importance in the body of family theory and practice. Additionally, it is difficult to place certain schools in Beels and Ferber's categories. Palazzoli and her colleagues (1978) would call themselves 'systems purists', but probably not 'reactors'. Minuchin, too, would probably see himself as a 'system purist', but he certainly is also a 'conductor'. The work described in the present book would fit most neatly into the 'reactor/ analyst' group. However, while there are certainly real theoretical similarities between the work described in this book and the works of those authors placed by Beels and Ferber in the 'reactor/ analyst group', significant and important clinical differences exist, such as the difference in emphasis on the use of the transference and countertransference, particularly as experienced in the 'here and now', and in the degree to which therapists will be directive. Thus, while the paper remains 'a classic', the actual classification proposed no longer seems useful.

Martin (1977) recently and more straightforwardly suggests that family therapists, faced with the difficulty of working in a highly complex field and aware that it demands a new orientation, but without the necessary framework, have tended in North America to resort to one or two polarized theoretical and technical positions. On the one hand, she proposes, there are those North American therapists who have stayed with, and tried to utilize, concepts and techniques both from classical psychoanalysis, and she suggest, from object relations theory (such as Wynne, Boszormenyi-Nagy, and latterly Stierlin). On the other hand, there are the group she labels system purists, who 'have tried to simplify matters and make them more manageable by discarding analytic concepts and turning to concepts derived from communications theory' (op.cit., p.55). As well as those system purists listed by Beels and Ferber, Watzlawick and Palazzoli should be included in this classification. Martin suggests that British writers, such as Skynner and Byng-Hall tend to make their frame of reference a bridge between the two groups, 'and are therefore less clear' (ibid. p.55).

Walrond-Skinner suggests a 'useful broad distinction seems to be between those schools of family therapy which concentrate on

helping the family group to change by acquiring some insight into
areas of its dysfunction (dynamic, Bowenian and experiential
schools) and those schools of family therapy which concentrate on
helping the family to change its patterns of behaviour without
increasing its awareness of dysfunctional processes (strategic,
communicational and behavioural)' (1979, p.2). Walrond-Skinner
is essentially taking the same stance as Beels and Ferber in
differentiating family therapists by means of what they actually
do. The theory which informs these different schools is given
less stress, Walrond-Skinner making it clear that she sees descriptive characterization of family therapists and their methods as
being most useful at the moment.

Bentovim, in contrast, states that 'although it may not be a useful task to attempt to produce a superordinate theory of family
interactions and intervention, it is ncessary to attempt to begin
to organize the increasingly large literature of family therapy and
theory' (1979, p.324). He proposes a particular classification of
theories based on the number of elements necessary for their
construction, considering dyadic, triadic and group theories of
family interaction. The elegance of this approach is that Bentovim
shows that at each level, dyadic, triadic and group, theoretical
concepts born in disparate frames of thinking can be related to
each other and indeed when juxtaposed appear complementary
rather than opposed to one another. Bentovim's contribution is
important since he demonstrates that concepts arising from a wide
variety of frames of thinking can be related to one another creatively. He has presented an interesting schema for such exercises
which is currently of value, even if, as with the classification
proposed by Beels and Ferber, the actual categories quickly
become redundant.

It would be most surprising, in fact, if it were not possible to
find rapprochement between the conceptual premises of the various
schools of family theory. Medawar (1969) and others have argued
that living phenomena, but in particular, human life, can be seen
as a series of hierarchically arranged open systems, so that family
therapists might speak of a hierarchy as follows: intrapsychic
object systems, individual, family, work group, community. So, it
is proposed that in discussing similar phenomena some writers
have developed their own descriptive terminology, others have
used the concepts of already existing theories, and others have
taken up the language of General Systems Theory. The crucial
difference between the various schools lies in the way theoretical
understanding of the family as conceptualized by each school is
applied in a clinical setting, and in the way each therapist chooses
to intervene in each family.

At this point it is important to stress that the effect of any form
of psychotherapy is difficult to assess. Frude (1980), commenting
on methodological problems in the evaluation of family therapy,
points out that this difficulty has sometimes led to the extravagant
and erroneous claim that effectiveness is simply not proven. The
measurement of effectiveness of family therapy does remain

problematic for many reasons, but in particular, because of the
difficulty in defining effectiveness criteria, and the difficulty of
designing studies which will adequately measure success against
such criteria, as defined. There is none the less a growing body
of research, extensively reviewed by Gurman and Kniskern (1979)
which gives empirical support for the belief that family therapy
is a meaningful way to intervene therapeutically in a family. However, Gurman and Kniskern (1978) question whether standard
empirical criteria are sufficient for studying the outcomes of
family therapy, proposing that indices based on patients' and
therapists' objective assessments must also be considered. They
point out that even the most concrete measures reflect a research-
er's ethics and values, the implication being that any outcome
criteria are full of value-laden questions, such as what it means to
be a 'healthy family'. These issues are highlighted in a study
designed to compare insight and problem-solving approaches of
family therapy (Slipp and Kressel 1978). The authors report that
when asked directly whether the therapy they received was helpful, the insight treatment group reported greater satisfaction than
the problem-solving group. In contrast, on various standardized
measures of family functioning, such as rating scales, the problem-
solving group showed 'higher levels of adjustment' as defined by
the scales. Such results clearly illustrate the difficulty in choosing meaningful outcome criteria in comparing or evaluating
approaches.

The central point here is that there is not, and there probably
never will be, any particular method of family therapy which has
been scientifically and empirically proven to be the effective
treatment methodology, although family therapy as a treatment
modality has been shown to be clinically valuable. There is,
similarly, no generally agreed upon aim of treatment. Choice of
school of family therapy must ultimately depend upon the therapist's own preference for method of working, and reflect his or
her own value systems, prejudices and theoretical orientation.

It is clear that fundamental philosophical differences do exist
between the various schools of family therapy which must be
examined and evaluated. Madanes and Haley (1977) offer seven
'dimensions' on which they propose therapists differ: past v.
present, interpretation v. action, growth v. presenting problem,
method v. specific plan for each problem, unit of one, two or
three people, equality v. hierarchy and analogical v. digital. In
the discussion of some of these 'dimensions', specifically 'past
v. present', and 'unit of one, two or three people', Madanes and
Haley are clearly making points against psychodynamic approaches
to family therapy. As discussed earlier they are criticizing a
standpoint which no longer applies in Britain, so that some of
their arguments are irrelevant to the current discussion.

However, two of their dimensions are crucial, and will be considered in greater detail here. These are the dimensions of
interpretation v. action and growth v. presenting problem. When
discussing interpretation v. action they write - 'whatever the

cause of the problem the therapeutic issue is what to do about it'.
The choice for the therapist is between facilitating awareness and
integration through interpretation and containment in order to
facilitate change (psychodynamic therapists), or encouraging
change either by providing alternative, structured experiences
within a family interview (experiential therapists), or by actively
requiring new, prescribed behaviour outside the interview in the
real life of the family (directive therapists). Further, therapists
differ in relation to their goals of therapy, that is, on the dimension growth v. presenting problem. Madanes and Haley write:
   Some believe that therapy should solve the problem which the
   client offers and think that therapy has failed if this problem
   is not solved, no matter what other changes have taken place.
   Others, although they are pleased if the presenting problem
   is solved, do not have this as their basic goal but instead
   emphasize the growth and development of the person. Family
   therapists are divided on this issue with some focusing upon
   the presenting problem and some emphasizing the growth and
   development of the whole family (ibid., p.89).

In Madanes and Haley's paper their therapeutic position is
clear. The main characteristic of their therapy is that:
   the therapist plans a strategy for solving the client's problems.
   The goals are clearly set and always coincide with solving the
   presenting problem. The therapy is planned in steps or stages
   to achieve the goals. The therapist must first decide who is
   involved in the presenting problem and in what way. Next he
   must decide on an intervention which will shift the family
   organization so that the presenting problem is not necessary.
   This intervention takes the form of a directive about something
   the family is to do both in and out of the interview. Directives
   may be straightforward or paradoxical, simple and involving
   one or two people or complex and involving the whole family.
   These directives have the purpose of changing the ways people
   relate to each other and the therapist (ibid., p.96).
The focus is upon change by directives.
   This approach is clearly antithetical to the approach illustrated
in the work in this book. The therapist using Haley's model takes
responsibility for deciding what change should occur in the family
system, and how this should be achieved. Understanding, in the
family, is considered irrelevant. One problem is focused upon.
Should another emerge, a further treatment contract is negotiated.
In contrast, the view expressed in this book is that therapy provides the offer of an experience which would allow the family to
gain an increased capacity to tolerate psychic pain, such that they
(the family) can then negotiate for themselves changes in the
family if appropriate. The debate between the proponents of these
two positions antedates the birth of family therapy, echoing, for
example, the heated arguments between the behaviourist school
and the psychoanalytic school from the mid-1940s until the present
day. It is here proposed that workers with different philosophical
beliefs will long have to co-exist, practitioners grouping together

with like-minded colleagues to refine and develop those particular approaches which they have found both effective and satisfying.

If different groups of workers adopt different philosophical stances, then, so too the question has to be asked: do different sorts of treatment suit different sorts of families? Clearly families present for treatment with a multiplicity of areas of dysfunction, presenting at differing times in their natural history and in differing family constellations. There are some families for whom family therapy is contraindicated (see Wynne 1968; Skynner 1969).*
Furthermore, it is proposed here that there are families who may experience therapies based solely on awareness, understanding and the toleration of psychic pain as irrelevant, leading to their prematurely leaving treatment unhelped. It was out of such experiences, for example, that Minuchin developed his 'structural family therapy', adopting a communication model in work with deprived, disorganized, lower-class families where traditional therapy had made no impact whatsoever. Further, it may be that families with extremely entrenched pathology, often going back several generations, such as those families with an anorectic or psychotic member, described so vividly by Palazzoli and her colleagues, can most profitably be helped by an approach which actively and directively uses the forces deployed by the family *against* change, to produce change.† In addition, Martin mentions those defensively verbal middle-class families for whom interest in the meaning of their communications may well be anti-task.

However, there is no doubt that there are many families who have a wish or need, even if unexpressed, to understand themselves or understand how things became as they are. Families with unresolved mourning, for example, families in crisis and in need of being contained before any change can happen, families stuck in particular pathological patterns of neurotic relationship, scapegoating families, many disparate groups where action or structural change are only part of the desired solution.

Family therapy is now established as a well-recognized treatment modality. Its limitations, indications and contraindications clearly need clarifying. Each school's unique contribution values elucidation and consideration. However, it is hoped that the future will also see more cross-fertilization of ideas and concepts, for all these developments can only lead, ultimately, to increased efficacy of intervention in families, and to greater sophistication in theories of family functioning.

*This issue is addressed in Chapter 3, below (eds).
†The reader will recognize that this view relates to a different set of values than those implied elsewhere in this book (eds).

3 INTRODUCING FAMILIES TO FAMILY WORK

Beta Copley

In initial explorations with clients, knowledge of two different kinds develops. On the one hand one begins to learn something about the family itself, what the problems are and how the members relate to one another as the family dynamics unfold. On the other hand, alongside this, one tries to learn about the family's hopes and expectations of the clinic and begins to experience the use that is being made of oneself and what one says and does; in other words there is appraisal from the point of view of the transference and countertransference. These two strands are of course not necessarily experienced separately from each other in the course of the session.

In this paper, through the medium of a number of clinical examples, I propose to look at the interweaving of these two aspects of the work as a means to thinking about indications for further family interventions and their nature. I also propose to give detailed examples of how the interaction with the worker may help a family to develop its commitments to further understanding. (In the examples I give there was no one motivated to seek help as an individual or as a couple, so only further family work of some kind was in question.)

Mr and Mrs Smith came to the Counselling Service of the Clinic, saying they did not know what to do about their daughter Mary's behaviour; they added that she herself refused to come. Mrs Smith had made the appointment for herself and I had not expected to see the father as well. Mother was a neat, middle-aged woman, who initially seemed emotionally aloof and full of complaints about her daughter; father seemed more relaxed, puffing away at his pipe and speaking rather softly in a fairly offhand way, as if his intervention was absolutely expected, but at the same time giving a feeling of detachment. Mother spoke of what she presented as the basic problem, namely, Mary wanting to drop out of school where she said that, despite previous good academic achievement, Mary's work had fallen off. I explored this a little with them, but went on to query whether there were other areas of difficulty. I also asked if they both, in fact, viewed the situation the same way, Mother having done most of the talking.

In doing this I was attempting to make more sense of my somewhat puzzled feelings about the incongruity of Father being at the interview at all, while at the same time giving the impression of being very much at home there.

I went on to say that the appointment as I understood it had only been made for one parent and wondered if there were feelings that were relevant both to this and the fact that they both came. They looked at each other, and although they did not respond directly to my question, Mother, with some back-up from Father, went on to speak about Mary keeping bad company. They spoke of how she stayed out late with a group of young people and complained that they did not really know what she was up to. I wondered about their anxieties in this respect, and they said they didn't know whether or not she had had sexual relationships. On further discussion some of the family background emerged; for example, that the parents worked as insurance agents and were not at home as much as the children. They had added that there was also an older daughter, Sheila, whose image gradually unfolded during the interview as the 'good one' of the family. She was said to have a good relationship with Father and on my instigation we had an inconclusive but I think potentially useful discussion as to whether it was the father who treated her differently or she who behaved very differently to her sister in the family, or a combination of both. I tried to explore with the Smiths their views about Mary's 'bad friends', from which it emerged that Mr and Mrs Smith felt the problems were due to 'split parents' and a 'lack of respect for parental authority' among the friends with whom Mary mixed. I commented in low key, that they were talking about 'split parents' and a 'lack of respect for parents' and wondered if this struck chords in their own family in any way. They then said with some embarrassment that, in fact, there had been some kind of split between themselves about two years ago. I asked gently about this and was told that this was to do with Father having a relationship with another woman. However, they told me, rather quickly I thought, that this was all completely finished now and had been sorted out, although there had been considerable differences between them.

The above interchange seemed to bring the parents more into the interview as people with relationships of their own, as opposed to merely aggrieved parents complaining about their daughter's behaviour in the outside world. It thus became possible to look more at the interrelatedness within this family. I think one could say at this point that we were on the boundary of possible entry into some kind of family therapy.

Mother brought out some concern that they might have made mistakes, though Father tended to make light of this. They spoke of Mary's jealousy of her sister and also of the latter's good relationship with Father. I referred to the 'lack of respect for parents' they spoke of among Mary's friends and wondered whether there was anything like this in the home too. Mother spoke with feeling about how Mary would talk on the telephone to her friends at length, complaining about her mother in a denigrating way, as well as being directly insulting to her. She said that Father did not intervene and that she felt very unsupported.

I am trying to illustrate here how the parents had projected onto Mary's environment feelings of disharmony and inadequate parental functioning that had originally arisen between themselves. After being helped to give some recognition to this, they became more open to further explorations of the family relationships.

As the interview progressed a basic disagreement between the parents became more apparent; Mother resented what she felt was Father's indulgence towards Mary and Father criticized Mother for rigidity and having too high standards; for example, Mother felt Father condoned Mary coming home late while Mother tried to enforce what she felt were more reasonable hours. Earlier in the session one of the anxieties expressed was that Mary might leave home completely and stay with these young people they had mentioned earlier. They then related with some diffidence what they called occasional stealing by Mary of insurance money they sometimes brought home. They felt driven to lock their takings in their bedroom and this led me to ponder aloud if they felt their marital situation was really being raided by Mary, and they agreed.

What had by now emerged was a picture of a family to some extent at odds with each other, the parents feeling not only that Mary was falling into bad ways and might leave them as well as school, but also feeling raided and invaded by her. We were also in touch with marital discord and with Mother's feelings of being unsupported as a mother. In addition there was a picture of another daughter who was presented almost as 'too good', raising in one's mind the possibility that one might find that Mary was being seen as 'too bad'. It was possible to share this perception with them and suggest that a reasonable way into this situation would be for some kind of family intervention in which the family could come together and look at some of these issues. Despite their having said at the beginning they did not think Mary would come to the clinic herself they accepted fairly willingly and thought they would be able to get both children to come. The point I want to stress here is that, by trying to look with the parents at their own feelings and possible involvement they had been able to move in this brief intervention from parents 'complaining' about a daughter who was said to be unwilling to come to the clinic, to being parents with some recognition of a wish to examine their own difficulties and those they had with their children. This latter view of themselves may have enhanced the parental authority that would enable them to feel they could bring Mary. The invitation to bring the 'good sister', Sheila, may also have contributed to their ability to come as 'good parents' with a 'good' relationship to at least one child.

The family did come for family therapy with two of my colleagues, a man and a woman, as co-therapists. They were thought to make good use of it and it is interesting to note that the conflicts between the parents and Mary were fairly rapidly resolved.

I would like now to turn to the Brown family, members of which I saw twice in the setting of our Counselling Service.

Initially all I knew was that a mother, Mrs Brown, was coming about her daughter, of sixteen. I was surprised when I got to the waiting room to find the mother with a very young-looking adolescent standing behind her, making odd movements with her mouth and shuffling with her feet. Somewhat perplexed, I asked if they wished to be seen together. Mrs Brown said Aileen might as well hear what we said, did I mind? I suggested that they come to my room and we could talk, wondering to myself if Aileen was meant to listen to Mother and me talking about her. Mother immediately launched into an account of her difficulties with her daughter. Aileen was thought not to have done well in her examinations and might not be kept on at school. There was also trouble at home. She and her husband could talk to Aileen as much as they liked, but she would not listen. Mother continued forcefully and emotionally that it got her health down, 'making' her have ulcers and headaches. She had to go to the doctor, she said. Aileen had been a bit better since the doctor had a talk with her, and the latter had suggested that she might benefit from a talk with somebody else, for example here. Was this right? I felt that I was wanted by Mother to be some kind of medically prescribed 'talker' who would forcefully 'cure' Aileen, although she had some doubts as to whether I would fulfil this role. I also felt that I was to be some kind of inbuilt action paragraph in relation to the school, though not clear what. In addition, I was very aware of Mother talking to me about Aileen in her presence, while the latter sat silently, looking rather like a twelve-year-old. Trying to give attention to the feelings of both and to phrase what I was made to feel in some way that could be useful to them, I recognized with Mother that she felt very upset, but turned to Aileen and asked her what she thought, and also wondered what she felt about coming. She said she did not mind really. I wondered if she shared her Mother's views about the various difficulties and she said that she felt treated like a child younger than her years. I said I was in a difficult position because I was being asked by Mother, I thought, to 'give' Aileen some kind of talk, really a 'talking to', that was meant to produce considerable change and 'make her better'; if I could or would do this, Aileen might feel I was treating her as much younger than her age.

It had seemed to me necessary to interrupt the flow of Mother's complaints in order to bring Aileen into the interview as a person. The next step was to try myself to hold on to and then share with them what I perceived as their very different stances. If I had not done so I think I would have been in danger of colluding with Mother's projections and so rendering myself useless to the family.

I went on to explain that this was not the way we worked, but queried with them what they knew about the kind of service they had come to, and clarified how a joint exploration of problems, as opposed to provision of solutions, was offered. I also explained the Brief Intervention nature of this particular service.

In brief or exploratory work it also seems to me sensible not only to attempt to understand with clients something about the initial hopes, expectations and fears that they bring, including what is being projected on to the agency, but also to give some realistic information about what could be available. Apart from trying both to give them some indication of what I felt they were expecting of me and to clarify what could be offered, I hoped that if I could in any way hold on to and show them their opposing views it might be possible to bring what working capacity there was in them into the session.

I made some further allusion to Mother's view of Aileen not listening, which she felt ended up in illness in her, and Aileen's view perhaps of being talked 'about' or 'at' rather than 'with', for example, in Mother's conversations with the Doctor, the Headmistress and myself. Aileen then said that she did feel people talked about her too much. I asked her if she could enlarge on this but she suddenly left the room to go to the toilet.

Mother and I sat uncomfortably for a moment or two and then she said she did not think Aileen was taking it seriously and, I felt, put pressure on me to agree, as if we were two equal adults talking about a small recalcitrant child. In support of the method of work I had outlined, I began to put something to Mother about complications of Aileen being out of the room, but the latter came back in quickly and I referred back to the situation before she went out. She, however, said she had forgotten. It occurred to me that she may have attempted in a concrete way to evacuate her feelings down the toilet but I did not feel it appropriate to raise such a view at this particular time. I also thought it important to get into the open what she might have felt had been happening between Mother and myself in her absence as well as what had actually happened. I therefore reminded her that we had been referring to her feelings about people talking about her before she had left the room and perhaps she felt that her Mother and I had been doing just that during this time. She replied 'yes' with considerable gusto. I also made clear that in our work I thought that communications would have to be shared openly, and obtained Mother's permission to repeat what she had said to me.

We then heard a long account about the school situation, including Aileen's feelings that people, particularly other children, talked about her at school, and that she was not really interested in other children at all. This led on to her saying in her somewhat stilted manner of speech that she considered the purpose of education was not for the purposes of socialization but to enable one to take one's place in employment in the adult world. She then complained about the childish behaviour of children at a school she had attended for five years and from which she had been suddenly withdrawn by the parents, though apparently in some disagreement with each other at the time. There were then very concrete references to the adult bridge club nearby which Aileen attended, her consequent coming home late and the parents being worried; this culminated in Aileen saying in a pseudo-adult voice that there was no cause for any parent to be worried and in any case it was not their business and she really felt more like an adult than a child anyhow. On my exploring ideas about the future Aileen talked, rather grandly, I thought, about wanting to go to college with a view to going on and improving the world; she also said she would like to live in a room on her own where she could cook for herself, feed herself and be entirely self-sufficient. 'With no parents?' I asked. 'Yes', she said. 'What are parents for?' asked her mother. This led me to wonder aloud about the father and to query the disagreement between the parents about the previous school. Mother went on to say, 'Oh yes, we've had lots of quarrels', and Aileen replied in reproving pseudo-adult tones, 'You shouldn't quarrel, you really shouldn't quarrel; it's a habit you really ought to stop, it's not good for anybody.'

Somewhere in this discussion I pointed out the ongoing dispute in the family about the nature of adulthood and how it affected relationships between parents and children. I went on to say that it might be useful to look at the areas in which quarrels arose, to try and understand more about the feelings involved. I also pointed out that there were two of them here and we were talking about quarrels or differences that were said to arise between three people and went on to suggest that maybe Father should take part too. (Somewhere they had told me that Aileen's older sister of twenty-one had married and left home and that an older brother was away in the north so there was no question of inviting them to come too.)

After some discussion this was accepted, whereupon Mother turned to me with a confident air and said, 'Confidentially, before Father comes, I had better tell you...' I interrupted her and again took up my reluctance to receive a confidential communication in a threesome, indicating that this topic had already been broached in a twosome, and perhaps also was an issue for the family. She acquiesced and said, but no longer 'confidentially', that Father had had a stroke last November and did not like this being referred to. He had not quite accepted it and it was very difficult because Aileen wrote him such horrible notes which, on enquiry, included 'I hate my father' and 'my father is cruel.' She added that it was a cruel thing to have to come down to breakfast and to find such a note when you have had a stroke. I said, 'Yes, but maybe hate is also a difficult feeling to deal with' and Aileen said 'Yes'.

The interview ended in a more relaxed way and I think we all
thought something had happened in this session. Probably the
major feature was a minimum of holding on to and thinking about
Mother and Aileen's opposing and seemingly undiscussable views,
without, I hoped, my being pushed into collusion with either of
them. A setting as a basis for some further exploration may also
have been provided.

Father came to the next session and he too made strange movements with his teeth and body. There was quite some animosity
apparent between him and his daughter and Mother complained
that he did not exercise enough discipline. I also got the feeling that she did not give him much space to do so. We explored
such themes as Aileen feeling infantilized (which had already
come up in the previous session) and Mother feeling upset
because Aileen had threatened to hit her when she was old, and
claiming Father would no longer be able to protect her. To this
Aileen protested, however, with a highly 'reasonable' air that
she was only defending herself because Mother kept 'looking at
her at mealtimes'. This somewhat strange point I thought illustrated Aileen's view that Mother was 'getting at' her and controlling her by looking at her. It was now possible to relate
this to the feeling spoken of initially by Mother of being made
by Aileen to have ulcers and headaches, and to share with them
that there could also be communications within the family of a
non-verbal nature which were felt to be very powerful.

All three members of this family continued to express their viewpoints about a number of family disputes vociferously and with an
air of speaking the self-evident and only possible truth. It seemed
very clear that it was not only Aileen who 'did not listen' to the
feelings of others. Yet what from the beginning could be seen to
be a rather disturbed family had managed to come, do a bit of
work, and evince some interest in the proceedings. They seemed
at least momentarily relieved at having some discussion of their
unhelpful polarization, and having some of the infantile/adult
confusion given some recognition by me. This did not in fact
amount to much more than bringing to their joint attention that
there seemed to be very differing views among them as to who
might be being adult, and who infantile, but each one felt absolutely 'right' and that this seemed to be a very painful area for
them all. They may also have been helped to listen to each other,
however briefly. That there was some response to my attempted
holding, as opposed to the seemingly usual pattern between themselves of reacting to these interchanges, made me wonder if it
might be possible to work further with them. Against this there
was the concreteness of their thinking, the presence of projections,
probably on the basis of part object relationships, that were felt
to have strong physical effects, such as being causative of
physical illness in Mother. Altogether there seemed to be a predominance of what could be called paranoid/schizoid ways of
thinking with much of the so-called 'adult' behaviour of all of them
probably being an indication of pseudo-mature adulthood based on

projective identification (see Waddell, Chapter 1; Moustaki, Glossary). There seemed to be no indication for attempting individual work, because none of them seemed moved by curiosity about their inner world, nor wanted to be seen as patients. I did, in fact, refer them on for further family work, but in the view of the therapists who attempted to work with them in some depth, the family experienced this as attacking and although initially interested, withdrew after a number of interviews.

Looking back on the case it seems to me that the points about family psychopathology that I have outlined in the last paragraph were a contra-indication for attempting this latter work, viz., longer term family therapy using transference interpretations. It seems to me now that the work done with them in the Counselling Service was primarily that of containment. This concept as used here originated in the work of W.R. Bion (1962a); it is elaborated by Waddell in Chapter 1, Box in Chapter 5 and Moustaki in the Glossary. In family work it seems to me that a worker can open him or herself to the full impact of the communications coming from different family members, however bizarre, incompatible and painful, and attempt to give them some space within him or herself, and having borne and thought about them, relate them back again to the family in a more bearable form. Although I think I did offer the Browns some aspects of a containing experience attempting to give attention to, hold and relay back some of their contentious interchanges, I now think that I over-reacted to what I experienced as some use of what we did together and passed them on too quickly in an attempt to utilize what seemed to me to be some mobilization of energy for work. On reflection, I think it would have made more sense for me to have continued with them for a few sessions more, largely on the basis of an explorative and containing experience. I could have offered the possibility of a follow-up some time later if this had seem appropriate. As I elaborate when discussing methods of work below, I use my own feelings in the countertransference as a guide to understanding with such families. Although with this family I picked up early on Mother's wish for me to talk to Aileen as a means of controlling her, I now think I did not pay enough attention to the notion of my being felt, by Mother in particular, as being a powerful therapeutic tool 'prescribed' by her and the GP to fulfil a particular requirement in her mind and this may have led to my having responded with some degree of therapeutic zeal to the idea of a further referral. With hindsight, I also think I might have been more aware of the lack of feelings in the transference or countertransference of me as an 'object' with personal qualities; this lack was another factor which did not bode well for the family being able to sustain working in depth.

Although I would not call the foregoing accounts 'Family Therapy', they may be worth thinking about as being examples of therapeutic work with families. This kind of work can, I think, be thought about as a useful entity in its own right, as well as a possible introduction and entry where appropriate into more formal family therapy for the families concerned.

I should now like to gather together some thinking about aspects of the method of work that I use and its relation to psychoanalysis. In individual long-term psychoanalytical psychotherapy my main working tool is the transference relationship to myself which I attempt to gather in from the beginning of therapy with the purpose of using it to allow understanding of, and change in, the internal objects of the patients. In other words, in the session I am constantly attempting to relate material to myself in the transference. This would obviously, I think, seem inappropriate in brief work, whether individual or family. In this latter setting, while not making the exploration and interpretation of the transference the main working tool, it does, however, seem essential for the therapist to be constantly aware of its development, with a view to taking it up when necessary.

In this kind of work I see actual interpretation of the transference as appropriate in three kinds of instances which can, in fact, overlap, as they do in the examples that I go on to give. In the first instance, it serves to draw attention to material in relation to oneself as a means of illustrating something in the clients' external lives in a way that they might be able to use. For example, with the Browns I took up the possibility of Aileen feeling I was someone who was talking 'at' her, as in Mother's conversations with the doctor and headmistress. Secondly, it may be necessary to comment on something in relation to oneself to avoid a block in the session, that is, a negative transference reaction; the same example in relation to Aileen applies. The third instance is the use of oneself in the 'here and now', quite often in the form of a representative of the agency, as a means of relating to what the clients are hoping for, fearing or experiencing, this time with the aim of making the current experience usable by them. Taking another facet of the same example, when Mrs Brown quoted the doctor in a way that made me feel I was expected to take powerful action in relation to Aileen in order to give relief to her ulcers and headache, I think it was appropriate to take up what was hoped for from me. Although technically a transference reaction, it would seem to me to be inappropriate to take it up with emotional impact in relation to oneself, but better to try and understand their expectations of me as the person they happened to encounter in the agency. The initial interchange with the Brown family I think is, in fact, an example of what can be called pre-transference phenomena, in other words feelings that related to me not as in a particularly personal interaction, but rather based on the family's projections onto the agency before coming.

Here of course the countertransference is relevant, because one gets in touch with such projections by way of what one is made to feel; in that instance, for example, that I was to be a prescribed, forceful cure for Aileen. You may have noticed that in the cases that I have presented I have drawn very much on my own observations and feelings in the countertransference as a method of working and understanding. I am using the term to describe manifestations in the worker arising from interactions with patients and clients; the concept is further expanded by Margot Waddell in Chapter 1 and Errica Moustaki in the Glossary. To give another example, at the beginning of the first case, the Smiths, I both observed and experienced Father as a passive listener somehow 'in' the situation, yet not actively involved. This experience helped me to feel it was appropriate to try and open up the parental relationship and explore the relevance of Father's passivity to the difficulties reported in relation to Mary. It is clear, then, that the use of the countertransference is a major tool in all our work.

In longer-term family work it also seems to me useful to comment on the transference and by this means offer more opportunity to the family to understand their internal objects with a view to possible change. In the Workshop we are therefore attempting to find ways of using transference manifestations as a tool of family work. In this context I am referring to transference as the infantile feelings arising in the family experienced in relation to the therapists. Although aspects of transference in relation to the institution also arise and can be taken up, as in the earlier examples I have given in the context of briefer work, the transference can also be interpreted with reference to the therapists as they are felt to be perceived by the family in the 'here and now', say for example as a parental couple. This approach in my view also calls for the development of family interpretations, allowing insights of how the family use the therapists. This is illustrated in the following case of the Manner family.

It seems to me that when one is thinking about the appropriateness of offering the longer-term work to a family, one might think not only about the dynamics of a family, but also about their capacity to work, making use of a transference relationship as, for example, the Browns probably could not, though the Smiths and the Manners could.

I should now like to illustrate how, using such criteria, we decided to offer ongoing therapy to the Manner family.

Mr and Mrs Manner came to the clinic asking for family therapy for themselves and their nineteen-year-old daughter, Olga. A male co-therapist and I saw the three of them together. The parents explained that they had had family therapy in their own country, Denmark, and had been recommended to continue this during the period when the parents were on a work assignment in England. Olga had a long history of illness and had had various forms of therapy. Her current difficulties were said to include the inability to leave home or to take a job, and living very much as part of her parents' lives. Her parents expressed perplexity about how to view this, fluctuating between seeing her as ill and needing to be with them or as being lazy and requiring what they felt to be quite harsh treatment. Olga was unwilling to attend therapy on her own, though she was the one that the parents claimed needed it. We saw them first for a family exploration, without a commitment to ongoing therapy. Early on the parents told us firmly that therapists were equally

good anywhere and maintained that we were no different from
our Danish predecessors.

The nature of the family problems with areas of fusion and non-
differentiation within the family seemed apparent from what we
observed, as also from the history; in relation to us there was
the question of a non-differentiation from the previous therapists.
Although there may be some external similarity to the Browns in
expectation of the agency, this did not appear to be just a somewhat concrete pre-transference requirement that we should fulfil
a role for them, but a manifestation of their difficulties in separating and differentiation. This became apparent in several ways.
They, for example, in the exploration were able to become
interested and curious about us, both in relation to our style of
therapy and as people; this gave us scope for beginning to examine with them areas of differentiation between the two of us as
a couple and also between us and their previous therapists. In
the countertransference we had fluctuating perceptions of being
experienced at one moment as a conglomerate entity fused with
the institution, or at another moment, more separately, though
still as part of the Tavistock.
In the first family meeting we explained that we would soon be
taking a pre-arranged break. The family were unwilling to
believe that we ourselves could have made a decision to take a
holiday so soon. They preferred to lay this event entirely at
the door of the institution, seeing us simply as a part of it, and
thus unable to decide such issues for ourselves.

The fact that one could see, feel, comment and elicit interest
in relation to ourselves, albeit at that time denied, encouraged us
to believe that we could work in the transference. With so much
fusion present in this family, it seemed very appropriate to try,
where we could, to interpret in a way that was meaningful for the
whole family by means of family interpretations. In an attempt to
develop family interpretative work in this way, I find that I draw
on the experience of group work as developed by W.R. Bion
(1961).
In an early session, for example, the therapists made interpretations which the parents assiduously translated 'for' the daughter, the index patient. The latter could speak some English but
was basically inactive in therapy at that time. When we talked
about this, Olga rejoined that the therapy was for her (despite
the fact that she had not wanted to be an individual patient),
implying that her parents were doing their job correctly. We in
turn interpreted for the family that we were felt to be the
parental-therapist providers of mental food, Mr and Mrs Manner
acting as the 'ears' or 'hands' to take it from us and put it in
the 'Olga mouth' of the family body.
Working with this family, then, we tried to provide ourselves
as a basis for first understanding, and later disentangling,
family interactions. In this way we also made available the possibility of introjecting and identifying with unfused, differentiated objects. Observations of the family dynamics and our

perception of the transference and countertransference manifestations in the first few meetings led us to offer the family
ongoing therapy in which we used the transference relationship as a basic method of work. The therapy ended nearly
two years later, shortly after Olga, who by then was in full-
time work, had left home and was about to be married.

SUMMARY

In this paper clinical examples have been given of families with
whom it seemed possible to engage in some form of family work.
Problems referred to by these families or elucidated by the therapists included:

Difficulties experienced as occurring directly in family relationships	Smiths Browns Manners
Splitting, projecting and scapegoating	Smiths Browns
Fusion and non-differentiation	Manners
Families where a potential patient might not otherwise come	Smiths Browns Manners

This, of course, is not intended to be a comprehensive set of
criteria; and one has also to bear in mind that it has not been
appropriate to examine the alternative of individual therapy in this
paper. Interestingly enough, however, although it was not the
intention to find such examples when collecting this material, it
does overlap considerably with some of the indications given for
family therapy elsewhere in the literature, e.g., S. Walrond-
Skinner (1976); F.E. Martin (1977).
  I think these interventions illustrate that when deciding how to
proceed it may be useful to look not only at a family's symptom-
atology and internal dynamics, but also at how the family relates to,
and is experienced by, the workers in the transference and
countertransference. An attempt has been made here to illustrate
how one may decide about alternative kinds of family interventions
and their possible usefulness. One could perhaps postulate at this
stage of our thinking two somewhat different, but overlapping,
areas of work with families.
  1 Intervention with a family, or some family members, involving
  chiefly exploration, clarification and containment, with possibility of some work in such areas as projections and splitting.
  Such work would rely particularly on the use of observation and
  the countertransference with limited use of transference interpretations, but, in my view, should pay considerable attention

to the family's expectation of the agency. It might be brief, would not necessarily require any conscious commitment to therapy, but might give relief from family stress and allow some movement to take place within the family. This could well be sufficient for the needs or kind of involvement a family was willing or able to make or that an agency could provide. A family may also be helped by work done in this way to undertake further work (e.g. the Smith parents moving into family therapy with their children). For some families, based say in the paranoid/schizoid position, more interpretative therapy may be perceived as too persecuting and/or unfulfilling of expectations which may be manifest in the family (e.g. the Browns).

2 Family therapy, very likely longer term, where one is attempting to develop the use of interpretations geared towards the family meaning of what is being discussed, with the benefit of the interpretation of a transference relationship to the therapists as a working tool (e.g., the Manner family in this chapter and other families elsewhere in this book; Henry, Chapter 7 and Williams, Chapter 8). Working in such a way offers a family a chance not only of alleviating external distress but also of unravelling the distortions of its shared internal world. Hopefully it may also help one to experience and learn more about the use of a psychoanalytic approach in thinking about families, which might have further application in short as well as long term work.

4 RE-ENACTMENT AS AN UNWITTING PROFESSIONAL RESPONSE TO FAMILY DYNAMICS

Ronald Britton

The notion which is expressed in the title of this chapter is that
contact with some families may result in professional workers or
their institutions becoming involved unknowingly in a drama which
reflects a situation in the relationships of the family or within the
minds of some of its individual members; and that this is not
recognized but expressed in action. As the action appears to be
that of professionals going about their business, i.e., interacting
with the family, colleagues or other agencies, the fact that these
transactions are shaped by an underlying dynamic is unlikely to
be perceived. This may eventually call attention to itself by its
repetitious nature or by the impasse which seems to follow a
variety of initiatives. Indications of the presence of a prevailing
unconscious process influencing professional responses may be
the intensity of feeling aroused by a case; the degree of dogmatism
evoked; or the pressure to take drastic or urgent measures. In
other cases, in contrast to this, the professional 'symptoms' are
inappropriate unconcern; surprising ignorance; undue compla-
cency; uncharacteristic insensitivity or professional inertia.

This last characteristic is illustrated in the case of a boy referred to a Child Guidance Clinic by the school he attended, or more
precisely rarely attended. A new teacher at the school had
reactivated concern about an old situation. In the past the School
Welfare Officer had been very troubled about the boy who
appeared to be neglected by his mother, with whom he lived alone.
The Welfare Worker had involved the Social Services Department
in the case, as the boy could not learn at school and seemed
undeveloped emotionally and socially. A regular arrangement was
made for a woman social worker and the mother to meet to discuss
the problems of both child and parent. The outcome was the per-
petuation of this arrangement for a long time with its purpose
lost and its effect negligible. Frustrated by her own lack of impact
on the school attendance, the Welfare Officer had effectively
ceased to be involved in the case. Like the boy's father in the
early years of his life, she left the scene.

The psychiatrist at the Clinic, having gleaned this information,
felt his best course of action was to consult with the social worker
already involved with the family, a common clinical approach.
Thus began a protracted, desultory, 'consultation' with the social

48

worker, in which the 'work with the family' was discussed. For
a time the school showed signs of considerable frustration at the
lack of new developments but then seemed to lose interest, leaving the two professionals still involved with the case in a relationship very like that of the boy and his mother, or the boy and his
school, which was repeated with the mother and the social worker.
There seemed to be in all the situations related to the case the
emergence of a characteristic pattern of object-relations, i.e., a
pair staying together in an unsatisfactory, non-progressive
relationship from which frustration was nevertheless excluded and
instead felt by the person whose failure to make an impact eventually led them to withdraw or depart. A configuration like this
could be discerned in a number of interpersonal contexts. It
could also be a description of an intrapsychic situation in which
freedom from frustration and its consequences was achieved by
the elimination of any real desire or expectation from the individual
who thus became the cause of discouragement of others who were
provoked by this inertia into attempting to kindle some desire for
change. Here we seem to be dealing with repetitious actions which
transfer a pattern of relationships from one situation to another
in which new participants become the vehicles for the reiterated
expression of the underlying dynamic. The repetition compulsion
may be a dynamic in the sense of being a compelling force determining events but in another sense it is essentially static. The
basic situation remains unrealized and unchanged whilst new
versions of it proliferate. The cast changes but the plot remains
the same. This is well described in the psychoanalytic literature
as occurring in the lives of individuals; here I am referring to a
similar phenomenon in the lives of families and groups.

A number of psychoanalytic concepts are implicit in this account.
One is the recurrence of a specific pattern of events and relationships. This phenomenon referred to as the Repetition Compulsion
was first described by Freud in a paper published in 1914 called
'Remembering, Repeating and Working-Through' (Freud 1914). He
linked it to the established idea of Transference, which he said
'is itself only a piece of repetition... of the forgotton past, and
not only on to the doctor but also on to all the other aspects of
the current situation... the patient yields to the compulsion to
repeat... in every other activity and relationship... at the time.'*
In the same paper he described the tendency to replication of
unconscious ideas in action rather than thought for which the
term Acting Out was subsequently adopted (Freud (a)).

My characterization of a process in the case described above
whereby frustration is denied and extruded from the relationship
of the couple and provoked in a third party can be seen as an
example of 'projective identification'. Melanie Klein (1946) coined
this term to describe a phantasy of the self or more often parts of

*I do not intend in this chapter to explore the fuller meaning
given to the concept of Transference in subsequent psychoanalytical work by Melanie Klein and others.

the self entering into the identity of another person; if this is
preceded by denial of those aspects in the subject then they are
perceived as attributes of the object of the process. Thus in
this case the third party appears to be one who wants change or
development and the couple feel no urge to transform or clarify
their situation. The situation could be described as an omnipotent
unconscious phantasy that those aspects of themselves which
would experience such desire, and its associated frustration and
helplessness can be split off and located in someone else. However,
there is more to it as the behaviour and experience of others is
actually influenced by the process. Wilfred Bion (1974) commented
on this and together with other analysts who followed Melanie
Klein has enlarged the use of the term to include the effect on the
recipient of such 'projections'.

I am not sure [he says] from the practice of analysis that it is
only an omnipotent phantasy; that is, something that the patient
cannot in fact do.... I have felt and some of my colleagues likewise that when the patient appears to be engaged on a projective identification it can make me feel persecuted, as if the
patient can, in fact, split off certain nasty feelings and shove
them into me so that I actually have feelings of persecution or
anxiety (p.105).

This would then link the notion of projective identification with
that of 'countertransference', an older term defined as 'the
analyst's unconscious reactions to the individual analysand –
especially to the analysand's own transference' (Laplanche and
J.B. Pontalis 1973). As these two authors point out, some take
the countertransference to be that in the analyst's personality
which is liable to affect treatment, others to that brought about
by the transference of the analysand. Though this is an important
distinction (implying as it does that the analyst has a special
responsibility for the former) in practice, in the consulting room
the two may not be separable since the one plays on the other.
As Lagache (1964) points out, the transference and countertransference are reciprocal parts of a whole, involving both of the
people present.

One way that the analyst may remain unaware of his countertransference is that he, like the patient, may act it out, instead
of experiencing the psychic situation. A good deal has been written
about the way an analyst may increase his understanding of his
patient by scrutiny of his own irrational feelings and impulses in
the analysis. Rosenfeld (1965a), like Bion, has emphasized that
projective identification may be a form of unconscious communication from the patient. It may be, however, that it is in his
behaviour with the patient, including his choice of interpretation,
wording, tone, timing, etc., that the evoked 'countertransference'
may be evident, as a re-enactment of an unconscious object relationship in the analysis. Betty Joseph has drawn attention to
this, emphasizing that 'the more the patient is using primarily
primitive mechanisms and defences against anxiety, the more the
analyst is... used by the patient unconsciously and the more the

analysis is a scene for action rather than understanding'
(Joseph 1978).

It is a recurrent discovery that processes described as occurring in the microscopic world of psychoanalysis have relevance
outside it. I believe this to be the case with the concepts just
described: Freud in first describing Repetition Compulsion said,
'The patient yields to the compulsion to repeat - in every other
activity and relationship... at the time' (Freud, op.cit., p.150).

I would like to paraphrase this in relation to the ideas expressed
above and say that the more primitive mechanisms and defences
against anxiety are being used the more is every professional contact likely to become a scene for action and for the professional
to yield to the compulsion to repeat or re-enact an unconscious
situation. The term countertransference is commonly used to
describe the feelings the analyst becomes aware of, or what he
sees to be his emotionally determined expectations and apprehen-
sions in contact with his patient. I would like therefore to use
the words Complementary Acting Out to denote the counterpart
to countertransference in deeds rather than words; that is, the
enactment by the analyst of a reciprocal object relationship to
that acted out by his patient. By extension I propose to use this
term to describe unconsciously determined action (or inaction),
by professionals when this is evoked by their involvement in
certain cases.

I have been impressed by the way this may continue beyond the
immediate contact with the family and seem to infect the relationships of colleagues or different agencies. In some cases the pattern of response of education departments, schools, social services
or doctors takes on uncannily the shape of the family; quarrels
are pursued between workers who seem as incompatible in their
views as are the parents; highhanded intervention by senior
colleagues echoes the domination of a family by the intrusions of
an opinionated grandparent. In another case a succession of professional agencies not only failed to accept responsibility but
uncharacteristically failed to communicate with each other or
acknowledge other workers' existence, thus echoing the family
pattern of a child who had been at different times abandoned by
both his parents, long since separated, who related to him
independently without acknowledging each other's existence.

Such examples have become familiar in examining the circumstances of situations referred to the Tavistock Clinic for help
when there is disagreement, stalemate, or what are felt to be
intransigent problems. The sphere of action, however, need not
be so obviously related to emotional difficulty or disturbed
behaviour. The nature of Complementary Action may only become
evident when a particular configuration is seen to recur in varied
forms. The formulation of this may give a meaning which the
separate acts, by their apparent diversity, have obscured. Thus,
in the example I am about to quote, the way I choose to present
the facts already represents my view of the case, i.e., as a
coherent attempt to dispose of a psychological difficulty through a

particular kind of action. It is clear that the events were perceived at the time as a series of situations unrelated to each other
and demanding action in their own right. It is therefore evident
that my view may be mistaken and might appear arbitrary or
fanciful. As a hypothesis it can only gain strength if it has pre-
dictive value.

The case concerned a girl, her family and a hospital. It was
characterized by a preoccupation with removing some presence
felt to be dangerous to the girl. She was recently sexually mature.
One organ under suspicion was removed lest it contain the malignancy which had previously killed her grandmother. A second
organ, known to be diseased in her mother, was suspected of
causing the girl's symptoms and was excised only to be found quite
healthy. The girl attempted to remove life itself by suicide. The
hypothesis, that an unconscious phantasy was operative, that
something malignant and female must be got rid of, seemed plaus-
ible. If this hypothesis was correct this imperative, though unconscious, belief influenced the decisions and behaviour of the girl,
her parents and a number of professional advisers at different
times. One way of expressing this underlying phantasy would be
to say that there was a powerful anxiety that something catastrophic would follow from the development of a mature, female, sexual
presence (or in the psychoanalytic sense the emergence of a
dangerous, female, 'bad' object). In this family, you might say,
there was a shared phantasy that there was something threatening
about feminity; that women contained the seeds of destruction or
malignancy. A family history of women of two earlier generations
spending time in mental hospitals lent credibility to this version
when it emerged a little later.

The working hypothesis gained support, however, by subsequent developments. Further mystifying symptoms provoked a
superficially different but basically similar response within the
hospital staff. The malignancy was now located not in an organ
or tissue but in the girl's relationship with her mother; specifically
it was thought that the food produced by mother provoked the
disease. The solution was again removal, this time of the girl from
home, into care: I would emphasize here that this apparently new
initiative, which in a psychodynamic sense is so repetitious, came
from the professional staff as their response to the situation with
which they were in contact. If they were steered by unconscious
forces, these forces were operating in them, called forth as it
were by their experience with this family.

The quality of this story provoked the feeling that these events
belong in a dream. In a sense that may be true. To return to
Freud's notion of Acting Out - he says, 'The patient does not
remember anything... but acts it out. He reproduces it, not as a
memory but as an action' (ibid., p.150). We can substitute for
memory in this definition all other forms of mental activity. Hence
action seems not simply a substitute for memory but for 'realization'. If we follow Bion (1970) in seeing the endeavour to contain
emergent states within the 'mental sphere' as a constant struggle

for individuals and groups, the case can be seen as a failure of 'psychic containment'. First, within the girl whose phantasies were not expressed in thoughts, or dreams, but in the development of hypochondriasis and the location of a feared disorder in a body organ. Second, within the family whose anxieties were not expressed in ideas but enacted in the dramas which spilled over into the hospital. Finally in the professionals drawn into the case who took atypical drastic steps rapidly more than once and were stirred into repetitive action rather than reflection, even though very concerned about the case.

Bion's view (1967) is that thinking is a development forced on the psyche by the pressure of thoughts and that a breakdown in the apparatus for thinking or dealing with thoughts may lead to a psychopathological development. He suggests 'that what should be a thought becomes a thing in itself, fit only for evacuation.' We might add, 'and dramatization'. He links this capacity for thinking to the dominance of Freud's 'reality principle' and its failure as a regression to the pleasure principle. This, in turn, hinges on the achievement of what Melanie Klein (1975) called the 'Depressive Position'. As Hanna Segal suggests (1973, p.76), 'in the depressive position then, the whole climate of thought changes... capacities for linking and abstraction develop.' She points out that 'psychic reality is experience and differentiated from external reality, the symbol is differentiated from the object... in contrast with symbolic equation in which the symbol is equated with the original object giving rise to concrete thinking.' I believe that this latter state, characteristic of the paranoid-schizoid position, is linked to a greater tendency to action rather than thought· a more wholesale 'acting out' as Rosenfeld describes (1965a) and a greater tendency to evoke action in others.

The implication is that families whose mode of mental operations are characteristic of the *'paranoid-schizoid'* position (Klein 1975) rather than the depressive position are not only unlikely to see themselves as the agents of their own disturbances but are likely to evoke unconsciously determined action in those around them. The process of projection or projective identification within the family leading to the perception of one member as the source of difficulties is familiar as the scapegoat phenomenon and may lead to referral of this person. In many other cases, however, the principal manifestations occur around the family rather than in it. The members of a family whose relationships are experienced in the main in the paranoid-schizoid position as opposed to the depressive position, are likely to feel persecuted rather than guilty; ill rather than worried; enmity rather than conflict; desperation rather than sadness. They are liable to be triumphant or if not to feel squashed and to see others as either allies or opponents. Their tendency to take flight (e.g., by moving, changing partner, changing schools, etc.) is linked to their belief that psychic experience can be split off and left behind: by the same token there is a sense of being hunted and a fear of being cornered. For people with these characteristics a place like

a clinic where problems are focused on seems threatening and
even the collation of information is felt to be unwelcome. It is not
surprising therefore that they shun clinics; avoid meeting
teachers and become the chronically unsatisfactory cases of social
services if, as is by no means always the case, they are in the
lower-social classes. If the family are amongst the more affluent or
educated groups the dramatis personae tend to be different but
the kind of happenings are similar. The professionals then may be
solicitors, private medical advisers; family friends or relatives;
colleagues or partners at work; divorce courts; Members of
Parliament and so on. The risk of them becoming unknowingly
involved in an enactment is as great with even less likelihood of it
being recognized.

It is the recognition of these provocative or paralysing effects
in such cases which at least gives pause for reflection. This often
produces the painful discovery of the limitations of help or the
constraints involved in the situation. In turn it may lead to the
possibility of taking uncomfortable but necessary steps or accepting small, significant changes rather than cherishing unrealized
hopes for a transformation. The thesis which is argued here is
that 'realization', and change as a consequence of 'realization',
rather than change as an alternative to 'realization' may prevent
patterns which cross not only individual but generational
boundaries.

THEORETICAL DISCUSSION

The clinical phenomenon described in this chapter is of the repro-
duction amongst professional workers and agencies of a pattern
of 'object-relationships' which resemble those of some families with
which they have contact. The repetitious pattern or event may
take place between family members; family members and professionals; professionals and professionals; professionals and
social agencies.

It is argued in the chapter that the phenomenon of Repetition
Compulsion first described by Freud (1918) may be analogous to
this and that an essential element in this concept is replacement
of recollection (or any form of mental realization) by a blindly
repeated pattern of events. In the instances referred to, the
events transcend the individual's and his family's lives and rever-
berate amongst those associated with them. It is suggested that
some of the processes grouped under the concept of Projective
Identification, first used by Melanie Klein, may underlie the
phenomenon. Since it appears to occur even where there is no
direct contact (as may be observed in groups who simply discuss
these cases) the mode of operation would seem to be by identification and replication, mobilized by something psychic analogous
to 'resonance'. That is to compare it to the physical phenomenon
by which vibrations in one object can induce sympathetic vibrations in another at a distance, e.g., musical instruments. This

would seem to be a feasible metaphor if the assumption was made
that certain basic internal object relationships are ubiquitous.
Freud speculated in 'The Wolf Man' (Freud - 'From the History of
an Infantile Neurosis') that a knowledge of the 'primal scene'
might be phylogenetic, thus implying that a rudimentary form of
the oedipus complex would be innate. It is implicit in Melanie
Klein's writings that some basic phantasies are innate concerning
good and bad objects for example; and the 'primal scene'. Roger
Money-Kyrle with his description of 'imageless expectations' and
Wilfred Bion with his notion of 'innate preconceptions' make this
explicit.

In the passage of Freud's referred to above where he considers
the possibility of 'instinctive knowledge' as an hereditary endow-
ment, he uses the German word 'instinktiv' where the word he
usually used which is translated into the English as 'instinctual'
is 'triebhaft' which is open to the substitution of 'drive'. This is
of some significance in view of the later development of the concept of unconscious phantasy, particularly in Kleinian writing.
Susan Isaacs, in her definitive paper, 'The Nature and Function
of Phantasy', considers unconscious phantasy as the mental
expression of instincts; all impulses, all feelings, all modes of
defence are experienced in phantasy (1952, p.83).

Authors influenced by Melanie Klein, such as Bion, Jaques and
Menzies have described how groups may share such phantasies and
collectively react to them. In his paper on 'Social Systems as a
Defence against Persecutory and Depressive Anxiety' (1955),
Jaques describes institutions as having beneath a manifest structure and function an underlying 'unconscious function'. He sees
this as the maintenance of shared beliefs and activities which
collectively defend against basic anxieties. He describes this as
based on shared projections, i.e., 'when external objects are
shared with others but used for common purposes of projection,
phantasy social relationships may be established through projective identification with a common object... further elaborated by
introjection' (p.482).

Thus in the first example in this chapter the fundamental
anxieties associated with the oedipus complex would be mobilized
in the phantasies of those in contact with the case. Then the
defensive configuration mobilized of a sterile couple and a defeated
third party, enacted unwittingly. Whilst repetition prevailed and
and unwitting re-enactment continued, realization could be avoided,
constancy maintained and conflict averted. In the second case
described, change is threatening the family in the form of the
emergence of a sexually mature young woman and provoking
basic anxieties about such an object or past object. 'Malignancy'
is suspected and the 'malign object' sought in various anatomical
organs before being perceived by the professional group as the
mother herself. Here the shared phantasy of a dangerous, dis-
ordered, female object was collectively defended against by action
designed for removal.

Events involving families, and the elements of society in contact

with them, in such cases as I have described are thought about
by many family therapists in terms derived from 'General Systems
Theory', 'Cybernetics', and Information Theory. General Systems
Theory (GST) was founded as a general science of organization
and wholeness by Ludwig von Bertalanffy in 1940; it has a great
deal in common with Cybernetics, a subject which dates from 1942
and was named in 1947 by Wiener and Rosenbleuth to describe
the science of control and communication in the animal and
machine; it emphasized particularly that the laws governing control are universal and do not depend on the classical dichotomy
between organic and inorganic systems. This is expressed in GST
in the concept of 'structural isomorphism' or with an assumption
of 'dynamic equilibrium' (Schanck 1954); that is the maintenance
of an overall 'steady state' by any fluctuation in sub-elements
being compensated so the system remains in total balance. Thus
'a systems approach is an approach to the study of physical and
social systems which enables complex and dynamic situations to
be understood in broad outline' (Ackoff and Emery 1972). Systems
may have recognizable subsystems and the improvement of one of
these to the detriment of the system as a whole is described as
'sub-optimization', hence the warnings from some family therapists
about treating individuals; and from some sociologists about treating particular families rather than society. The ascending order
of systems inside larger systems like 'Chinese boxes' are often
referred to as 'hierarchies' and the rules governing patterns of
behaviour which is reproduced at different organizational levels
are called 'recursive'. This is a term borrowed from linguistics to
describe language rules which can be applied an indefinite
number of times in generating sentences. The phenomena which I
have referred to could perhaps be described as 'recursive' in
this sense. It is not my intention to describe the application of
these theories to family therapy in this chapter or to place the
concepts which I am endeavouring to describe in relation to a
'systems approach' to families. There is, however, one fundamental question raised by the notion of 'dynamic equilibrium'
whether applied to individuals or families which has a place in
psychoanalytic theory and I would like to pursue that as it
influences the way the social system (whether it be a family or an
institution) is perceived.

This notion of 'dynamic equilibrium' is enshrined in a very
influential 'systems approach' to sociology in the work of Talcott
Parsons in the 1950s and the related school of 'structural-
functionalism'. This is a mode of theorizing in which particular
features of social structures are explained in terms of their contribution in maintaining a self-equilibrating system as a viable
entity. I find it of particular interest that sociological critics of
this approach object to it on three particular grounds: one, that
it is tautologous; two, that it explains stability and not change;
and three, that it ignores essential conflict. Critics of other
schools who particularly make this last point are known as 'Conflict
Theorists' and may in general be either 'pluralist' or 'Marxist'

sociologists who regard conflict as inherent in society.

It is of interest to a psychoanalyst, I think, because it covers similar ground to that which Freud explored in the 1920s; in particular in 'Beyond the Pleasure Principle' (Freud 1920) and 'Civilization and its Discontents' (Freud 1930). In these two books he re-examines his earlier ideas about the basic forces underlying man's behaviour and social relationships. He had previously followed the idea that the basic determinant was the 'pleasure principle' - this he derived from Fechner's 'constancy principle' or 'tendency towards stability'. Activity was therefore directed to restoring an earlier state of things. It looked like movement but sought quietude: the dominance of the pleasure principle was opposed, he had suggested, by the reality principle. He realized therefore that if this - which we could perfectly describe as 'dynamic equilibrium' - was the only force the 'elementary living entity would from its very beginning have no wish to change; if conditions remained the same it would do no more than constantly repeat the same course of life.' He linked, therefore, the 'compulsion to repeat' in the behaviour and experience of people with this tendency which he described as 'the inertia inherent in organic life'.

> The dominating tendency of mental life... is the effort to reduce, to keep constant or to remove internal tension due to stimuli - a tendency which finds expression in the pleasure principle.

This he named the 'death instinct' since he saw its ultimate goal as returning in ways 'immanent in the organism itself' to inorganic existence. He was careful to point out that self preservation and mastery were component instincts whose function it was to ward off any other possible ways to death and were themselves manifestations of this status quo seeking instinct. There was only one inherent source of opposition which existed because it was a living system and that was the urge to reproduce. The disturber of the peace therefore in the case of the human being was Eros, his capacity for object love, which in the individual stood in opposition to his narcissism. As Freud put it, object instincts were in opposition to ego instincts.

In 'Civilization and its Discontents' he went further, more clearly equating the life instincts with the disturbers of the peace within the individual and the death instincts with a 'primary mutual hostility of human beings' which he saw as perpetually threatening civilized society with disintegration. The satisfaction, he thought, which derived from the exercise of this destructive urge lay in the fulfilment of the ego's old wish for omnipotence; aim inhibited, i.e., 'moderated and tamed', he saw its satisfaction lay in control over nature.

Freud, therefore, came to see conflict as inevitable and expressed in ambivalence towards love objects who were both the source of desire and dissatisfaction; the origins of hope and the end of omnipotence. Melanie Klein later was to describe in the 'depressive position' the attempts of the individual to resolve this basic ambivalence to the primary object and its consequences. An object relations theory which incorporates this basic conflict and its attendant persecutory and depressive anxieties sees social conflict as inevitable and social institutions as attempting to contain them.

As Freud described it, the compulsion to repeat unthinkingly was an expression of that tendency to constancy, to inertia, which he thought innate. The counter tendency - to experience, to seek, to relate - he associated with the life instincts and the urge to change. We could argue therefore that the struggle to 'realize' rather than 'repeat' takes place within this basic conflict and that an element of discomfort, strain or anxiety is inevitable in the process. When professional workers therefore are called upon to resist unconscious collusion in order to become aware of the existence of an underlying dynamic configuration, they will find themselves 'going against the grain' of their own emotional inclinations.

5 WORKING WITH THE
DYNAMICS OF THE SESSION

Sally Box

'A lot of people come to philosophy wanting to be told how to
live - or wanting to be given an explanation of the world,
and with it an explanation of life - but it seems to me that to
have at least the former desire is to want to abnegate personal
responsibility. One shouldn't want to be told how to live... And
therefore one shouldn't come to philosophy looking for definitive
answers. It's an entirely different thing to seek clarification of
one's life, or clarification of the issues involved in particular problems which confront one, so that one can more effectively take
responsibility for oneself and make decisions with a fuller, clearer
understanding of what is at stake.'

This comment was made by the philosopher, Bryan Magee, in an
impressive series of television conversations called 'Men of Ideas'
(1978). It has helped to highlight for me an important aspect of
the approach to family therapy that is the subject of this book,
and that may differentiate it from many others.
I would like to explore here some of the technical implications
of this way of thinking as it relates to working with the families
who come asking for help. How do we deal with their wish 'to
be told how to live' and their subsequent bewilderment at the lack
of advice and suggestions that we offer? For even when the conscious wish in coming to the clinic is to 'seek clarification of
the issues involved' they may find themselves immersed in the
very opposite of the rational processes anticipated. It is one of the
most difficult but inescapable realizations emerging, especially
from psychoanalysis, that such issues are not necessarily susceptible to meaningful clarification on a purely rational basis.
Problems based on unconscious, long-established emotional conflicts require a shift of emotional stance if there is really to be a
fuller, clearer understanding. Moreover, the question for us has
been what sort of method can provide the opportunity for such
a shift to take place. Is it possible for these unconscious conflicts
to surface and be enacted in such a way that they can be better
understood and perhaps experienced differently in the light of
a new response? It is the issues involved in providing such a
method, suitable in the context of family work, that constitutes
the main theme of this chapter; and with the help of material from
two rather different sorts of families, I would like to focus

particularly on the way that the problems of handling the implicit
anxieties are highlighted at the critical times of beginnings and
breaks.

THE METHOD

If we accept that a major aspect of the therapeutic task is to
promote the chances for genuine choices to increase then the
methodological task becomes one of engaging with the compulsive
qualities, patterns and reactions, that constantly qualify or impede
those possibilities. It becomes one of providing a space in which
the obstacles to independent thought can emerge in the interaction
of the session and can be met anew.

As I see it, it is possible to think of the session as such a space
in which a kind of microcosm of one patient family's world can
exist and in which they can experience, in relation to each other
and to us, some of the crucial conflicts that concern them; that is,
the family can use the boundaries that we provide for the members
to demonstrate their particular patterns and preoccupations through
the way they are with us; and we, as therapists, may draw upon
our experiences with them in the sessions to help us understand
these patterns and to interpret the underlying conflicts to which
they relate.

In this sense, it is a setting which provides for significant
internal dramas to be re-lived here, with the therapists not taking
a history or reconstructing a picture of the early lives of the
patient, but trying to create a situation in which the history is
recalled spontaneously when the living internal relationships
associated with it are experienced in the present.

The reader may understand that behind this lies a particular
view of therapeutic interaction: such that if the therapist can
in this way be available for the powerful feelings invoked and can
help to articulate the internal dramas that have the family in their
grip and that interfere with their capacity to move freely in their
lives, it may be possible for feelings previously unmanageable
and extruded to find some means of expression and some possibility of being re-owned. There is a chance that whatever the
immediate reaction, the overall experience will be one of relief
and a little step towards integration of each one's world, a living,
learning experience as it were, with the therapists and the
session serving as container – or, in other words, as a medium for
working on unmanageable aspects and a mediator of family projections. The implication is, of course, that the increased scope
implied in such integration carries with it the capacity to own
aspects of the self hitherto split off and disowned, although the
awareness of limitations and conflicts which this involves may at
times seem a high price to pay for the enrichment it enables.
Those who are familiar with it will recognize in the description of
this process the debt it owes to Dr Bion's concept of 'container/
contained' (1962a, 67, 70).

Briefly, in terms of the treatment situation, the notion of

containment refers to the way the impact of an experience - one's
own or another's - can be registered and dwelt upon sufficiently
for it to take some shape in the mind and be put in words which
can help the patient to manage it.

In 'A Theory of Thinking' (1962b), Bion suggests as a model, the
idea of the mother or her breast, as the container for the infant's
intolerable feelings:

If the infant feels it is dying, it can rouse fears that it is dying in the mother. A well-balanced mother can accept these and
respond therapeutically; that is to say, in a manner that makes
the infant feel it is receiving its personality back again but in
a form that it can tolerate - the fears are manageable by the
infant personality. If the mother cannot tolerate these projections the infant is reduced to continued projective identification
carried out with increasing force and frequency (1967, p.114).

During their sojourn in the good breast they are felt to have
been modified in such a way that the object that is reintro-
jected has become tolerable for the infant psyche (1962, p.90).

Put in these terms, the issue would be what kind of containment
or container is available for the painful, conflictual or other
'undigested' feelings and what happens to the family member or
therapist who is the repository for them. The difference between a
mother who can bear and somehow 'metabolize' her baby's fear
and pain, and one who, for example, is herself terrified of them,
is a crucial element in the child's development and in his own
subsequent capacity to bear and digest such feelings for himself.
Similarly, perhaps, for the patient family.

What do these principles mean in practice? How are they observed
in action and what is the process of transformation implicit in the
idea of the therapist as the prime object for projections?

TECHNICAL ISSUES RELATED TO THE EARLY MEETINGS

It must be said that in many of the families that we see, no one
has come acknowledging a wish for help for themselves as an
individual and there is great uncertainty as to whether they dare
engage in the kind of exploration together that is on offer. Many,
as in the first case to be discussed, are actually coming more or
less explicitly because of difficulties in living together or because
a delicate and hard-won balance in the family is collapsing. A
death in the family or the onset of adolescence is often enough to
topple it, but, in practice, it may seem to be the referral itself
or the experience of coming to the Clinic that is felt to represent
the final tip of the scales: the extremely precarious tolerance of
anxiety in these families tends to lead to its being converted
immediately into action or short-circuited altogether, so that all,
including the therapists, may feel extremely inhibited about
voicing uncomfortable perceptions for fear of provoking impulsive
or violent reactions and destroying the possibility of treatment

before it has begun.

It is not surprising then that the initial meeting is filled with anxiety - for therapists as well as patients. The very virtues of the setting and of a reflective, rather than a directive stance seems also to present its greatest problems and make the most exacting demands on the worker: to reflect on, rather than react to, is a hard transition to make at the best of times for therapist as well as family. In my experience it is a major task in itself to recognize the pressures to enact the family's projections and the resulting tendency to start behaving like a stage director, or a judge or some other significant figure from their inner world - especially if it finds a corresponding figure in our own. (The theoretical aspects of this process are discussed in the previous chapter.)

In practice, the problem is not only to recognize when and how this is happening and what is the particular constellation of which one finds oneself a part, but then to recover sufficient space in one's mind, to discover a way of formulating the experience for the family so as to provide them also with a corresponding sense of space.

Particular problems arise from the fact that it is often in the most troubled families that the dynamics are most naked, and it may be easy for a therapist to observe a pattern in the family and then voice it to them in the hope that they will be able to learn from it and change accordingly. But many patients, because of their great emotional fragility, have developed defences so pervasive that they are not able to use an observation put to them in this way. As therapists we often find ourselves, with these sorts of families, caught between being persecutors driving them away, on the one hand, or in some comfortable collusion, that fails really to engage with the ill or problematic part of them, on the other. This is a major reason for the value set upon the discipline of working in the transference, where the dynamic patterns are taken as they occur in the relationship to the therapist. Contributions from psychoanalytic work with psychotic and borderline individual patients have spoken very precisely to both aspects of this dilemma and have helped towards understanding and responding to the projections involved in ways that I have found most relevant to our work with families. See for instance papers by Rosenfeld, and Steiner on Borderline Patients (1977 and 1979). In relation to excessive feelings of persecution they highlight, for instance, the importance of the therapist(s) being prepared to experience themselves and be experienced as the 'bad' object or to represent some unwanted aspect of the self which the patient himself cannot as yet entertain. So in families, while it is clearly a crucial part of the therapist's work to identify what he may be 'carrying' for the patients, it may be necessary for him to be identified himself with it first and let himself be the focus for its examination, if he is not simply going to persecute the patient and drive him away. The efforts to struggle with these issues may be discernible in our interaction with the families to be described.

BEGINNING WORK WITH THE DUN FAMILY

In the Dun family, the fear of dependency and the taboo on neediness, or feelings otherwise considered childish, did not exclude concern and sympathy between the members but made it very difficult for them to be at all tolerant of their own pain or available in practice for that of each other. This family has consisted of five members. The father, a lawyer, had recently died, leaving an older son, no longer at home, and two teenage daughters, Jane and Patricia, who lived at home with their mother. It was the younger of these two girls who was the referred patient though her family had agreed to come together with her, after a number of previously unsuccessful attempts at individual treatment. In fact, 'unsuccessful' was the operative word for Patricia. She felt unable to work and enjoy life - unable to get out of bed much of the time - and a hopeless failure compared to her sister who was viewed as active, happy and successful, and only later revealed her own worries about herself in terms of 'drugging' and, as she herself put it, 'running away' from all depressing things.

The therapists were a man and a woman who planned to see the family once a week. (It may be worth adding that the time for beginnings and ends of sessions, as well as the consistent arrangement of the room is adhered to as precisely as possible by the therapists and represents the physical boundaries of the setting within which other variables can then be more clearly identified and observed.)

The family members were intelligent and articulate and could tell us a great deal about themselves. So it was not too difficult to gain a vivid picture of them as a group and of the polarization and fights between the two girls, with mother in the middle, herself frustrated and hurt at their rejection of the meals she provided for them but seeing it as her job to be brave and keep her spirits up, even if, as it emerged, she had to turn to the spirits in the bottle to do so.

But besides the more obvious picture the family conveyed with their words, our interest as therapists was to observe and experience the ways in which such a picture might get enacted. This enabled us to understand some of the very painful aspects of the family's relationship together which had crystallized since Mr Dun's death; and what patterns they had developed to deal with them. As with other families, the enactment sometimes came before the words, sometimes afterwards. But always the problem was to engage with the feelings entailed. For instance, it was from their difficulty in coming all together to the session that we experienced the intensity of the struggle in living together at home. In an early session, before a regular time had been settled, the older sister, Jane, had not appeared, and while the other children blamed mother for this, it seemed that her absence served a purpose for them all. When we spoke of the difficulty for them of coming here together, especially in view of the rivalry they had reported, we not only heard in a more immediate way about

the fights, but it actually emerged that Jane had been given the
wrong time for the session, not by her mother as Patricia had
suggested, but by Patricia herself: Right at the end of the hour,
she acknowledged in an almost inaudible whisper that it was she
who had told her sister the wrong time!

In terms of the family dynamics, one might almost depict the
two girls as representing opposite sides of a manic-depressive
coin, one virtually immobilized by depression, the other extremely
active, excitable and physically taking flight - both from home and
from the sessions. The session itself at times took on an atmosphere of drama and excitement in stark contrast to the frustrated
and difficult air it often assumed when the therapists attempted
to get more in touch with avoided feelings. The work was to stay
with those feelings without being ourselves immobilized by them.
In this way, the meaning of the defensive behaviour might be able
to make itself known. It soon emerged that the younger members
of the family were extremely worried about their mother's unhappiness and the drinking associated with it. In fact, Patricia's
depression seemed very much to reflect that of her mother and we
began to be powerfully aware of the kind of despair that lay
behind the fights and the drinking. Obviously, it is not for nothing that such despair is dealt with in this way and we soon got
a very clear idea of Mrs Dun's hatred of those feelings because of
her way of reacting in relation to them with us. She was able to
give us a fluent, though detached account of her husband's illness
and death, of how this had upset the balance between the girls,
and led to the increasing divergence between them which culminated in extreme depression, but when we felt the impact of this
and recognized aloud how sad and unhappy they might all be
feeling, trying to tune into it with them, mother's reaction was
most marked. First she could not hear; then when our words
were repeated, she looked absolutely blank, uncomprehending;
she pushed the therapists right away and was quite contemptuous,
starting shortly afterwards to talk about a boring neighbour of
hers and his boring girlfriend. She told us that the one time the
family could be at peace and have a quiet evening together was
when there were outsiders like that whom they could unite about.
It seemed the boring couple quite clearly stood for the boring
therapists, and in terms of countertransference feelings, one
actually did feel a bore and very crass and unstylish to be talking
in such an unaffected or unscintillating way about sad or unhappy
feelings. Perhaps, we suggested, they were feeling they might at
least have a quiet evening together this evening, that we were
like the neighbour and his boring girlfriend, and, if nothing else,
we might serve the purpose of the outsiders they could unite
against.

More important to recognize, however, was the way that it was
really the depression that was being termed boring and then
located immediately outside - in the neighbour/therapist couple.
It seemed that we were felt not only to represent the unwanted
feelings called 'boring' but also to be boring in the sense of push-

ing back to the family the sad feelings that were seen as so contemptible to Mrs Dun and had usually to be rationalized or drowned in drink.

I think this illustrates the kind of unconscious processes of projection involved when unwanted feelings find a refuge elsewhere than in their owner's mind. But it also serves to highlight the importance of the therapists' attention to the distinction between the family's readiness to talk about their unhappy experiences on the one hand, and their readiness really to get in touch with the feelings of sadness and grief associated with them on the other.

Betty Joseph, in a particularly useful paper on 'The Patient who is Difficult to Reach' (1975), has examined the problem of getting into what looks like a therapeutic alliance, which is actually inimical to a therapeutic alliance because it is with a 'pseudo-adult' part of the patient:

> The patient talks in an adult way, but relates to the analyst only as an equal, or a near-equal disciple. Sometimes he relates more as a slightly superior ally who tries to help the analyst in his work, with suggestions or minor corrections or references to personal history. If one observes carefully one begins to feel that one is talking to this ally about a patient - but never talking to the patient. The 'patient' part of the patient seems to remain split off and it is this part which seems more immediately to need help, to be more infant-like, more dependent and vulnerable. One can talk about this part but the problem is to reach it. I believe that in some of our analyses, which appear repetitive and interminable, we have to examine whether we are not being drawn into colluding with the pseudoadult or pseudo-cooperative part of the patient.

I think this process is often very clear in families and Miss Joseph's emphasis on the patient's method of communication rather than simply on the content, is of course correspondingly relevant. In this case, it alerted us again to our family's extreme sensitivity and proud defence against their vulnerability.

The question for the sessions was: could they bear to get in touch with such feelings here and stay with them? Moreover, could the therapist help the process by being available as a temporary refuge for the hatred and contempt stirred up in the process - a place where the presence and management of such feelings could be observed and possibly learnt from, at a little distance, so to speak.

Perhaps some further examples will serve to clarify. An important theme, for instance, was that of feeding - both in terms of what the family were telling us about themselves and the way they were behaving with us. In the lengthy discussion about why the children insisted on making their own meals, Mrs Dun spoke of having to pull the food out of the deep freezer. It reflected the sense we had already of there being insufficient ready nourishment to go around. It seemed that all of them felt in desperate need of comfort and not able to bear each other's distress. We saw mother, for instance, dismiss with instant words of advice and

reassurance her daughters' tentative efforts to convey their
difficulties and we felt very strongly the shared anxiety that we,
like them, would be unable properly to register their distress as
a family and would misunderstand or misinterpret their communication to us. We perceived what it was like to be trying to communicate with such an object, one that was felt to be so thick and
dense.

At the same time we could experience the despair and helplessness of being like that and, of mother especially, at being found
wanting and unable to meet the hungry demands. What food or
what help was offered never seemed to be quite right. We were
grumbled and griped at for the kinds of interpretations that we
made, lectured at and reasoned with about not being more social
and more like human beings with them, and while Mrs Dun talked
of her own depression when she had no one to feed, she showed
us very clearly what it was like to have our interpretative food
rejected and spat out.

But the family did make it possible to work with this; and when
we interpreted that we, as therapists, were being given an idea
of what it was like to have one's offers rejected in this way,
Mrs Dun, with the children's encouragement, followed by spontaneously beginning to recall her own experience as a mother and the
awful time she had had feeding both children as babies. It seemed
to be the direct response to the emergence and identification of
such feelings in the session, and in relation to the therapists. It
is an example, perhaps, of the process referred to earlier, in
which the space provided can enable the obstacles to independent
thought to emerge in the interaction of the session and be engaged
with in the transference to the therapist.

Taking the experience from the other side of the relationship
in this same sort of interaction, the therapists could take up the
fear that the point would be missed and the connection to the
family need not be made. The pervasive image of an impermeable
object or unsatisfactory relationship was terribly distressing for
all concerned, but especially for Mrs Dun who would get into the
most awful kind of impasse with one or other of the therapists.
But again, when I suggested on one occasion, that the current
dissatisfaction was with me, as the dense one who misses the
point, Mrs Dun came back the next week saying that she thought
some of the difficulty in the relationship with her husband was
because she had not properly listened to him and had always had
an answer for everything he tried to say to her. In fact, rather
movingly, she seemed to have registered how she herself could
behave in this unreceptive way. It was an example of the very
sort of behaviour that they kept accusing us of and that we had
interpreted the week before, as if the possibility of the therapist
owning such attributes and acknowledging them could render
them much less insufferable and potentially overwhelming.

But such moments of linking are not always so easy to observe
and often continue to be interspersed with periods of intense
frustration for everyone. In this case, there were times when the

girls were anxious that their mother would want to abort absolutely the contact with us, instead of coming to an agreement to
make a commitment to therapy as they increasingly seemed to
wish. In the second session, for example (a week after they
started) there was a reference to a row between Patricia and her
mother the evening before; it was about abortion and the family
got quite worked up as they talked about the value, or non-value
of human life and babies, of a week-old baby, in fact, compared
to a plant; for it seemed to Patricia that Mrs Dun would be prepared to kill a week-old baby in the same way as she would be
prepared to chop off a plant or cut a flower. The question seemed
to be whether this week-old interaction between us could produce
something new or was it to be aborted before it could develop
and could we really bear the struggle to take care of such a baby
and all the mess and the pain and the difficulties involved in that.
The interpretation of this led Patricia to say that she knew it was
silly but that when we talked earlier about their skirting around
things, she had felt, 'Oh dear, if we go on doing that, they will
decide not to see us.' This enabled us to discuss thoughts about
starting in therapy and to agree upon the practical arrangements
for this.

In such a way the family show us the fears and hopes they have
in relation to the possibility of this new undertaking; and we can
try to recognize and voice them as part of the process involved in
their choosing whether to engage in it or no. The members of
this family were clearly painfully aware of the conflicts in their
relationships with each other and, fight it though they often did,
they were evidently interested and able to grasp the meaning of
the interactions at an emotional as well as intellectual level in a
way they could use.

In some families, however, it may seem well-nigh impossible to
get in touch with the meaning to the family as a whole of the
presented problem and with the fears and phantasies that underlie
it; or to know if anything at all is being achieved. The material
on which I am drawing next is from a family in which there is
again polarization between the parts, but this time one which is
more value-laden and absolute as well as being accompanied by a
striking lack of space for entertaining the conflicts implicit in
bringing the two parts together. It may be interesting for the
reader to consider the differences between the two families and to
identify the kind of criteria that are relevant for evaluating their
functioning from a dynamic point of view.

I will describe some interactions from early sessions before
going on to try and look at the processes being discussed here in
the light of the effect of changes and breaks in the treatment.

THE O'BRIEN FAMILY

This was a family of seven, referred because of the behaviour of
the two oldest children. Father was a semi-skilled labourer who

had been absent from home a great deal. An illness of the mother's
had necessitated these two boys, David and Martin, being placed
in care when small. The family had recently become reunited and
stabilized amidst great hopes of a new beginning. But the main
complaint, that of bedwetting, was one in a long list of items
about the boys: they were presented as dirty, lazy and in every
way intractable; besides Martin's bedwetting there were hints of
stealing. Mrs O'Brien was declaring herself in despair.

The three little girls, born after the mother's illness, seemed
absolutely the opposite of their brothers: clean, rather grown-up,
well-behaved and beautifully dressed. Father was eager to co-
operate and conveyed feelings of great anxiety and inadequacy
while mother presented as competent, determined and clearly seeking allies in her battle with all this incompetence and mess.

The remarkable polarity between the two groups, which was
even expressed in the seating - male and female - was clear and
one might expect to find that each group was carrying some features and characteristics for the other. It was equally clear that
the boys had been brought by the parents, particularly mother,
in order for the therapists to alter their behaviour and especially
to stop the younger boy, Martin (sixteen) from bedwetting.

The family's view of the therapists (again a male/female couple)
seemed to come with them, so that even before they saw us in
action at all, they clearly looked to the female therapist to take
the lead in the sessions, just as the female partner dominated the
situation at home. It is difficult to convey the extraordinary
passivity of those boys in contrast to Mrs O'Brien's bewildered
impatience and unquestioning assumption that they would want the
same of themselves as she did. It was not, for example, a matter
of Martin wanting to stop his bedwetting because he was distressed about it. It was as if neither he nor anyone else would worry
about it much if it was not for Mother's great expectations and her
unremitting pressure on the boys to change. Even then it seemed
that it was only the discomfort of this pressure that he minded
rather than the bedwetting itself. When he eventually came asking
if he could have help with it, the reasons he gave were to do
with the nuisance of changing and washing his sheets himself.

More strange still for the therapists to witness was the way in
the first session that both boys sat listening to their mother
itemizing a catalogue of their faults, their stupidity, dirtiness,
laziness, etc. and yet showing absolutely no reaction to it. There
was no sign of resentment, anger or offence - nothing. In fact,
the boys said practically nothing at all except that when the
therapists tried to explore their feelings about coming here
together, the older one, David, managed to say that they had not
known they were coming until the day before. He was quick to
add, though, that if his mother wanted him to come, then he was
prepared to. It was the beginning of a repeated demonstration of
how Mrs O'Brien especially saw herself as thinking and planning
for these boys and how they simply let her do that. Now, here
they were, obediently coming along and sitting impassively, almost

as if deaf and dumb - or at least subnormal.

Meanwhile the little girls sat listening intently until the youngest one started to play with the toys we had put on the table; and Mr O'Brien, solid, anxious, good-humoured, appeared to be in general agreement with what his wife was saying, if a little embarrassed by it. The inescapable impression was that the two boys were damaged in ways that felt quite irreparable. In view of their histories this would not be surprising. But striking though the picture was, the question for the therapists was how could one start usefully to work with it? How, also, could one avoid getting caught in the pressure to take sides in what increasingly came to feel like a very intense tug-of-war between Mrs O'Brien and her two sons whose most difficult quality was the fact that even when their resentment was voiced, their major expression of it seemed to be at a more or less unconscious level and of a totally passive unaware kind. Plied as we were with historical accounts of the series of traumatic events they had all experienced, it seemed clear to us that no amount of verbal engagement with that history could in itself hope to reach the sense of despair and futility that it had engendered. Furthermore, the relentless pressure to reform from one side of the family seemed only to entrench the resigned and intransigent behaviour patterns of the other.

The therapists seemed to be expected to operate like auxiliary parents, in rather the same way as the grandparents apparently had, i.e., to reinforce the parents' own constant efforts to impress upon the boys the behaviour that they were certain was right for them. We were expected to behave in an authoritarian way through the medium of criticism, advice and prescription as did Mr and Mrs O'Brien themselves.

As it was, we could only comment on the boys' lack of response and suggest what might lie behind it. For something suggested to me, perhaps the intense searching look I was getting as I started talking, especially from the older boy David, that he was more alert and more in touch than he had seemed; and we eventually suggested that really to allow themselves to have feelings, or even thoughts, about what was happening, might seem to them too dangerous - too potentially explosive. It was David again who nodded and said, very timidly and warily, looking from his father to his mother and back, that, 'it might upset people.' It seemed there might be currency in this family for the assumption that uncontrolled behaviour would be preferable to outspoken disagreement or criticism.

It became increasingly clear to us that as long as the boys were so apparently unconcerned about their own behaviour - not at all convinced why they should change it unless through some external, almost magical, medium for which they need take no major responsibility, then all current efforts directed towards changing specific bits of behaviour such as the bedwetting would go the same way as previous efforts in which pills, mechanical devices, etc., had failed for lack of proper use. Also it seemed that the parents had some investment themselves in maintaining the status quo, as if by firmly attributing all the problems to the boys and locating them in their pigsty bedroom, the marriage could be kept ideal and absolutely problem-free in the way that both so desperately wanted.

The following example from an early session may give some idea of this process and of the pressures that the family put on the therapists to join in their way of operating.

After expressing a rather eager interest at the beginning of the session to start where they had left off the week before, the family soon dropped that idea, and reverted to the subject of Martin's bedwetting. It seemed he had been dry for a few nights and Mrs O'Brien then informed us, in a very secretive way, that he was having a 'tonic' that the doctor had given him, very clearly implying that it was actually some drug he was getting. Then looking directly at the doctor here, she said in French, 'Comprenez vous?'

My partner was completely taken aback. It was as if he was meant to be the father having a private discussion with mother about little three- or four-year-old children, incapable of understanding; and the boys again behaved as if they were quite oblivious. But it was an opportunity to point all this out and to show how Mrs O'Brien was wanting the doctor here to join in a secret about what she was giving this boy of sixteen years for his health, as if he was far too infantile to know or take any responsibility for himself. At the same time, it was also very clear how the boys invited everyone to speak for them, act for them and think for them. As we suggested, Martin, in particular, was like a child whose extreme slowness made it easier to do up his shoelaces for him than to help him to do them up himself. The discussion of this led David also to take his courage into his hands and relate it to a similar situation he was in with father and mother. It seemed that they deemed him incapable of managing the money that he had earned in his job; and after he had clearly demonstrated his practice of spending it all, they now insisted on keeping it for him, giving him pocket money from it and putting the rest into a savings account for him. It was another example of an invitation to infantilism being more than readily complied with. And the problem for the therapists was not to get drawn into one or other side of this struggle. Indeed, it was interesting to see how easy it was to fall into a similar kind of dependency mode of behaving as the family itself had - preaching or lecturing to them much as these parents did to their children; or joining with one part to discuss the other so that neither were actually engaged in being the patient or the problem. Technically this would be an example of the kind of enactment spoken of at the beginning - an 'acting in the countertransference'.

There was a great deal of pressure on us as therapists to direct them, instruct them and judge them in the manner of specialists who could provide the formula for cure without them having to do the work or face the conflicts and pain involved in undergoing change themselves. For it became increasingly clear that all the arguments about the stupidity and dirtiness of the boys served to avoid the extent of the depressed and rejected feelings they were suffering. With all the emphasis in the sessions on the closeness between the parents, it took quite a while to bring into the open, first, how pathetically pushed out and forlorn the boys felt and, second, how really tense and loaded the fight for space, possessions and attention could become when they gave up their servile positions, and when the atmosphere of rather hopeless resignation gave way to one that included a hope of something different.

The combination of a 'dependency' culture such as this, on the one hand, and the difficulty of acknowledging the dependence or any of its implications, on the other, provides a set of conditions which are bound to highlight the problems associated with changes, separations and breaks in the therapy. Later material from sessions with this family may help to illustrate some of the technical issues for the therapist in managing such changes.

Attempts to contain reactions to change and the implications of rejection
The first major change I will mention in the work with the O'Brien family was the necessity, on the part of the therapists, to change the session time. And it is the family's reaction to this, linked to the events of the ensuing Christmas break that I will describe.

The significant thing about our proposal to change the time was that although it was clearly inconvenient for them in terms of all their other evening engagements and activities, they took the attitude that it was up to them to fit in with us, Mrs O'Brien with angry resignation and Mr O'Brien saying in a comforting tone that their need was such that they must expect to make sacrifices. In fact, we had left a number of sessions to negotiate the change of time and we commented on their unquestioning acceptance of our proposal with no explicit objections. At some point Mrs O'Brien actually said 'are we allowed to criticize?' We tried to show them how their feelings of dependence on us, and that they must comply, really made them squash and restrict their complaints, criticisms and disappointments out of all awareness in much the same way as they expected each other - especially Martin and David - to do at home.

The work that we did on this heralded a phase of much more interaction and participation on the part of all the family, both with each other and with us. Mrs O'Brien, in particular, questioned the whole value of the therapy and they all made their ambivalence to it very clear. But the power of the attack and apparent rejection of our help also seemed to represent their way of dealing with the feelings they had of being pushed about and rejected by us. Notwithstanding some easing up, the emerging degree of hostility and the continuing difficulties of tackling us directly with their dissatisfaction led to various forms of representation in action - absences, latenesses, etc. - accompanied by verbal material about strikes and go-slows, as if the more direct way of complaining could not be sustained by the family as a whole any more than by the boys, and was again denied and enacted instead.

But the theme of being unwanted was poigantly presented in
some interaction around the older boy, David, in the sessions
before the Christmas break. David had been talking about leaving
home and going to America but he had actually done very little
about it and one's impression was that he longed for people in the
family – especially, perhaps, his father – to explore this idea with
him, perhaps to ask him why he wanted to leave home or to show
some regret or concern about it. Instead of this, however, Mrs
O'Brien attacked him scornfully for dithering about so much and
not going ahead with his idea. It seemed that it was she and
Mr O'Brien who were most keen on his leaving home. If David had
wanted reassurance that he was after all wanted at home, in fact
he got the opposite! When we took this up it led to Mrs O'Brien
saying that there was no point in talking about your feelings, for
instance, the depression she felt herself, because no one would
understand. That seemed to be the crux of it for all of them.
There was very little idea of an object who could really pay attention, with the wish to understand and take in and help their
particular problem. The dynamic pattern being demonstrated by
David was one of dealing with the terrible sense of not being
wanted by threatening to leave in the hope that people would then
show a wish for him to stay, thus demonstrating his fear to be
unfounded (only to find the opposite, in fact); and it was this
pattern that the whole family unconsciously seemed to re-enact in
relation to the therapists and the break.

For then came the Christmas holiday and on the day of our first
appointment afterwards, we received a letter from Mrs O'Brien
essentially saying that they would not be coming to their therapy
anymore. It had not resolved Martin's difficulties and we had not
offered him any kind of answer to his problems individually.

It was not possible to contact the family in time for that evening
session but we did respond with great care, acknowledging their
sense of frustration, etc., but also stressing the importance of
discussing together before finishing the therapy, in terms both
of this and of any alternative that might seem appropriate. We
said we would expect them the following week. Well, it did seem
that they might be dealing with their feelings of rejection by rejecting us, much as the older boy, David, had done in talking of
going to America. But if, as a family, they were functioning like
him, we might expect them also at some level, to be testing our
readiness to give them up and let them go away, just as he had
been testing theirs.

Even with this possibility in mind, however, we were surprised
at the alacrity and apparent enthusiasm with which they responded to our letter, Mrs O'Brien ringing up immediately to say that
they would be coming for their appointment. The ensuing sessions
were spent discussing their doubts and resentments and considering their wish to terminate. But, in some way, this episode did
seem to present a milestone in the treatment and it was clear by
the third session after Christmas, not only that they wished to

continue, but that there was actually a very different atmosphere
and feel about the interaction with us. They began to show much
more explicitly their interest in us. Do we see other families and
what do we think of them in relation to these other families? It
seemed, somehow, more possible to work in the transference. The
elder boy presented a dilemma about changing his job and the
notions of change did seem to be in the air. There was a sense of
them standing on the threshold, debating whether to go over it.
As if to emphasize the more positive feeling, the little girl gave
to each of us a drawing she had made during the session. Altogether the general despair, despondency and discouragement
which usually prevailed did seem now to be a little tinged with
hope from time to time and even with occasional surprising moments
of genuine concern in the family. Of course every sign of hope or
movement like this is subject to all too easy undermining; each
break seems to put the treatment in jeopardy again and face us
with the question, what are we really doing, attempting to work
with such a situation in this way?

It is notoriously difficult for individuals as well as families in
treatment to be in touch with the significance of interruptions and
changes in the sessions and, of course, it is often those most in
need who find it hardest to know about or think about it. So that
efforts to prepare for impending breaks tend to feel forced or
futile - just as attempts to make links between other experiences
and the feelings they evoke seem often to be falling on barren
ground. We can begin to identify a constellation of associated
features which characterize a family like this and give substance
to questions about the appropriateness for them of engaging in
this form of treatment.

The concreteness of thinking, constant pressure to action and
extreme dissociation from any awareness of the real sources of
behaviour can all be seen as expressions of the difficulty for each
individual - as well as the family as a whole - to suffer their own
and each other's feelings.

This mode of response in the family to the need for their feelings
to be entertained and suffered is reflected in the difficulties for
the therapists to provide such containment in the treatment. It
does seem possible to provide some sort of containing experience -
if only through finding contact with the relevant feelings by their
evocation in the therapists themselves; it is clearly when this
sense of containment fails that the increased tendency to act out
ensues. But the question of feasibility remains and the possibility
of providing adequate containment for a family such as this
depends partly on our skills in managing their experiences of
loss and change in the treatment. There is a tendency for us to
underestimate the effect of breaks on all families who are engaged
in ongoing therapy, but especially those who may seem to care
least about them. I have been trying to indicate the significance
of these breaks in highlighting the family's way of functioning
(concretely I think it is evidenced by the number of families who
drop out, or whose therapy seems to stagnate at such times).

While in individual therapy, we seem to be more tuned in to the subtleties of reactions that are provoked by these interruptions and more skilled at working with them as an important part of the therapeutic process, yet the corresponding need for such attention in work with families is obvious.

Most, if not all, of the families we see have quite severe problems related to mourning - often crystallized through an actual death in the family, but usually dating much further back and representing a major aspect of their functioning in general. If we can be alert to it, the breaks can provide an important opportunity to work on this with the family, instead of simply being the occasion for more drastic actions, as so often happens.

SUMMARY

I have tried to convey in this chapter how we seek to use the therapy setting to enable a process of meaningful experience to take place, and to discuss some of the problems of handling the anxieties of the families we see, particularly as these problems are highlighted at the critical times of beginnings and breaks.

With the help of material from two families I have suggested some of the issues involved in enabling family members to get in touch with the pain and conflict in themselves that they had hitherto denied. I have tried to indicate how such denial may be to the detriment of their own individuality as well as to the discomfort of those around them; and hence the importance of the struggle to get to grips with it; I have also pointed to some of the features that differentiate the families in these terms and may help us to think about our work with them.

The philosophy behind this approach is not one that promises any panacea or freedom from distress. If it does offer freedom, it is of the kind that arises from beginning to get to know and to be with one's distress and with the other experiences that resist integration, sufficiently perhaps to own them and work with them.

6 MAKING A SPACE
FOR PARENTS

Anna Halton and
Jeanne Magagna

In this chapter we will be concentrating specifically on work with
parents. This will include observations and thoughts in relation
to the parents' experience of bringing their child to a clinic for an
assessment for psychotherapeutic treatment and the dilemma which
they face when the child is accepted for treatment. In the latter
part of the chapter there is an account of psychotherapeutic work
with one parental couple whose children were in individual treatment.

Since a major part of this book is concerned with aspects of
work with whole families, either in assessment or longer-term
treatment, perhaps we should explain why we have chosen to focus
exclusively on one part of the family system in this way. The reasons are twofold. Firstly, given that we draw on an underlying
family point of view, in which the family relationships and problems are carefully taken into account, there is always a certain
flexibility in our thinking about the best way to approach any
given family. It is not ipso facto the case that they are seen
together as a group, because it is not always appropriate, advis-
able or desirable as far as the particular family is concerned.
Secondly, when a decision is made, for whatever reason, to offer
individual treatment to a child, it is our experience that the
impact on the parents is not always given the recognition it
deserves.

In 1932, Melanie Klein, speaking from the position of a child
analyst, wrote of the parents' dilemma:

The child is dependent on them and so they are included in the
field of the analysis; yet it is not they who are being analysed
and they can therefore only be influenced by ordinary psychological means. The relationship of the parents to their child's
analyst entails difficulties of a peculiar kind, since it touches
closely upon their own complexes. Their child's neurosis weighs
very heavily upon the parents' sense of guilt, and at the same
time as they turn to analysis for help, they regard the necessity of it as proof of their guilt with regard to their child's
illness. It is, moreover, very trying for them to have the
details of their family life revealed to the analyst. To this must
be added, particularly in the case of the mother, jealousy of the
confidence which is established between the child and its analyst.

In this chapter we hope to throw some light on these issues of
guilt, ambivalence and jealousy, and to illustrate ways in which
parents might be helped with their own difficulties in their own
right.

PART I - INITIAL EXPLORATION AND ASSESSMENT

A child is identified as troubled in some way and he is referred
usually by the general practitioner, sometimes by the school or
social service agency and sometimes by the parents themselves.
So the parents will have been involved to a greater or lesser
extent in this referral process, and they are likely to expect the
child to be the focus of our attention. They bring him along,
sometimes reluctantly, expecting to tell us about their worries
about him, or to give us information or simply to wait quietly in
the waiting room while we make our 'diagnosis'. Whether it is
immediately apparent or not the parents are usually in some distress, having anxiously anticipated their meeting with us.

Society places a high value on child care and 'proper parenting'
and while the child remains a child he is usually thought of as the
innocent or wronged party if he gets himself into difficulties. It
is likely, therefore, that the parents approach us expecting to
be blamed or criticized. It is even more likely if their own internal
worlds are peopled by blaming and blamed figures. We have in
mind those who have internalized their own parents as highly
critical (Klein 1932). We, as the authority figures, 'the people at
the clinic', will be expected to behave in the same way.

During the assessment we are concerned to listen, to observe,
to receive the impact of the family disturbance and hopefully to
provide an experience in which their anxieties will be shared and
attended to carefully and considerately. The issue of 'who is to
blame' is likely to be a central concern of the family at this stage
and we would like to consider some of its manifestations in more
detail. Of course, the very word 'assessment' is problematic in
that it carries all sorts of connotations of being judged and
scrutinized. It would probably be better to describe this phase
of the work as a mutual exploration.

Adolescents, like Suzy in the following example, often prefer
the opportunity to be seen individually.

Mrs Allen, divorced mother of Suzy, aged sixteen, saw a
psychiatrist for two interviews during the assessment phase
whilst Suzy was seen twice by a social worker. One of the
presenting problems was the fraught relationship between
mother and daughter and the workers decided to offer a joint
appointment to both on the third occasion. Mrs Allen was an
intelligent and capable woman who ran a successful secretarial
agency. She arrived for the third appointment with her daughter carrying a shorthand notebook which she proceeded to open
at the beginning of the session. Pen in hand, she looked expec-
tantly at the social worker, enquiring politely as to her diag-

nosis of Suzy's problems. This surprised the workers because
during her individual sessions with the psychiatrist, the mother
had been able to talk fairly freely about her worries in relation
to herself and to Suzy. It was suggested to Mrs Allen that she
might be very frightened of her first meeting with the social
worker and that she might feel the social worker was party to
all Suzy's accusations against her, and would then be wishing
to put her 'on the spot' having taken careful note of all her
misdemeanours as a mother. This seemed to free Mrs Allen to
close her book and join in. Later in the session she was able
to talk about some of her guilty feelings about putting her job
interests before her children. She also spoke of her feelings
of rivalry towards the social worker who she had assumed was
some sort of 'perfect mother figure' rather like her own mother
who made her feel she could never do anything right. It did not
surprise the workers when Mrs Allen said that her only really
happy times in childhood were when she had father all to herself.

In that example Mrs Allen was all set to put the social worker 'on
trial' in the same way that she anticipated being put 'on trial'
herself. Sometimes parents may deal with their discomfort in other
ways. For example, Mr Y said of his son, 'I just don't know what's
the matter with him. We've always done our best, he's had everything he wanted from us' or Mr and Mrs X, speaking of their
daughter, 'It seems as if she's never liked us. Even when she was
a baby it seemed we could never do anything right for her.' Such
statements help the workers to understand the extent and nature
of the distress felt by the parents because they convey a sense of
grievance and a feeling that all this suffering is the fault of the
child. The worker may even experience pressure from the parents
to make an alliance with them against the child as if to say 'we
adults try to help and look what the child does to us'. We might
see this pressure as arising from anxieties in the parents that the
worker may join with the child in some accusation against them.
If so, we would share these thoughts with the parents in the
session – as the Social Worker did with Mrs Allen – in the hope
that we would be able to alleviate some of the anxiety by acknowledging it.

Perhaps it would be useful here to differentiate this sort of
approach which addresses itself to the underlying anxieties from
another in which we might allow ourselves to be seen as helpful
by making 'reassuring' comments. The parents of a referred child
are likely to be feeling not only guilt about real or imaginary
harm done to the child but also a sense of shame in relation to the
exposure of this. The wish to be reassuring is in some ways a
natural response to someone greatly troubled by feelings of guilt.

Mrs Bond came to the Clinic because of the referral of her
daughter, Rachel aged 8, who had been suffering from night
terrors for several years. Mrs Bond was seen on her own and
was quite distraught in the interview and said she could hardly
remember when she had last experienced a peaceful night's

sleep. She was alone, her husband having left her soon after
the birth of Rachel, her only child and they lived in inadequate cramped accommodation. She cried profusely as she
recalled violent feelings towards Rachel. Mrs Bond's therapist
was extremely sensitive and receptive to her distress. So much
so that she felt quite overwhelmed and was prompted to tell
Mrs Bond not to worry so much. The therapist felt sure that
Rachel's fear (of being murdered in the dark) would soon be
overcome and said so. Then, in response to an urgent question
from Mrs B., the therapist offered some advice in relation to
the management of Rachel's bedtime. To the therapist's con-
sternation Mrs Bond simply became more distraught. The reason emerged when she said that she had been telling Rachel
every night for almost two years, that there was nothing to
worry about, and that there wasn't really anybody trying to
murder her.

The point of this example is to demonstrate that the therapist's
efforts to 'reassure' were interpreted by Mrs B. to be due to
the same inability in the therapist to bear the anxiety that had
led her to make similar comments to her daughter. It had also
led her to seek the advice which flowed naturally from family and
friends, but it had brought the mother little relief from the
anxiety about her child's terror and her own violence. Instead the
reassurance and the advice tended to increase her despair.

If we, as therapists, hurry in with reassurance, it is likely to
be in response to our own discomfort as if to say 'please don't
feel so awful because it makes me feel so awful.' Our need to offer
advice may arise from similar motives, although the parents, in
their anxiety, may urgently request it from us. It is the anxiety
underlying their request, rather than the request itself, which is
crying out for attention.

There is also the problem of truth, or putting it another way,
of our own ignorance in the face of a new situation. We actually
don't know who did what to whom, when and why. We don't know
who is to blame, if indeed anybody is. We don't know to what
extent the guilt or the regret or the worry is based on fact or
fantasy. Reassurance can be experienced by the client as our not
wanting to hear or to know.

Transition from assessment into treatment
During the assessment phase the task of the therapist is to help
the family members to locate and identify the areas of pain and
stress. When some mutual understanding has been reached, it is
then possible to think with them about what form of help would be
most appropriate, whether, for example, the child should be
offered individual therapy or whether the family as a unit should
be the focus of treatment. These decisions obviously depend on
the experience of the assessment work, the family's own preference, and degrees of disturbance and/or motivation in individual
family members. (These points are referred to by Beta Copley
in Chapter 3.) There are also other factors such as the prevailing

attitude of the clinic team towards particular methods of work, as
well as individual preferences and staff availability.

Often when individual treatment for one child is indicated,
parents are offered an opportunity to continue to explore their
own difficulties in relation to the child. They may feel ambivalent
about their own involvement in treatment for a number of reasons.
Since the role of the 'referred patient' in the family is very often
one of holding and representing disowned conflicts and anxieties
for other members, parents often feel quite exposed and unpro-
tected when seen on their own in the absence of the referred
child who would normally be the focus of attention, concern or
attack. We have found this especially to be the case when the
assessment phase is completed too quickly and there has not been
sufficient attention given to the exploration and understanding of
the parents' own distress. Those of us who work in 'child-
centred agencies' are probably familiar with the situation in which
the psychiatrist or child psychotherapist sees the child and the
social worker sees the parents. While this may be a rational and
appropriate division of tasks it can, and sometimes does, develop
into a sort of two-tier system of intervention in which the child's
therapy is regarded as of prime importance and the work with
the parents is some sort of back-up resource where information
is gained from and advice given to the couple. (Sometimes the
father is not given sufficient encouragement to attend the Clinic
and therefore by implication his role in relation to both mother
and children is often overlooked.)

This may have to do with issues of role and status within the
agency. The social worker may be regarded as someone whose
primary task it is to protect the therapy of the child from parental
intrusion or sabotage. The implicit message would be that the
social worker is also responsible for protecting the psychotherapist's work. This might involve her in various activities such
as contacting the child's school to exchange information, arranging therapy times, transport, etc. In this case the actual work
with the parents could develop along similar lines - reminding
them about therapy times, asking for historical details and for
accounts of the child's behaviour at home. It is possible that the
parents will then experience themselves as united into a co-
operative management role with the social worker, forming a sort
of sub-system supporting and supplying the therapist-child
couple. In one sense this may fulfil a need in the parents to feel
useful and helpful in the situation but it may also in the longer
term undermine their own parenting capacities in a less obvious
way. This emphasis on their management role leaves very little
space for exploring their own feelings, for example any resentments about the clinic workers appearing to have taken over
responsibility for the child, jealousy of the relationship between
child and therapist, feelings of envy towards the child for all the
personal attention he is receiving. The worker too may have to
deny similar feelings in herself about working in this auxiliary
role and the inevitable limitations it places on the use of her own

professional capacities. The following example illustrates the way in which a child's treatment was nearly sabotaged when parental feelings of jealousy and redundancy were not recognized.

A social worker was seeing Mr and Mrs Davies during the therapy of their daughter Tracy, aged 5. They came on the fifth week full of news of the marvellous improvement in Tracy's behaviour at home. The social worker knew from the child's therapist that she had made good contact with the child and felt optimistic about alleviating some of Tracy's anxieties. The social worker was therefore extremely pleased to be able to share the parents' expressed feelings of relief and gratitude. Mr and Mrs Davies, who had met the therapist briefly on one occasion, went on to express their great faith in the child's therapist, extolling her experience, wisdom, patience and other virtues. They seemed quite unable to talk about anything else, in fact the social worker found it difficult to get a word in edgeways.

When she discussed this in the workshop later she remembered a sensation during the interview, that her jaw had begun to ache from smiling. She also remembered that she had felt quite depressed following the interview, although she had, at the time, attributed this to other factors. She had felt sure that the parents had little further need to come but in discussion she was able to see that they had, in fact, idealized the child's therapist and caused her, the social worker, to feel quite redundant.

Mr and Mrs Davies cancelled their own and Tracy's appointments for the next week. The following week Mr Davies brought Tracy to the Clinic, telling the social worker that his wife had 'flu and was still unable to come. The social worker, remembering her own feelings after the last interview, enquired further as to Mrs Davies' state of mind. Mr Davies said that she had been crying a lot which was 'natural after 'flu' but she had been further upset by Tracy who talked of nothing but 'the nice lady at the Clinic who gave her toys to play with.' When Mrs Davies had cancelled Tracy's appointment Tracy had told her that 'she didn't love her Mummy any more.'

The social worker recognized the feelings of depression and redundancy in the parents and was able to help Mr Davies to bring his wife to the next session, where their feelings were discussed and shared. They later admitted to a considerable jealousy of Tracy's therapist, but had felt unable to express this as it seemed so 'ungrateful when everybody was doing their best to help'.

This example highlights the way that the workers' countertransference experience served as a useful signpost to the underlying feelings that were opposing the parents' conscious wish to co-operate. If the child himself is reluctant to come, or hostile to the therapy, then of course it is even more difficult for the parents to maintain their conscious co-operation in the face of their underlying reservations.

It would seem appropriate here to share some thoughts about
the parents' experience of 'handing over' a child to a therapist
and how this situation might be managed. In our experience it
has been helpful for the parents to meet with the child's therapist
before treatment starts, even when another team member has seen
them and plans to work with them. Such a meeting allows the
parents to see and talk to the person about whom they are likely
to have many anxieties and phantasies, and it is an opportunity
for them to perceive the therapist more realistically. Also it
reinforces in a practical way a respect for the parents' responsible and decisive role and the necessity of their co-operation. It
gives the therapist an opportunity to discuss therapy times and
arrangements for bringing the child to the clinic. It is a chance
for the parents to ask questions, to give factual information and
to prepare themselves for some of the difficulties that they may
encounter in the handling of the child at home as therapy pro-
gresses.

Sometimes it is appropriate for the child's therapist and the
parents to meet during treatment, e.g. to discuss a change in
the child's therapy times or to share some important information
concerning the child. This possibility of direct communication
does have the advantage of maintaining space for the work with
the parents, a space freed from the interference of message-
carrying functions.

However, it is always important first to explore the meaning of
such a meeting for both parents and child and for the therapists
to clarify their own respective positions. It is not uncommon for
therapists who are treating different members of one family to
become caught up in the family dynamics in such a way that they
begin to act from their own countertransference experiences.
They may find themselves in relationships characterized by
rivalry or intrusiveness which mirror the family members' current
difficulties with each other. It is often helpful to have one member of the team who is not involved in direct contact with family
members and who, in discussion, contributes a more objective
and overall perspective which represents and supports the
integrity of the team. (See Chapter 4.)

PART II - ASPECTS OF ONGOING THERAPY WITH PARENTS

So far we have concentrated on the problems of beginning, of
initial exploration, assessment and transition. Now we would like
to describe aspects of work with parents in various stages of
treatment. To illustrate this, we will refer to the therapy sessions
of one parental couple, Mr and Mrs Garcia, who were in joint
treatment with two therapists for several years. They were
parents of two children referred for individual therapy.

Mr Garcia was a highly successful Spanish middle-class businessman, and Mrs Garcia, also Spanish, an active, talented and
articulate woman. They appeared socially confident and capable

people with a wide circle of friends and a variety of interests.
They were extremely concerned about the behaviour of their two
children (a boy aged eleven and a girl aged nine) who were
underachieving at school and who had become increasingly clinging, demanding and generally unhappy at home. The parents
readily agreed to therapeutic help for the children and also responded favourably to a suggestion that they too should be provided with an opportunity to discuss their difficulties on a regular
weekly basis with two therapists.

Immediately following their decision to have treatment for themselves and the children, but before treatment began, there was a
short holiday break. During this time, the couple made a brief
and rare visit to Spain and while there Mr Garcia had an acute
and near fatal illness. This seemed highly significant in that
Spain, while being their country of origin was also the country
in which their own families had been severely persecuted by the
government during the Spanish Civil War. The fathers of both
parents had been killed and Mr Garcia's mother had been badly
beaten. Mr and Mrs Garcia had both escaped to England as teenagers and had met in London in their early twenties.

So the treatment began, after Mr Garcia partially recovered,
with a marked contrast between the still confident and capable
appearance of this couple, and the shared knowledge that, when
faced with a concrete reminder (Spain) of their parents' immense
torture, they had almost collapsed through the near death of the
husband. Even before they met the couple, the therapists found
themselves experiencing a fear of helping them look at their
difficulties. The fear was that something painful, even a painful
reminder of the past, could result in a catastrophe of some sort.
The therapists were acutely aware of the connection between
father's anxiety-provoking illness and the finalization of arrangements for treatment. They wondered if the illness was a kind of
communication in advance, demonstrating anxiety and guilt about
having things brought into the open in therapy.

The unfolding of shared anxieties in the transference
It would seem useful here to describe what we mean by working
in the transference before going on to illustrate this with clinical
material.

The therapist's aim is to focus on the emotions that are most
immediate and pressing in the experience of the therapy session,
the idea being that internal change can best be facilitated through
interpretations which meet anxiety at the moment at which it is
being experienced. So the material that the couple bring is
scrutinized by the therapists with a view to the clues it offers
to what is actually happening in the session. The therapists avoid
introducing topics or making judgments about the rightness or
wrongness of the parents' actions or attitudes. Instead, they aim
to provide a situation in which the couple can talk about whatever
is on their mind, however insignificant it may seem to them, or
however controversial they fear it will be (Strachey 1934).

The focus of the work is the transference relationship between the couple and therapists. In facilitating the unfolding of the transferences the therapists are concerned with matters of (a) place – relating to the experience as it emerges inside the therapy room, and the way in which it links with other relationships outside, (b) time – relating to what is experienced at the moment rather than yesterday or in the last session and (c) receptivity – a capacity to accept and bear the presenting anxieties, however uncomfortable or painful for the therapists. Within these parameters there are also more specific considerations. It is not so much the content of the communication but more its meaning and significance which is of concern to the therapists (Meltzer 1967). It is important to focus on the method of communication, the way the patient actually speaks and the way in which the patient reacts to the therapists' communications, in order to provide an understanding of the immediate experience (Joseph 1975).

Once it has become evident that a particular anxiety exists, its true nature may only become apparent in a careful observation of not only what is going on between the therapist and patient but also on what is going on inside the therapist, what it is that is being transferred and what exactly it feels like. It is through the therapists' ability to discriminate between the different emotions evoked in themselves that a clearer picture of the internal world of the patients emerges. The figures (or objects) of the internal world and the relationships of these objects, one to another, are projected onto the therapists who receive them and provide an opportunity for them to be re-experienced and re-tested against the reality of a new and more favourable relationship. The parents' eventual capacity to face and bear their own emotions, respond to each other's needs, and help their children depends on the internalization of the experience of being helped to bear their emotions with the therapist couple.

During their first few meetings with Mr and Mrs Garcia, the therapists experienced powerfully and dramatically the impact of the fear and the anxiety which the couple themselves could not tolerate. At that time, it seemed, they could only evacuate it into others or express it in the form of stress-induced physical illness. So the anxieties that were denied by the couple were experienced by the therapists, who found themselves feeling fragile and tentative in the face of Mr and Mrs Garcia's lively and excitable accounts of their daily life.

The therapists also experienced a merging of identities. Mr and Mrs Garcia would often arrive late and come straight to the room without informing the receptionist of their arrival. On entering the room they frequently enquired as to the therapists' health and state of mind, and generally behaved as if they were at a dinner party telling amusing anecdotes and paying exaggerated compliments to the therapists, referring to them as 'charming young ladies' in a patronizing way. They talked almost continuously and often simultaneously.

The therapists found themselves feeling bombarded and

unable to think. When one of the therapists managed to interrupt to make a comment, the other therapist noted that she had
been just about to make the same comment.
After the sessions the therapists tried to make sense of their
countertransference experience in order to understand what was
going on. They felt undifferentiated one from another, having the
same thoughts and experiences, closely identified as if clinging
together for survival, like 'babes in the wood'. It seemed as if all
boundaries were being disregarded. The therapists found it
difficult to comment on the Garcias' late arrival to the sessions,
feeling that the couple would feel humiliated and treated like
children. It was also difficult to end the sessions on time and the
therapists, although relatively experienced, were somehow made
to feel like fumbling and nervous students. The parental couple's
anxieties about the exposure of any vulnerability in themselves
was being experienced by the therapists by means of projective
identification (Klein 1946). If all boundaries were merged and
confused, then it was impossible to see or think clearly, and seeing and thinking seemed to imply the revelation of something quite
terrible. The therapists had to acknowledge and work with Mr
and Mrs Garcia's intense feeling of humiliation in relation to coming to therapy and also their dread of what therapy might involve.
Gradually the couple felt safe enough to begin to talk about some
aspects of their family life and in particular their worries about
the children.
    In the initial stage of therapy parents naturally tend to talk
about their children, since they have usually been a focus of
anxiety and the ostensible reason for their approaching us. As
they discuss their children the therapists try to provide them
with the experience of containment for their distress in which the
therapists listen and try to understand rather than give advice
or provide 'good solutions'. (See Chapter 5 above for further
elaboration of the concept of containment.) Often the description
of the child will include many references to what has been split
off and denied in the couple's own personalities. We could see
this as 'the child in the parent', i.e., some sort of unresolved
pain from their own past experience of being parented, which
remains alive in their current relationships and gradually becomes
apparent in their relationship with the therapist. It is important
that the parents are given enough space initially to air their
grievances about their children and each other, in order that the
specific nature of their own unmet needs may be understood.
    After discussing their shared worries about their children for
several weeks, Mr and Mrs Garcia started to express their
impatience with each other. Their attacks on each other did
not provide any relief of anxiety, instead they appeared to
become more guilty and more distant from the therapists who
seemed to be increasingly perceived as judges. It was as if
their disagreements had become a way of avoiding contact with
the therapists, who were so feared by them.
    Early in a session Mrs Garcia spoke of how futile it was to

come to the session and speak to her husband. Then she said
he felt it was very difficult for him to talk to her because she
always said he was angry. Mr Garcia said he doesn't like talking
to her because she always says she knows how he feels. She
said she read in a magazine that it is reassuring to say 'I
know'. The therapists interpreted the couple's fear of the
therapists' criticisms, and the feeling that they might apply
psychoanalytic knowledge from books in a dogmatic or purely
judgemental way.

When the therapists, rather than the other partner, receive the
complaints about such things as coldness and unresponsiveness
and do not respond in a revengeful or hurt manner, the parents
discover that it is all right to complain and then may begin to
explore the way in which they experience the therapists as meeting
or not meeting their needs.
Mr Garcia described how his wife felt that coming to the therapy
was like a prison sentence and Mrs Garcia said that she felt
there should be a point in their lives when they could stop looking at themselves and asking where they had gone wrong. At
the end of the same session they said 'See you next week'.

Now that the couple's transference feelings were becoming more
explicit in their relationship with the therapists, it became clear
that the Garcias viewed the therapy as a punishment for the
damage which they felt they had inflicted on the children. These
intense feelings of persecutory guilt were extremely distressing
and as yet they could only bear to locate the distress in each
other, rather than speaking for themselves which seemed to feel
too direct and too much of an exposure.
Mrs Garcia described how her husband had been unable to cope
with the pressures of family life. He had cut himself off from
emotional things because he had been through so much as a
child.
Mr Garcia described his wife's near breakdown when she
heard some upsetting news. Later he described the current
relationship between his wife and her mother saying, 'You
can feel the tension when they are both in the same room. It's
hard to describe because the actual behaviour can't be faulted,
but her mother is dogmatic, sterile and narrow-minded and my
wife dare not criticize her in any way.'
This image of a severe mother who is at the same time too fragile
to be criticized, appeared again and again in their material. It
seemed to match the therapists' countertransference experience
which was a feeling of having to be gentle and careful so as not
to confront the couple with 'powerful' interpretations, but at the
same time feeling incompetent and rather hopeless about being
able to help, rather like a mother who could hurt but who could
not hold the child. Much later in the therapy, after these feelings
had been further explored in the transference, it became evident
that this was how Mr and Mrs Garcia had both experienced
their own mothers as children.
The other way in which the Garcias avoided a direct confronta-

tion with their own distress was to locate it in their referred
children.

At times they said that they were only coming to therapy 'for
the children's sake' with Mr Garcia adding 'for the children I
would do anything'. Mrs Garcia cried profusely after a discussion with one of the children's therapists who had said that
the treatment would last three or four years. She was worried
about having to tell the new school about the child's treatment,
feeling that he would be ostracized, stigmatized by friends and
treated like a 'nut case' by the teachers. Mr Garcia wondered
if the difficulty in talking with others about the children's
treatment had to do with his wife's own difficulty in acknowledging that the children needed treatment.

These were understandable and genuine concerns in their own
right, but they also reflected the couple's fear for themselves and
their worries about what the therapists would see and discover in
them. Mr Garcia himself touched on this anxiety in the above
example.

To summarize, this first phase of therapy was characterized by
intense feelings of persecution which were defended against in
the following ways: by a merging and confusing of boundaries, by
a massive projection of feelings of inadequacy and neediness into
the therapists and by attempts to locate distress elsewhere - into
the other partner and/or the referred children. We have shown
how projection into the therapists rather than each other enabled
the parents' therapy to progress.

The use of manic defence
As the therapists became more in touch with the couple's difficulties, they came up against a mutual defence of a very manic kind.
We have already alluded to the fact that both Mr and Mrs Garcia
had suffered considerable deprivation as children with experiences
of parental separation and loss. Although they did not speak of
early childhood memories, they conveyed an experience of parental
figures who were preoccupied with intense anxieties for their own
safety in an actual situation of political persecution. As we have
shown, the therapists experienced in the countertransference
something of the anxiety which the Garcias sought to avoid. Mr
and Mrs Garcia, meeting and marrying in England, but with a
shared traumatic past in Spain, had clung together as survivors,
determined to make a new and better life. (We have already described how the therapists experienced the 'clinging together' in
the countertransference.) For thirty years this couple had been
developing a psychic structure for surviving together. The
structure which had evolved seemed to be heavily reliant on the
notion of a 'super parent/spouse', a father/mother or husband/
wife who was highly idealized as successful, capable, impervious
to criticism or self-doubt, able to tolerate and administer to the
needs of the whole family. As we will show, they both strongly
identified with this omnipotent 'super parent/spouse' at different
times and continuously reinforced each other in this identification.

For example, they were both engaged in fund-raising and various philanthropic activities on behalf of refugee children while at the same time their own feelings of childlike vulnerability were denied and thus cruelly neglected. This was, of course, directly related to the actual difficulties they experienced in parenting the children. They encouraged the children to grow up and be 'strong and capable' long before they were ready. It was also likely that this had been Mr and Mrs Garcia's own experience as children. They had both, at an early age, assumed parental responsibilities in their families of origin as a consequence of the premature death of a parent.

This kind of projective identification with a 'super parent/spouse' with omnipotent powers to obliterate painful experiences could be likened to what Winnicott (1965) has described as the 'false self' or Helene Deutsch (1942) as the 'As if' personality. In Mr and Mrs Garcia's case, this identification with a 'super/parent' was a way of coping with helplessness, neediness and rage. Because of their difficulty in holding and bearing these painful states of mind which were exacerbated by the external traumatic events of their childhood, they became identified with a parent who is a model of tough self-sufficiency, one who could bear anything. This identification was a way of avoiding, however temporarily or precariously, the pain of mourning the lost parents.

The therapists' task was to try to help the couple to differentiate between what was real and actual in the experience of being marital partners and parents as opposed to what was merely being inside this omnipotent 'super parent/spouse' and therefore quite out of touch with their own dependent needs and those of their family. If the therapists explored the necessity for this 'super-parent' structure prematurely, i.e., before the parents had sufficient inner resources to face these anxieties, they felt more persecuted and retreated even further inside this defensive structure. For example, Mrs Garcia in response to an interpretation would sometimes 'become' one of the therapists to look at her husband's difficulties – to, as it were, get inside the therapists' skin both for protection and as a way of staying in control. This was an example of the use of projective identification. When a therapist drew attention to this, Mrs Garcia temporarily relinquished her reliance on the defensive structure and experienced panic. She gave a vivid example of how she felt at that moment in the session:

She described sitting in a car at the traffic lights, with the window open. A group of youths were walking down the street in her direction. They did not look tough but as they got near her, her heart beat rapidly; she panicked and immediately shut the window. She was worried that they would beat her up.

This example demonstrates the panic that Mr and Mrs Garcia experienced whenever there was felt to be even a slight crack in their 'super-parent' armour. When Mrs Garcia experiences a space in which the youths, containing her own projections of an enraged, deprived, young self, can touch her she feels threatened. Being

in contact with the therapists' helping capacities involves letting
in this rage about previously unmet needs. It is humiliating and
she wants to 'wind up the window', stay inside the car/therapist
identity and keep unbearable parts of herself out. In this primitive state, the excluded part of herself is concretely felt to be a
'tough enraged youth'. She fears that getting in touch with her
needs would mean actually becoming a violent youth.

> She told the therapists that incidents like that often happened.
> Mr Garcia quickly intervened to say that he knew all about his
> wife's anxieties and added 'the point is can anything be done,
> can anyone help?' He went on to describe an American presi-
> dent's lack of understanding of the needs of the Cambodian
> people and the cutting off of American aid and supplies to these
> people.

When Mr Garcia starts to wonder if someone can help, he is immediately confronted with fears that his needs (placed in the Cambo-
dian people) will not be met and that a catastrophe (his protest)
will follow. It is worth mentioning here that one of the therapists
was American and this particular session was shortly before a
holiday break, so support was actually being withdrawn from the
couple at that time.

The above examples clearly show the important characteristics
of the object relations which the couple shared in their respective
internal worlds: a highly idealized, super-capable, all-knowing,
totally self-sufficient parent and a desperately needy, enraged
child, unattended to and unheard. Being in touch with the needy
child inside themselves threatened an explosive overthrow of their
coping, adult selves, and was to be avoided at all costs or treated
with contempt. So when one parent expressed painful feelings, the
other would deny the problem, or trivialize it by making a joke
or behaving in a generally manic excited way. The therapists too
were experienced by the couple as either 'up' (trying to expose
the couple's weakness in a cruel way in order to be superior and
triumphant) or 'down' (naive, young, inadequate and inexperienced
people).

In discussion after sessions the therapists explored their
countertransference feelings and often one of them would feel
pleased, almost excited about having done some useful work in a
session and the other would feel hopeless about the prospect of
any change. The therapists themselves seemed to find it difficult
to stay in touch with their capacity to offer something helpful in
an ordinary way because it became so easily converted into a kind
of naive optimism or deep pessimism. The therapists became more
critical of each other and at times felt quite competitive. They
no longer felt merged or united but were more aware of their
differences and disagreements. This seemed to reflect the process
of differentiation that was taking place in the parental couple.

The following example illustrates the cruelty to the self and to
the other which is implicit in the omnipotent manic denial of
vulnerability.

> Mr Garcia came to a session feeling depressed. He said that he

had 'come down with a bang', that he felt 'near to tears' and
'redundant'. His wife, finding this intolerable, quickly interrupted, saying that they had to get on with life, it was no
good filling themselves with doubts. She spoke briskly and in
a matter-of-fact-way, indicating by her manner and expression
that it was simply a matter of putting on a brave smiling face.
Mr Garcia attempted to join her in this mood, saying that he
could not wallow in these feelings, he thought he would go
back to work full-time the following week.
Mr Garcia had, in fact, been strongly advised by his doctor to
work part-time. Since his serious illness (in Spain) the previous
year, he remained at some risk and needed to rest and take care
of himself. So his wish to rush back into full-time work, at this
moment encouraged by his wife, represented a denial of both
internal and external reality. They again take refuge in the
omnipotent idea that through some exciting activity, feelings of
depression and humiliation, experiences of damage and dependency
can be obliterated. The concern about the cruel neglect of the self
and, in this case, an actual risk to life is not acknowledged by
them but projected into the therapists who find themselves extremely concerned and anxious about Mr Garcia's health.
It is important to mention that due to limited availability of male
staff at the time of referral, both therapists were women, and in
some ways, this made it more difficult for Mr Garcia to stay with
his depressed feelings at the times when his wife was disowning
hers. It was felt as humiliating for him to be seen as a man in a
'weak state', particularly in the presence of three women and it
was necessary for this to be openly acknowledged. Two women
therapists tended to reinforce the phantasy that one parent could
'do it all', as if the therapists were actually demonstrating that
the male role in the parental functioning was a redundant one. Of
course, as is usual in co-therapy, the actual experience was that
aspects of 'maternal' and/or 'paternal' functions were fulfilled by
both therapists. Nevertheless, it was extremely important to discuss with the couple the meaning they attached to the absence of
a male therapist.
We have described the therapeutic work with the couple's shared
psychic structure, which we have called 'super parent/spouse'.
We have suggested that this structure was based on denial and
projection of intolerable, painful feelings and was characterized by
manic and omnipotent behaviour. This phase of therapy was
characterized by an increasing sense of differentiation and some
acknowledgement of vulnerability.

Emergence of the 'child in the parent'
With a lessening of the need to maintain the defensive structure of
the 'super parent', and with an increased capacity to bear deeper,
more painful feelings, Mr and Mrs Garcia became ready to re-experi-
ence childhood anxieties under the more favourable conditions
provided by the therapist couple. Now that they were more able to
experience the therapists as having something good and useful to

offer them, they were confronted with their anxieties about sharing. These included jealousy of each other's relation to the therapists, jealousy of the therapists' relation to each other and anxiety
about there not being 'enough' for both of them. (Experiences
which they were later able to link with the behaviour of their own
children in early infancy.) Mr and Mrs Garcia would often demonstrate jealousy by a withdrawal of interest.

    For instance, when Mr Garcia described his difficulty about
    being a father, getting close to his children, and his flight
    to helping charities and long hours of work, Mrs Garcia sat
    immersed in her own thoughts, sealed off in a world of her own.
    Similarly, when Mrs Garcia dramatically described some of the
    difficulties which she experienced in managing the home with-
    out help, Mr Garcia appeared inattentive and uninterested.
Progress in the therapy could almost be measured by the closeness
or distance that one partner felt towards the other, when one of
them was voicing a worry. The therapists focused their interpretations on the mutuality of the problem, i.e., the effect of one
partner's difficulties on the other in their shared life together.

    Mr and Mrs Garcia's jealousy of the therapists' 'togetherness'
was sometimes expressed by their talking simultaneously, both
urgently addressing themselves to the therapist sitting nearest
to them. The splitting of the therapist couple was particularly
evident in their respective countertransference experiences, when
they sometimes felt divided in a quite radical way.

    After a session, one therapist felt that she had been 'soaking
    up' the intensity of the couple's distress in such a way that
    she had felt quite unable to think or to comment on what was
    happening. The other therapist felt that she had been reeling
    off 'textbook' interpretations, responding to the discomfort of
    being out of touch with feelings by intense intellectual activity.
Bion (1959) has demonstrated the nature and function of attacks
on linking and the detrimental effect they have on the therapist's
helping capacities, particularly in relation to the therapist's ability
to think creatively. In the previous example, the therapist couple
were experiencing not only an attack on their individual ability to
think, but also an attack on the link between them, their co-
operative effort as it were. In fact, the parents' unconscious
jealous attacks seemed to be directed against three different creative links - the link between the mind of one therapist and the
mind of the other, the link between thought and feeling and the
link between activity and receptivity.

    Another difficulty in sharing occurred when Mr and Mrs Garcia
experienced positive help from the therapists and were then
faced with the anxiety that there would not be enough to meet
their overwhelming needs. They were worried that the therapists
were not strong enough, capable enough or caring enough.

    During one session they talked rapidly about their anxieties
    about themselves. They frequently broke into each other's con-
    versations. At one point Mrs Garcia remarked that her husband
    was 'greedy as a pig', ostensibly referring to his attitude to

food. They later had difficulty leaving the session, still talking
while putting on their coats, saying 'we've got buckets more'
and finally as they walked out of the door 'we hope we haven't
bored you to death'.

Although they were so preoccupied by their worry about 'there
not being enough', they were now more in touch with their anxieties and able to talk about them, rather than simply projecting
them into the therapists.

At other times, the difficulty of sharing their good relations with
the therapists as well as the pain of the damage and loss was
masked by an eroticization of their positive feelings towards the
therapists.

Mr and Mrs Garcia would come to the sessions in yet more ele-
gant and colourful clothes, Mrs Garcia beautifully made up and
Mr Garcia transmitting the piquant aroma of some expensive male
cologne. They would comment on each other's appearance and
generally appear to be excitedly competing to be 'the best' at
winning the attention of the therapists.

At one stage in the therapy when this excited behaviour was a
recurrent feature, there were again somewhat unexpected repercussions in the countertransference.

In discussion after a particularly difficult session, one therapist
remarked that she could not understand why the couple ignored
a seemingly important comment that she had made. The other
replied in irritation that it was possibly due to the fact that she
was wearing a rather tightly fitting dress and therefore could
not expect to be taken seriously.

This kind of sexual rivalry between the therapists who usually
worked co-operatively and easily together, related to the phantasies
apparently aroused in Mr and Mrs Garcia whenever they experienced the therapists paying more attention to one of them than the
other. In Mrs Garcia's case she behaved as if she were having to
bear the humiliation of her husband flirting with two other women
before her very eyes. In Mr Garcia's case he seemed to anticipate
the humiliation of three women 'ganging up' against him and threatening his masculinity. So the good contact between the therapists
and 'the child in the parents' could easily become spoiled by
rivalry, possessiveness and greed, masked by adult sexual seduc-
tiveness. It was necessary for the couple to understand that the
frustrations of the 'needy child' and the intense competition that
this aroused was experienced as so unbearable that it was converted by them into a more exciting sexual relationship with the
therapists which was felt as more bearable.

It was noticeable that in the later phase of therapy when the
good contact with the therapists was more easily maintained, it
sometimes led to a resurgence of jealousy. It was only through the
couple's repeated experience of the therapists' capacities to tolerate
and understand the jealous attacks, that they were able to face
the nature of the rage inside them about previously unmet needs
and to understand the way in which this rage and jealousy threatened to sabotage the helping process.

Gradually they became more in touch with their feelings of loss and unhappiness and were able to express a genuine and increased concern for themselves and each other. The following example is from a session near the end of the second year of therapy.

Mr Garcia said that a friend's father had recently died and he had offered to paint a portrait of the father as he remembered him in his prime. He said it would be an epitaph. When the portrait was completed he saw that he had portrayed the friend's father as an old man dying. Since then he had been unable to paint anything. Mrs Garcia spoke of her husband's paintings, describing how beautiful some of them were. She had never been able to talk to him about why he had stopped painting.

Later, and in subsequent sessions, Mr and Mrs Garcia were able to relive some of the acute pain about the premature death of both their fathers and Mrs Garcia talked freely about her concern for her husband's health, and her fears that he too would die. This also led to an increased awareness of, and concern about similar fears in their own children.

This is not, and cannot be, a complete account of the Garcias' therapy. In fact, this last example indicates the beginning of a more fruitful phase of the work. Mr Garcia's health did improve gradually and the couple made considerable use of their therapy, as did the children. The developmental relationship between the parents' and the children's therapy was, of course, a significant feature. If the parents' difficulties had not been attended to, the children's treatment could not have progressed.

CONCLUSION

The purpose of this chapter has been to examine some aspects of assessment and psychoanalytically based therapy with parents. The necessity of reaching an agreement with parents for treatment as patients in their own right has been noted. The possible detrimental effects of superficial reassurance and advice has been illustrated and attention has been drawn to the fact that work with parents may suffer from the interference of having to carry messages and make practical arrangements on behalf of the child's therapist.

The method of work described here includes delineating the child and adult parts of the parents' personalities and noting how each parent encourages the other to function as a part of his/her own personality in relation to the therapists. The parents' shared internal objects are shown through their response to the therapists' interpretations and examined in the light of the therapists' counter-transference experiences. Obstacles to growth such as jealousy, guilt, the use of the manic defence and projective identification are illustrated. Interpretations based on an awareness of the 'child-in-the-parent's' shared experience with the therapists in the sessions are considered as the basis for growth in the parents' relationship to each other and their children.

7 PSYCHIC PAIN AND PSYCHIC DAMAGE

Gianna Henry

I am going to describe in some detail a short period of co-therapy that a male colleague and I conducted with a family residing briefly in England. Concepts that we had both found useful in analytic work with individuals were used as a frame of reference in the therapy. At the end of this chapter, I would like to discuss the usefulness of transferring a model from one setting to another. In particular, I shall try to differentiate depressive anxiety from depression and to focus a particular type of 'psychic damage' - that is the crippling consequences of defences against psychic pain. In discussing these issues, I shall refer to material in the more descriptive part of the paper.

From the beginning of our contact with the Johnsons the sense of 'ending' was a salient feature, and what emerged as one of the most relevant problems in the dynamics of this family was separation, loss and endings and the difficulties associated with them. The fact that my colleague and I knew from the outset that our work would be short-term probably enhanced our opportunity to explore this area.

THE INITIAL CONTACT

Father wrote to the clinic asking for help because of his own and his wife's concern for their seventeen-year-old daughter Paula. In his letter he described Paula as 'depressed'. A week later Mr Johnson telephoned asking with some urgency if an appointment would be offered and conveying the feeling that the situation had deteriorated since he first wrote. My colleague and I offered an appointment for Paula and her parents with a view to possible family therapy.

No other members of the family had been mentioned prior to the first session. But to the second session the parents also brought their nine-year-old son, Simon. We knew that father was Australian and mother was Scottish. The referral had been received at the beginning of March, and the family was to remain in England until the end of December.

I will give a detailed account of the first session in order to share the experience of getting to know this family.

The predominant feeling during this first meeting was one of tremendous urgency. Father made himself the spokesman for it. As soon as we sat down, he began speaking in a slow, but very insistent voice about Paula's symptoms and his anxiety about them. Paula did not enjoy her present school, she had lost all interest in studying, she hardly ever went out, and she didn't seem interested in sight-seeing. Mother nodded in agreement, but remained silent during most of this session. At first, Paula seemed to conform to her role as designated patient. A tall, rather obese girl, her face totally masked by a hood of dark hair, she was observing us unseen and seemed not to want to be involved in any way. When my colleague remarked on this, Paula slightly opened the curtain of hair and in a soft, but very angry voice, said very explicitly that she herself had no wish to come and see us, but that father had been 'adamant'. She could see no point in it, and she hated being pressured, she was pressured enough at school; at home they pressured her about sitting with the family at meal time, while she was on a diet and didn't want to sit with them at the dinner table. Father intervened, saying that indeed there was a point in coming, and that we had to find a way to engender some 'joie de vivre' in Paula as she took pleasure in nothing, 'adolescence will be over before you know it', he said.

Father's words had an urgent ring to them, and their impact was very strong. I felt that the pressure to engender instant hope was weighing very heavily on us and that a strong feeling of hopelessness was being evoked. I thought that this projection might be a significant communication in terms of the countertransference. Perhaps we could come to know the feelings this family could not tolerate only by having them engendered in ourselves. I acknowledged the urgency of father's request, but said that we were bound to fall short of the family's expectations in terms of 'instant hope'. Paula said it was absurd anyhow to feel hopeful about anything when the world was going from bad to worse. She spoke with great feeling about ecology and pollution and seemed much more angry than depressed. Mother intervened then and somewhat dismissed what Paula was saying. Mother expressed her concern about the imminent arrival of Sonia, a friend of Paula, who was going to stay with them. Sonia's outlook on life was, if possible, gloomier than Paula's. 'We should bring her here too, Sonia and Paula together will really get into the doldrums.' Mother's intolerance of Paula's gloomy communications suggested her own fear of 'getting into the doldrums'. It was becoming increasingly clear that a brief was being given to the therapeutic couple: the brief of very quickly exorcising this dreaded feeling of depression, to engender 'joie de vivre' in Paula, and to take care of the sombre Sonia. As we voiced the perception of being given a brief by the family, father said in a detached tone of voice – as if he wished for the information to go on record – that he himself knew about being 'in the doldrums', because he had gone through a bad spell of depression three years ago; he had received some help, and 'it was now completely over'. By the end of this first session,

Paula still looked very sullen, but now we could see her face, because she had emerged from her hood of hair.

During the first meeting and the subsequent two sessions, it became evident to all the family that, although we acknowledged the pressure, we were not going to provide an instant cure nor yield to their urgency. We defined the boundaries of our initial contact by saying that we were willing to continue exploring the family's problem together with them, to see if it might be useful to embark on a prolonged period of treatment.

All their voices remained very soft throughout, but resentment and disappointment made themselves heard in other ways. We were told of another absent-present member of the family who could profit by coming to us for help, a maternal uncle. He was very prone to violent tempers, but whenever he got angry and felt like 'yelling' he lost his voice completely. He had been given many physical examinations but no organic causes could be found for his symptoms. We were probably being told - through the suggestion that someone else 'should join the session', like Sonia in the 'doldrums' - about a significant problem in the family, i.e., difficulty in dealing with hostility and aggression. We had been struck, for instance, by Paula's particularly soft tone of voice when at the height of her anger.

The fourth member of the family, nine-year-old Simon, was probably the one who least lost his voice when it came to expressing negative feelings. In the third session, he told us about a teacher he hated and put a great deal of feeling into saying so. This teacher, he said, cannot control his temper and shouts at the children all the time, or else 'he just puts you outside the door for no reason at all.' Mother confirmed that this teacher was indeed very highly strung and suggested, with a laugh, that he too might benefit from our sessions. We were getting used to this type of message, and mother may have laughed, I think, because she too was beginning to notice the recurrent suggestion: 'someone else should join us'.

Although the maternal uncle and the teacher seemed chiefly to represent split-off aspects of family feelings, Simon's complaint about the unpredictable man who 'just puts you outside the door' might have had something to do with the family's uncertainty during this period, when they were 'put outside the door' at the end of each session. (We had not yet offered to embark on treatment.)

At our third meeting we offered regular weekly sessions for the remainder of the family's stay in England. We realized that, despite our falling short of their expectations, they all experienced considerable relief when we agreed on a longer-term contract. It was then that mother said our work must have been of help already, because Paula appeared to have come out of her shell a little. She was going out more and had enrolled in an Art class. Mother was pleased, but she regretted that the Art class met only once a week.

Once we had decided to offer a treatment contract, we felt freer to work in the transference and to connect mother's 'only once a

week' to our offer of weekly sessions. Before we had decided on a
longer period of treatment, we were more cautious in interpreting
infantile feelings.

THE TREATMENT

Reaction to the first holiday break
As I have already mentioned, the brief duration of our contact
loomed large from the beginning of our work. Mother was the one
in the family most in touch with feelings about the brevity of the
treatment.

The Easter holiday came shortly after we agreed on regular,
weekly sessions. Mother was very aware of the fortnight break
and said it was a pity to have an interruption so soon after we had
started. Father seemed to ignore our mention of the holiday, and
Paula and Simon did not take much notice.

The first time we saw the family after the Easter holiday, it was
Simon who spoke with great feeling about not liking his parents
to go out and leave him at home with a baby-sitter. Paula would
baby-sit sometimes, but she sounded much less disposed than
Simon to being in the lonely corner of the Oedipal triangle. Her
friend Sonia was now staying with the family and Paula was not
left alone when the parents went out; she had a friend of her own
age. It did not sound as if Sonia and Paula were at all getting
'into the doldrums'; they seemed to be getting on very well, going
out often and having a good time. Paula's attitude seemed to highlight Simon's much less privileged position. I described how, in
the third session Simon had spoken for the family in expressing
resentment at being left outside the door which had probably
reflected his predicament as the youngest member of the family.
Now he was voicing perhaps on behalf of the others as well, how
it feels when parents go out with some reference to the break in
the treatment and to the therapists as a couple that had gone away
and not been available.

In reply to our interpretation about the holiday, mother said
that during the break they had a very frantic time. She spoke of
a very hectic period of sightseeing and complained that father had
to do everything fast, 'as if life was slipping away'. She also mentioned his concern that they would not have seen everything by
the time they return to Australia. She said that she didn't mind
for herself. She enjoys what she does while she is doing it. There
seemed to be a link between this communication and the fact that,
indeed, we would not be able to look at everything that needed
looking at and working through during our brief period together,
but the sense of urgency seemed to have been shifted onto sightseeing.

At one of the subsequent sessions it became apparent that the
family equated the therapeutic relationship with sightseeing, for
defensive purposes. I will report in some detail the material that
led to our discussion of this crucial issue.

At the beginning of a May session, father told us in a rather
off-hand way that the family had been visiting a number of
museums, and the tone of the communication suggested that we
might be one of the sights they were visiting. While talking about
the British Museum, I was struck by the word 'mummy', and I
tried to figure out what connection there was between the museum
material (and these particularly dead exhibits) and my feelings at
that moment of the session. I felt particularly inhibited and had
difficulty in talking during the first part of the session. Could
there be a link between the mummies Paula was talking about and
my sense of being somehow deadened at that point? Was the
Tavistock being turned into a tourist sight and I into a museum
piece, some sort of mummified mother-mummy? In subsequent
conversation with my colleague, who had felt much freer to interpret during the first fifteen minutes of the session, we concluded
that the dead feeling had been lodged chiefly in me during that
part of the session.

The family's perception of the Tavistock as a museum to be
visited served many defensive purposes. The uniqueness of
specific museums seemed to be obliterated – the message appeared
to be that there are museums in every town, and they could go
on with their sightseeing even after they had left England. It was
also significant that this devitalizing transformation of therapists
into museum pieces occurred immediately after the holiday when
our deciding to have a fortnight's interruption and behaving like
a live therapeutic couple, who can come and go, had been resented,
not only by Simon, but by all the family members. Another aspect
was that by deadening an object before it died on them, that is
before separation occurred, feelings of loss and mourning were
bypassed and avoided. When we had interpreted this deadening
process to them as a particular defensive manoeuvre, mother said,
quite sadly, that there actually was very little time before treatment came to an end. She had counted the weeks that remained.
She did not know how many weeks we intended to take off during
the summer, but she knew that they had to leave England by the
end of the year.

It was only when the mood of the session shifted in this direction that the family could examine with us some of their more frequent defences for avoiding psychic pain. A certain capacity to
hold depressive anxiety was required if one were to examine
defences rather than employ them. The frenetic element implicit
in moving from sight to sight had also been present in the family's
relationship with us. At times we were given a wealth of material
and were kept on our toes if we were to distinguish significant
'content' from significant 'process' in the interpretive work.
As the atmosphere became less frenetic (hopefully, through
containment of anxiety), we could begin to talk more about the
frenzy.

It was important to clear Mr Johnson of the charge made by the
rest of the family, that he was the only 'compulsive sightseer'
who needed to speed from one sight to another. Indeed, they had

all willingly joined him during those holiday activities. In this context we spoke of the joint defence that was implicit in treating us as one of the sights to be rushed through. My colleague and I felt that this was the point at which father really became involved in the treatment, and it is interesting that on this occasion he spoke for the first time about his own parents and family. It was the first time, too, that he appeared in the role of someone's child. Mr Johnson had much more difficulty than the others in acting like someone who had had a childhood himself. One might give some thought to the significance in family therapy of the point at which either of the parents or both are able to cross this threshold and talk about their relationship to their own parents.

Father spoke of his mother, who had been dead for three years, and said that his depression had followed her death. He said that he could not forgive himself for having avoided contact with his mother during her long illness. He lived in a different part of the country and very seldom visited her, less often than he might have. He was sure that his mother's ill health had got worse when his sister left home, never to return, because her marriage had not been approved of. He seemed to imply that his absence and his neglect had contributed to the deterioration of his mother's health. He had been away when she died, and still had not yet put a tombstone on her grave. Father spoke with much feeling and sincerity about his difficulties in sustaining pain, mourning and loss. Simon was sitting next to him and drew very close to his father. This was one of the sessions in which the whole family, at least for a time, could sustain feelings of sadness, loss and regret, i.e. depressive rather than pathologically depressed feelings.

It was a good opportunity for us to link their difficulty in dealing with feelings of loss and mourning with the way they were attempting to negotiate the ending of their relationship with us. When we spoke about deadening the relationship, mother had a very spontaneous response to the interpretation. She said that she very seldom forgets people's names, and she was surprised that none of the family could remember my colleague's name when they got home. All they could say was 'Doctor ...what?' The whole family seemed to agree that this was another defence against the risk of losing somebody valuable. It might be described as 'out-of-mind before out-of-sight'.

In this and subsequent sessions we worked steadily on the themes of both sadness and anger. Father showed some concern about his tendency to lose his temper, especially with Simon. He wanted his son to be perfect and probably set very unrealistic standards. As father climbed down from his usual position of rigid authority, there was the risk that the family might take this as a moment of weakness and gang up on him. Mother said she found it extremely difficult ever to be angry when her husband was present, but she could be very angry indeed when he wasn't there, to the extent of occasionally doing mental, if not physical, violence to the children. Mother had never presented an excessively

idealized picture of herself, and this acknowledgment did not
evoke the same kind of attack that the pricking of father's bubble
had. Father merely said that he found it easier to tolerate his
wife showing anger than painful emotions. When visiting relatives
had left for Australia she cried at the airport. Father could not
bear open tears. Both my co-therapist and I felt that this remark
contained an implicit accusation against us, as if we were seen as
wanting to put the whole family in touch with tears that had not
been shed.

Persecutory feelings
I have illustrated some of the defences this family adopted against
painful feelings and depressive anxiety, especially the manic
defences involved in the hectic sightseeing and the drastic deadening measures that were taken against the possibility of mourning
a live object.

I should now like to focus on the emergence of persecutory feelings which seemed to indicate a shift from depressive anxiety back
to a much more schizo-paranoid dimension. These shifts occurred
at different times during the treatment. Two specific examples
seem particularly significant, although they did not emerge in
close sequence.

The first very persecutory image we encountered was in the
extremely vivid description of a woman cousin of father who was
coming to visit the family. We were struck by the possible link
between this overpowering relative and the therapeutic couple,
because the woman was described as 'always full of good advice',
about rearing children and sorting out family problems. She
always acted like an expert, and her expertise seemed to extend
to many fields. They found it very unpleasant to go to museums
with her because she always knew so much more than anyone
else. They also remarked on her accent. She always affected a
very pure English accent in Australia, so they could well imagine
how hard she would try to speak perfect English on her visit. It
was not clear whether this particular remark was aimed at me
(and my foreign accent) or at my colleague, the only one in the
room who spoke with an English accent. What did seem clear, however, was that the links between the cousin and the therapists
suggested that we were perceived as overpowering people who
flaunted their expertise and knowledge of families. Something was
perceived as very persecutory, probably not in our accents but
in the content of our communications. A significant reference to
the cousin seemed to coincide, in the here and now, with what
was happening in the session: father told us that when his cousin
phoned recently from Australia, he so much disliked the sound
of her voice that he held the phone away from his ear and didn't
really listen to what she was saying. During the same session,
twice when my colleague tried to speak, father drowned his
voice with his own. Father seemed unable to listen, even before
he knew the content of the message.

It proved harder to deal with the summer holidays than with the

Easter holiday, because the family had been looking more closely
at some of the defences they used to shield themselves from missing someone. Their defences, then, were less operative and they
were more exposed to painful feelings. After the summer break
another relevant person was mentioned, someone who had never
been mentioned before. This was the maternal grandmother, who
had moved from Scotland to Australia and was described by each
member of the family in turn as somebody they did not look forward to seeing when they returned, indeed the feeling of persecution seemed to be shared by them all. She was described as a
domineering person; she had helped them financially and therefore
felt entitled to organize their lives. They feared her proximity
when they returned to Australia. The family saw her as someone
who was willing to offer a great deal, but for a high price, the
price of their freedom. What seemed to emerge in terms of the
family's relationship with us was anxiety about the strings that
might be attached to whatever we gave to them, and fear of
becoming dependent on us. The holiday break had been difficult
to tolerate, and heightened the feeling that we might be imposing
a rather high price on them.

Dependency and independence seemed to be in the air in this
session. We learned from Mrs Johnson that Simon had taken the
Underground alone for the first time. The whole family seemed
extremely happy and proud of this achievement. Another relative
was also mentioned, a maternal aunt who had difficulty going any
distance from her home and entering unfamiliar surroundings.
She had planned to visit the family in England but was afraid to
leave her home environment. The adventurous Simon and the
almost house-bound aunt seemed to represent the two poles of
independence and extreme dependency. The main anxiety apparent
in this session was fear of being enslaved in a relationship of
utter dependency.

Conclusion
During the last weeks of treatment, feelings of persecution lessened considerably as we interpreted them in the transference.
The parents - more than the children - were particularly able to
sustain feelings of loss and to prize what was going to be missed
with the end of our contact. Father had often spoken of resuming
family therapy when they returned to Australia. Although we
agreed that further help might be desirable at some point, we
thought it might not be helpful to replace us immediately with
another therapeutic relationship, because of the family's specific
problems of working through their feelings of mourning.

Some months after the family went back home, we learned that
they 'were giving themselves time' before seeking further help. The
homecoming had been fraught with difficulties, but they seemed
to have coped without serious crises.

It is hard enough to interpret a communication in the immediacy
of a session, so my hypothesis about the written communication,
'We are giving ourselves time' is very tentative. We had certainly

not offered this family answers or solutions. We had tried to give
them a taste of allowing and valuing a 'space for thinking' rather
than resorting to fast action or other pain-killers. This internal
space is also the essential prerequisite for keeping experience
alive. I think there are grounds for hope that we have been
granted a space in their mind and that we are not totally out of
sight, out of mind.

It is evident that I have described the dynamics of this family
as if I were speaking of an individual struggling with a problem.
Indeed, this was an hypothesis we were testing out in our work.
As I suggested at the outset, we were trying to apply an individual
model in a family setting. To clarify this frame of reference, I
shall continue to discuss the Johnson family in terms of dynamics
that could apply to work with individual patients. Whether this
transposition is feasible or not, our working hypothesis gave us
much food for thought.

At the first session we were presented with a designated patient
whose father had described her as 'depressed'. Our first perception of Paula seemed partially to confirm this. Perhaps this was
a problem of pathological depression, but whose depression was
it? The feelings of great hopelessness engendered in both therapists in the countertransference shed some light on this and it
might be helpful, at this point, to refer to Meltzer's (1978) distinction between hopelessness and despair. One may be hopeless,
without hope, but still painfully yearn for hope. Or one may despair, give up hope and no longer feel pain. If we call the former
'hopelessness' and the latter 'despair', hopelessness seems closer
to feelings of depressive anxiety, while despair (often accompanied
by anger and grievance) seems more typical of pathological
depression. In this context pathological depression can be seen as
a defeat in the struggle with depressive anxiety. 'Depressive
illness arises as the result of the inability to face or adequately
deal with the conflict aroused in the depressive position'
(Rosenbluth 1965).

At the outset Paula was probably so weighed down by the family
projections that she had given up struggling and 'grasping after
hope'. Our sense of hopelessness was engendered chiefly by
father's urgency in delegating the struggle to us. Father asked
for an injection of 'joie de vivre', he was afraid that 'adolescence
would be over before Paula knew it'; and mother wanted us to
keep Paula and Sonia 'out of the doldrums'. The whole family seemed
to be making meaningful communications and suggesting that the
problem was one they all shared. The countertransference message
seemed very clear: the co-therapists were being asked to keep
hope alive, because the family could no longer sustain the psychic
pain involved in the struggle to save hope.

The urgency of the request was probably proportional to the
weight of the intolerable anxiety. We must act quickly and provide
a fast remedy. A specific psychic pain had to be held and be given
meaning, so that it could be borne instead of massively projected
into one member of the family. It sounded as if Paula had given up

the struggle and was 'in despair' when she said that it was absurd
to feel hopeful when the world was going from bad to worse. But
there were also signs that the projection was not too firmly lodged
in her. For instance, when father alluded to his own 'bad spell
of depression', although he needed to add that it was now a thing
of the past, and it was completely over, Paula seemed only too
willing to shed the role of designated patient. Her initial appearance, with her hair masking her face, suggested a 'character in
search of an author', a frequent feature of family therapy, but
she soon emerged as a character 'in fear of an author', an unwilling receptacle of projection. No need to engender 'joie de vivre':
she found her own once the role assignment was lifted.

It was technically very important that the therapists open themselves in the countertransference to the projections that were
present and thus discover what the pain was about, rather than
redistribute the pain at a distance, as if checkmating the different
family members in turn. The projection of deadening in one of the
sessions served many defensive purposes, but it made us concretely aware of the anxious feelings and sense of paralysis involved in identifying with a lifeless object. This, of course, is a
significant feature of pathological depression.

There was abundant evidence that depression was accompanied
by massive persecutory anxiety. This is another feature that
differentiates pathological depression from depressive feelings.
There was a shared nightmare in this family. The individual members might feel the anxiety to different degrees, but there seemed
to be a shared internal object that took different guises; the
image of a damaged, and potentially vengeful mother appeared in
the very first session, when Paula spoke at length about ecology:
the polluted earth, like a neglected mother, might turn vengeful
and starve humanity. Paula's communication seemed to be a nut-
shell version of a problem we were to hear about later: father's
own mother had not been looked after during her long illness. She
had been neglected during her life and had not been mourned
after her death; no tombstone had been put on her grave. This
unmourned persecutory object appeared to be at the core of
father's 'bad spell of depression' and to have weighed him down
into the doldrums.

Until very near the end of treatment, the transference could
shift to very persecutory feelings in the family's perception of
their relationship with us; the therapeutic couple might become
the persecutory object. My colleague's voice became as threatening as that of the formidable cousin. There was indeed a risk of
becoming persecutory and act in the countertransference unless we
were vigilant. We must not march ruthlessly over the family
defences and prescribe compulsory mourning and compulsory psychic pain. We tried to contain the anxieties underlying the defences
and thus make the latter less necessary.

The family we worked with employed several defences. There
were attempts at quick solutions and a search for analgesics as a
defence against psychic pain. Manic defences were abundant,

e.g., the frenetic sightseeing, and it was important that these be
seen as a family pattern and not delegated to father. The casual
transformation of a valuable object into a dusty museum piece might
recur when the Johnsons went home, were they to embark at once
on a new contract of family therapy. Every member of the family
employed projective identification, e.g., the sense of hopelessness
engendered in the therapeutic couple at the first session and the
communication about Egyptian mummies, and there were cross-
projections within the family: Simon was made to bear all the
Oedipal pain; he was the one 'left outside the door' or left at home
when the parents went out. It was important that these aspects
be picked up in the transference, so that the family could see
them as a shared predicament that recurred in their relationship
with us. It was equally important not to collude in making mother
the spokesman for all the depressive feelings the family could
allow itself. She seemed to have assumed that function. She was
the only member of the family who openly commented on the Easter
break. She counted the remaining weeks of therapy, and she
expressed gratitude for Paula's improvement.

Father resented her because she could afford to cry when a
relative left. This frequently happens when a desirable aspect of
internal structures is lodged in one member of a group, because
that person might easily become the five-star patient, the one who
is 'really making use of treatment'. I find this kind of projective
identification, the opposite of scapegoating, extremely frequent in
group processes generally and in family work in particular. It
might elicit a very undesirable preferential attitude in the therapist.

Given the brevity of our work, we could not expect to help our
patients replace a persecutory or idealized object by a good object.
But we could guard against taking a judgmental (persecutory)
stance, and we could refuse to collude in idealizations of the kind
represented by requests for instant solutions. To grasp the
urgency of the request to fulfil an idealized role (a frequent
demand when persecutory anxieties are present) it might be useful to consider the specific element of persecutory anxiety in the
process of mourning.

In 'Mourning and its Relation to Manic Depressive States' (1940)
Melanie Klein says:

> The poignancy of the actual loss of a loved person is in my view
> greatly increased by the mourner's unconscious phantasies of
> having lost his internal good objects as well. He then feels that
> his internal bad objects predominate and his inner world is in
> danger of disruption.

I think this helps clarify the predominance of persecutory feeling in pathological depression, and the link between an impaired
capacity to mourn and sustain feelings of loss and depression was
a predominant feature in the Johnson family's psychopathology.

Severe states of depression might lead to such deadlines that no
attempt is made to restore 'joie de vivre' and there is a total
abandonment to 'joie de mourir'. No such gross pathology was

present in our patients. Consider for instance, father's urgency
in grasping all the good things in life, 'because life is slipping
away'. The manic edge is evident, but there is also a recognition
that life offers good things that are worth grasping. Persecutory
anxiety led to the request that we become an idealized object that
could counteract the dread of deadlines. We could not meet this
brief which would imply collusion at a schizo-paranoid level where
persecutory and idealized objects remain split, but it was important that we understand the anxiety that exerted such pressure
on us to fulfil that role.

In the last weeks of our work, depressive feelings increasingly
emerged and pathological depression diminished. It is natural
that depressive feelings fluctuate, and we tried to draw the
family's attention to the problem of holding psychic pain. Our
hypothesis, derived from work with individuals, was that there
is a close relationship between psychic pain and psychic damage,
and that impoverishment of the enjoyment of life and relationships
can derive from an intolerance of psychic pain. As Kahlil Gibran
said, 'the deeper that sorrow carves into your being the more joy
it can contain' (1926). We feel that we gave some help to this
family to increase their capacity to bear psychic pain without feeling too persecuted. Moreover, it is possible that the psychic
damage resulting from intolerance of psychic pain may also have
been lessened.

8 THE MICRO-ENVIRONMENT

Arthur Hyatt Williams

During ten years of therapeutic work with families, it has become increasingly impressed upon me that the family is the link between the individual and the wider social and cultural milieu. It is the prototype of all small groups. How does it impinge upon the young person who is developing as an individual? It becomes clear practically, as well as making therapeutical sense, that the impact of family upon the developing individual young person both facilitates and also restricts. It is a push-pull system and there are other functions too. If we regard the family as the basic eco-system of human beings, ideas about such phenomena as pollution, stasis, change, self-cleansing arise. When the family interactive eco-system is working satisfactorily, we, in the caring services, are unlikely to be given a chance to observe it, but we are called in when something goes wrong and the family functioning becomes impaired, distorted or comes to a full stop.

Like other relatively safe situations which facilitate development by being to some extent cordoned off from the wider environmental milieu, there are limits so that the sanctuary aspect of the family may, and often does, slip from its facilitating function, first into stasis and then into an increasing restrictiveness, so that what was a sanctuary becomes a prison.

Only after a considerable time did my co-therapist and I realize that the family about which I am now writing had slipped into a closed prison-like restrictiveness. To pre-empt what is to come later on in this chapter, one cause of the situation, which prevailed when we were called upon to give family therapy to the members of the Stone family, was the way in which both parents, but especially the mother, needed to keep the adolescent members of the family as if they were babies, even though they were almost grown-up. This attitude, of course, was unconsciously determined.

The reasons for the referral of the Stone family were that the eighteen-year-old son was said to be violent and unmanageable. Also, the family doctor said that the whole family reverberated with turbulence allegedly set into motion by the disturbed young man in such a way that the doctor was given no peace. Previously, psychotherapy had been given to the index patient - once a week over several years - but though there had been some temporary

lulls, the benefits of the treatment had not withstood the effects
of breaks in the sequence of sessions. At the time of referral to
us, the situation was stated to have reached crisis point.

The Stone family consisted of father and mother in their early
forties, Simon, the son, aged eighteen and Carole, the daughter,
aged sixteen. The father was a highly-verbal, intelligent business man who nearly always started off speaking in the sessions
by recording a catalogue of the depredations of Simon, complaining how Simon made impossible demands arrogantly and then
became abusive verbally when the demands could not be met. After
the words came the violence which was expressed by physically
aggressive assaults upon father, mother or sister or upon any
article of property which was immediately accessible. Simon would
sit listening to all this with rapt attention, nodding his head in
affirmation or shaking it in disagreement. It was clear from his
facial expression that Simon enjoyed being the object of attention.
However, if something was said which touched him at any depth,
he would explode into verbal abuse and follow up the violent words
with deeds. Simon customarily tried to set one person against
another and by seductive eye movements would try to gain an ally.
He would set his mother onto his father or onto one or other of the
therapists. In general he was softer and more ingratiating to the
males and harsher, nastier and more denigrating to the females.
Retreat on the part of his mother or sister seemed to evoke further
nastiness, at least in the early stages of family therapy, often
including scorn and mockery of a sadistic and insulting kind.
Counter-attack on the part of mother or sister resulted in violence,
often in the form of crude physical attacks aimed at inflicting pain.
For example, on one occasion Simon verbally attacked his sister,
Carole, and she shouted back at him, whereupon he got up from
his chair to hit her, saying, 'That'll teach you not to speak like
that to me.' Carole was thus reduced to tears of pain and humiliation. Simon attacked his mother violently on one occasion. He did
not initiate an attack upon his father but during his father's
attempts to restrain him, on one occasion my wife, who was my
co-therapist, designated the toddler part of him as being in a
tantrum and unable to bear any 'adult' advice from a more grown-
up part of himself or from either of us or from any other family
member. He was particularly enraged by this, and father then
intervened at a moment when I was feeling anxious about the
threat of actual violence to my co-therapist. Simon mocked me and
also imitated me without mocking but never threatened me with
violence.

CO-THERAPY

Before going on to recount the history and vicissitudes of the
therapy, I would like to discuss the effect of the fact that the two
co-therapists were related to each other as man and wife.

On previous occasions when she and I have worked together as

co-therapists with families, it has become clear that there are
special features about there being this actual relationship between
us. In most kinds of co-therapy, families tend to try and incor-
porate both therapists as family members. Sometimes they polarize
the co-workers, designating one of them as good and rejecting
the other as bad. The situation usually fluctuates. Family members
almost invariably have phantasies and suppositions about the
relationship which exists between the two co-therapists - that they
are involved in sexual orgies, are quarrelling and fighting. When
the two therapists are actually married, there are even more
efforts to set one of them against the other but there is also a
tremendous feeling that they are in fact inseparable. The link
between the therapists in this case did provide a firm holding
framework within which the family could be contained. But as well
as the family's feeling of confidence that the therapists who are
married to each other are able to withstand any attacks, consciously or unconsciously designed to split them apart, there was
in this case the shared feeling of being confronted with a powerful therapist gang-up against them. Power was experienced by the
family and sometimes omnipotence and/or omniscience were felt to
reside in the two therapists together. The supposed use to which
these persons would be put depended upon how the family viewed
them, and if the family members felt persecuted by the situation,
they saw it as being precipitated solely by the therapists. On the
contrary, if the therapeutic couple (viewed as one) was experienced as a helpful combination, they tended to be idealized. It is
not intended to suggest that the attacks by family members upon
the formal linkage between the co-therapists had no effect. Alternatively, it was clear that at least two things happened to us:
(1) We each experienced the family member or members differently
and, (2) What was actually projected into either or both of us,
if insufficiently worked through by us after the sessions with the
family, made our work less effective. On the other hand, when we
were able to work through both our similar and our different
experiences in relationship to the Stone family something like a
stereoscopic view became possible. It may be that the two co-
therapists who are actually married can find greater opportunities
to reach a more digested and, therefore, more integrated view of
the family in therapy than the unrelated couple where their only
meeting-time may be the therapeutic session with the family. It is
to be emphasized that in family therapy the co-therapists should
arrange to meet at least once between one session and the next
one to discuss and review what went on in the last one, referring
back to previous sessions in order to keep in touch with the trend
of therapy. With family therapy carried out by co-therapists who
are married to each other, however, many meetings occur between
sessions and often issues are brought up and discussed as they
occur to one or other of the therapists.

FAMILY ECOLOGY AND THE MICRO-ENVIRONMENT

While I was thinking of a way of looking at the Stone family and
the violent member who was regarded as their prevailing problem,
I was impressed again by the need to look at individual psychology
and group pathology in order to see what kept the family together
within a micro-environment.

Ecologically speaking the family consists of a small unit. It
starts off with the marriage of two people and begins to crystal-
lize some identity when the couple set up home together. Further
development takes place with the advent of each child. Contact
with the extended family and with various other ecological systems
in the wider environment is established. The situation which
develops is far from being a static one.

Looking at the family as a micro-psycho-social and economic
environment brought to mind the memory of seeing a micro-
environment in the English countryside. It was as follows: many
years ago I saw a large excavation made in the course of extract-
ing gravel. After the end of the marketable gravel had been
reached and the workmen had departed, leaving a large, wide
cavity, changes began to take place. After each rainy period a
pond was formed. At first, it dried up between storms but then
ceased to do so as an impervious layer of diatom and other skele-
tons of microscopic creatures accumulated. Thereafter a very
impressive micro-environment slowly developed, eventually reaching an ecological balance. There were trees, not only round the
edge, an array of plants and a wide variety of fresh water creatures from water voles to frogs, fish and dragon-fly larvae.
There had been formed an oasis which facilitated the settlement
and breeding of diverse forms of life, under conditions which
favoured growth and development. It was less exposed than the
world around it. It was comfortable though eventually to some
creatures it must have been restrictive. I began to think of the
similarity between this micro-environment and that of the family.
There is often the same protection from the outside world, inter-
activeness, ecological balance and ultimately restrictiveness.
When the balance has been disturbed by forces acting within the
micro-environment or impinging from the world outside the
environment, homoeostatic processes are set into motion to restore
it. In the case of the family where this effort has failed, there
comes a point at which they need therapeutic help.

The difference between the natural history of the two eco-
systems, the pond and the nuclear family, is demonstrated by the
way in which they break up. In the course of time, the deep-
rooted sallow bushes will pierce the impervious bed of the pond
and the water will leak out, leaving only an area of damp land.
The nuclear family ends when the growth to independence of the
children results in their leaving home at an appropriate time so
that only the two middle-aged parents are left to reconstitute
themselves in the two-person relations with which they began their
married life together. It must be emphasized that the development

of the children from infancy, toddler stage, latency period
to adolescence and finally adult status poses problems for the
family eco-system. These problems affect the parents differently
at each crisis of the growth and development. This applies whether
the crisis is about physical growth or educational achievement.
Transformations destabilize the family eco-system. In some families
the main efforts of the family members are directed to the task
of negotiating the destabilized periods. In other families, and
particularly in the Stone family, the energies of the parents are
concentrated on the restoration of stability. These efforts are often
successful in reducing strain. This can, however, be at the
expense of the more desirable growth through difficulties towards
independence and separateness within the overall framework of
continued interrelatedness.

In this family it will be remembered that Carole remained childish and Simon rebelled against retribution but they colluded with
each other and often even demanded total service and subsidy.
When the children leave home, fresh adaptive efforts are required
on their part, each in turn of course, and on the part of the
parents whose role has changed and become more limited.

It became clear to us that the Stone family was in the course
of such a period of change, with Simon having reached the age
of eighteen and Carole, sixteen. There was a resistance to the
process of growth towards independence in both the adolescents,
and a resistance to change in and reduction of the established
ecology of the nuclear family which was shown in the behaviour
and attitude of the parents. Thus there was a collusive effort
on the part of the whole family to perpetuate the status quo, and
to prevent what was regarded as the prospect of the death of
the family.

There was a collusive idea in the family that keeping in was
safer than letting out because letting out might be tantamount to
letting die. Fear of persecution coming from outside was exempli-
fied by the fact that both mother and Carole always locked all
the car doors when they were driving anywhere. In line with
this attitude was the way in which they treated my wife and myself during the early part of the therapy. They reacted as if to
say 'We will complain. That is why we came but you must not say
or do anything to anyone of us even if it only seems to be critical.'
The point of this seemed to be that they could put into us any
disturbing state of mind of an individual member of the family
as a whole, but once this was done we must not hand anything
back to them. If we did, one or all of the family members experienced what we said either as a persecution or as a rejection or
both. Having felt incorporated into the family 'pond', we were
being used as therapeutic lavatories or dustbins and only after
considerable work did this situation become modified.

ASPECTS OF ONGOING TREATMENT

It is difficult to describe the atmosphere which began to develop
but both my wife and myself became aware of an atmosphere of
brooding threat. I had known this before when dealing with people
who were in a murderous state of mind. The murderousness of
which we became aware was not in direct form but associated with
a complete lack of care about life – care about the lives of other
people – and we were left filled with anxiety about what might
happen during the period between sessions. My wife made our
anxieties explicit in one particular session but there was then
no time to open up the subject before it ended. The brief mention
of possible attack on life did not mitigate the anxiety of the two
therapists. I would like to stress a point of technique, namely
that brief mention may do more harm than good and that working
through a difficult state of mind, individual or shared, takes time
and work.

At the next session there was an atmosphere of gloom and fear.
The story emerged that Simon had parked his car, opened the
door to get out and a drunken cyclist had struck the door, skidded
and fallen heavily on the road, struck his head upon the hard
road surface and died in minutes of an intra-cranial haemorrhage.
Simon was prosecuted and found it impossible at that time to feel
sorry for the dead man. He was bogged down at the paranoid-
schizoid end of the anxiety spectrum (see glossary). To us this
indicated that Simon, in particular, and the Stone family, in
general, were in a state of mind in which there was no thought
for others, no real regret over irremediable harm done, but only
a shared wish to get away with it without blame or punishment.
The implication of this was that there could be no learning from
the experience of this awful incident and without such 'learning'
the catastrophe might be repeated. By this it meant that Simon
was not feeling guilt or remorse. He was not feeling sorry for
the man who had lost his life but, on the contrary, was angry
with the victim for 'causing' him so much trouble. He felt aggrieved
and wronged. This state of mind is characteristic of that of the
very young infant, and in a young man of eighteen years of age
is indicative of a severe degree of emotional immaturity.

The family were only marginally more concerned but mainly
protective towards Simon. My wife and I were shocked and sad.
Also we wondered how much this was an overdetermined situation,
and how much it was an entirely fortuitous disaster to which the
Stone family, in general, and Simon, in particular, were responding in a way which characterized them. The sadness we felt may
have been that which Simon and the rest of the Stone family could
not face in themselves. The state of mind that eluded them at
this stage was that of feeling depressive anxiety in which sadness
and regret are tolerated and from which arises attempts to make
amends for harm done (see glossary).

When the court case was over the family relaxed, and there was
a good deal of rather macabre jokiness. It was at this point that

we were able to point out the shared attitudes of the Stone family.
Other people did not really matter at all except in so far as they
were useful to them. When family interpretations were made there
was an immediate scurry to load that which was experienced as
blame or accusation onto Simon. It was constantly made clear that
Simon was repeatedly set up as the executive agent of all the
family violence and aggressiveness. The elements of family interaction in the session consisted of accusations used as missiles,
mockery and devaluation with the aim of deskilling a family member
or either therapist. Soft soaping, placation and threats were all
elements which were used in dealing with the therapists, but
self-accusations were experienced as if they were coming at one
or other family member from either or both of the therapists.

COUNTERTRANSFERENCE EXPERIENCES

Quite early in the family therapy as we observed the undercurrent
of incestuous sexuality between the two young people we drew
attention to it but it was denied. We, the co-therapists, designated
as grandparents, were nearly always set up as critics but not in
a straightforward way. My wife who is about the same age as Mrs
Stone was loaded with anger and disapproval, the anger and
disapproval was that which Mrs Stone would normally have felt,
while I experienced a mixed response. On the one hand, I could
see what dreadful things Simon said and did, but at the same time
I responded to a certain comic quality in his behaviour. The
response would have been appropriate had I been watching a comic
play but to Simon's burlesquing there was a more serious and
ominous side. I used to feel embarrassed when I found myself
smiling or even laughing at what was going on, especially when I
looked across at my wife and saw that she was angry with me. I
later realized that I was being 'conned' by the shockingly amusing
aspect of infantile behaviour which was a result of Simon's switch-
ing on to one of his joke-selves - a practised parade of the
naughty little boy. My wife, however, was filled with disapproval
of the manic current which had taken over with its mockery and
cruelty - another aspect of Simon's behaviour. In the discussions,
which we had after the session, we reached the conclusion that
we were being 'programmed' differently, probably by means of
projective identification, so that we became possessed by different
feelings. We had not experienced the different responses to
specific family issues in this way before. Since treating the Stone
family, however, we have had further co-therapy experiences
with other families which suggest that what we thought was
happening to us then really belonged more to the Stone family
than being part of our own individual psychopathology. We were
being projectively identified with differently.
There is a likelihood that adolescents project differently into
parents (and other authorities) and as a result often do see them
at loggerheads with each other. Our different responses to a family

may have been related to the different feelings experienced by
different family members at a given moment in time, with the
implied taunt being added in the form of the question 'How do
you cope with this?' The projection into another person of a state
of mind belonging to the projector was first described by Klein
(1946) and named Projective Identification. The object or projectee
experiences what has been put into him, and the projector, the
subject, is freed, at least to some extent from a state of mind
which is unbearable in one way or another. The equation can be
and often is reversed, so that what has been put into someone
is returned, and this is what Simon appeared to do - returning
what had been put into him as well as much of his own violence
(which was added to it). I must emphasize that projective identification is not the same as projection. In projection a state of
mind of the self is ascribed to someone else, not actually evoked
in him.

We realized after some period of time that the Stone family sometimes communicated as a whole and sometimes as individuals. When
they did so as individuals by means of projective identification,
it followed logically that we as therapists were likely to 'be taken
possession' of by states of mind which were quite different from
each other. The different feelings which had been evoked in us
had the effect of driving us apart so that we had the problem of
attempting to bring together and to understand the differences.
It will be evident that those differences really belonged to members of the Stone family and were the ones which they had been
unable to harmonize. How we, the two co-therapists, coped with
this situation was to try and work upon our own states of mind.
This was particularly important in the intervals between the
family therapy sessions in which we differed. When we had been
able to do this, and to respond to what was happening in the
following sessions, we noticed that the family members were able
to work better with us and also with each other to some effect
between the family therapy sessions. This exemplifies the need
for co-therapists to work over together, after sessions, the often
painful experiences, so as to provide a basis for further work
with the family.

STEREOTYPING TO AVOID INTRAPSYCHIC CONFLICT

Nevertheless each family member behaved in his or her individual
and characteristic way and the pattern was fairly fixed and constant. Simon listened to everything but was more prone than the
other family members to externalize what he had learnt from the
therapeutic session, and to apply it to the others rather than to
himself. To some extent the other family members also behaved in
a similar way, but less exclusively so. Father intellectualized
everything, mother felt accused of being a failure and wept
copiously. Carole, when she felt accused, accused somebody else,
usually Simon, but at times she quarrelled with her mother or her

father or with either of the two therapists. She had a high-pitched
voice and a babyish expression. These individualized roles which
the family members took meant that there was no individual feeling of responsibility for any aggression. What was the most
troublesome was a serious quantum of non-contained violence
which floated about and for the convenience of the rest of the
family it continued in the main to be settled upon Simon. He in
turn was susceptible to this loading upon him of all the awfulness,
and his response was complicated. He was angry and outraged but
also excited and exhibitionist like the actor in melodrama who plays
the part of the 'baddie'. Being the recipient of what the other
family members put into him gave a sense of importance as in the
well-known children's game 'It'. By 'it' I mean that he was singled
out by the family to act upon their behalf as a receptacle for, and
perpetrator of, all the family violence. But as well as being pleased
at being 'it', Simon was persecuted and aggrieved by having that
role thrust upon him. The enjoyment of being 'it' is a more serious
feature as it is perverse and is alienated still further from normal
healthy functioning.

At this stage we began to interpret the way in which the family
violence and anti-developmental aggressiveness were put into or
upon Simon and how, despite all protestations to the contrary, in
many respects it suited the rest of the family for this to happen.
It relieved them of guilt, externalized the responsibility, and gave
them all a cherished grievance together with a comfortable sense
of their own virtue. It also fitted in with the vain and exhibition-
istic aspects of Simon as he basked triumphantly in the notoriety
of every tense and reproachful family situation. This was a perverse aspect of his character. At other times he was able (with
some justification) to feel persecuted at being set up as a scapegoat by both his parents and his sister; and this attitude it must
be stressed, was an indication of the more healthy aspect of him
which developed further during therapy, albeit slowly.

One of the features which we noted in all members of the family,
but especially in the two adolescents, was that introjection (i.e.,
the taking into the self of experiences, communications, or
interpretations of either or both the therapists) seemed to constitute a psychically indigestible meal. This in Simon usually resulted
in an action or a series of actions by means of which he disbur-
dened himself of what had got into him. It also meant that nothing
in the way of an interpretation - or any kind of experience, say at
work - was ever retained in his mind for long enough for it to
'mature in cask' so to speak and thus lead to some development
and personal integration.

There was another aspect of not learning from experience shown
mainly by Simon but also by his sister and to some extent his
parents. This was the addictive nature of the relationships affect-
ing not only the nuclear family but being markedly manifested
in the relationship with both therapists. By addictive I mean a
need and a dependency but without a growth towards freedom,
ultimate independence and personal sovereignty.

MUTUAL EXPLOITIVENESS

Among the situations which we thought were important was the
sibling rivalry between the two young people, characterized by a
tyrannical, controlling attitude on the part of Simon towards his
sister and a more subtle manipulation stemming from her. Both
young people seemed to have an infinite expectation of service
and devotion from their mother, but Carole did not attack mother
with the same fury as Simon did. Remarkable also was the greedy
and demanding love Simon expressed in relationship to his father.
Cuckoo-like, he had successfully pushed Carole out of the
relationship with his father. He was also peremptory and arrogant.
I think that need and greed displayed in this way without care
and responsibility in relationships is why we thought of him as a
parasite. He extracted all the goodness that he could and appeared
to be unable to benefit from it. When the hosts upon whom he was
parasitic rebelled or refused him he became violent and destructive. Mr Stone appeared secretly to share his son's view of women
as slaves to be exploited and ill-treated, though his view was
expressed in a more muted way and in more diplomatic terms by
him than by Simon.
   Whenever some concern for family members or either therapist,
girlfriend or person at work began to be felt by Simon, the pain
aroused by the dawn of insight into the way in which he behaved
towards them immediately became intolerable and designated as
persecutory. Depressive anxiety based upon guilt and remorse
thus was rapidly replaced by persecutory anxiety based upon a
sense of aggrievedness. Simon then acted upon his feeling that
he had been wronged and tried to punish the object of his concern
so compounding the attacks upon other people. This aspect of his
relationships with other people was very important in the early
stages of the family therapy and it was characterized by exploita-
tiveness and an absence of regard for the individuality or personal
sovereignty of any other person with whom he was in close contact.
   One feature of Simon's arrogance was his expectation of enormous success at his work in business. He managed to arouse
expectancy of great things from him in his employers and usually
began to do a new job with application and initiative which brought
a degree of initial success. This did not last long. Trouble started
when he became discontented and bored because his rise was not
meteoric; he began to treat the people who worked with him very
badly, so that sometimes a spirited secretary would refuse to do
what he told her to do. At other times he would be reported for
rudeness or arrogance. Eventually he would be asked to leave,
and then having saved no money, again he would become a total
charge upon his father. Gradually it dawned upon us that Simon's
identification with his father included an imitation of his father's
attitude towards other people, especially his subordinates at
work. What Simon did, however, was to caricature and distort his
father's attitudes and behaviour. In this there was an attempt to

'be' his father, but also at the same time an attempt to 'guy' him.
In the therapy he did not do this to my wife, but certainly he did
it to me, and to give him his due, he put up a very creditable,
comic impressionist act. But the caricaturing and guying was part
of a defence against really experiencing being dependent, lonely
and envious, and what was unproductive was the way in which the
caricaturing stultified any real learning, from that particular facet
of experience. In order to learn from an experience it has to be
borne for some considerable time and this was very difficult for
Simon to tolerate. In contrast, when Simon became angry and
destructive, paranoid processes predominated with escalating
intensity. When he was in a manic psychic current he was mildly
grandiose, condescending and quietly mocking. It was an 'I'm all
right, Jack' attitude.

Both of these states of mind defended him against psychic pain.
He could not sustain the approaches to the depressive position,
because of the pain associated with that, and any brief reparative
activities consisted of manic reparation which is associated with
the avoidance of painful personal feelings despite glib protestations of regret or good intentions. There was for some time little
ability to learn from what was going on in the therapy until he
gradually developed the capacity to own some of his parasitic and
destructive aspects and painful state of mind without immediately
rushing into action. The first steps towards this improvement
followed on from our being able to relieve Simon of some of the
projections and projective identification put onto and into him by
other family members.

SHIFTING OF VIOLENCE

The course of family therapy seldom does run smoothly and if it
does so one should suspect that nothing is happening. Usually it
goes from crisis to crisis with scattered intervals of comparative
calm. At one point there was a misunderstanding between father
who was unwell, his daughter and wife – Mrs Stone indulged in a
bit of mischief-making, contradicting what Mr Stone had said to
Carole. Suddenly Mr Stone flew into a violent rage and threw his
whole meal together with the plate containing it at his wife's
favourite picture. Then he proceeded to throw everything everywhere, wrecking the room. This episode of violent and destructive
behaviour was recounted in detail in the next session by Mrs Stone
while her culprit of a husband listened sheepishly, and looked like
a small boy in the headmaster's study, at school. On this occasion
Simon, very much alerted by the smell of trouble, quickly made
a take-over bid for my therapeutic role and interpreted with less
caricature than usual father's regression and childish anger.

My wife drew attention to the way in which the mantle of
violence had now fallen upon Mr Stone and wondered what would
happen next. She speculated about how long it would be before
violence was forced back into Simon. We had not long to wait, and

it did not really surprise us when the next session began in the
old familiar way. Simon had lost his job and broken up the
drawing-room at home. A contributing factor had been jealousy
which was intolerable to him and which was roused when Carole
announced that she was going to marry her boyfriend. It appeared
that the marriage was to be many years in the future, but Simon
had felt upstaged by it. He had had a succession of girlfriends.
The relationships had not lasted because each girl after a brief
infatuation had found him to be quite intolerable. The clear statement of disapproval of Simon's unacceptable behaviour, instead of
acting as a guide and helping him to moderate it, goaded him to
further nastiness even amounting to violence and that finalized
his rejection by the particular young woman of the moment.

The next shift to violence was to mother. Carole spoke rudely
to me and her mother remonstrated with her, but was then
answered even more rudely by Carole. Mrs Stone with no warning
stood up at this point, quickly crossed in front of me, and hit
her daughter hard four times. Again my wife drew attention to
the way in which the violence had settled upon Mrs Stone who, for
that moment, carried all the family violence on behalf of everyone
in the family. One of the problems which confronted the therapists
was the way in which the work done in a family therapy session
was undone during the time gap between two sessions. It was like
Penelope's tapestry - woven by day and then dismantled by night.
At times the violence floated round in a very unstable state, waiting until it settled upon some family member. There was always
something of a relapse during our periods of holidays, or when
Mr and Mrs Stone went on holiday leaving the children to cope for
themselves on their own in the family home. Against the backcloth
of improvement and relapse changes of a more ongoing nature
eventually did begin to show themselves as is usual in treating
families.

ASPECTS OF MANIC DEFENCE

Before recounting the last phase of therapy with the Stone family
as a whole, it is important to discuss some of the ways in which
mockery, guying, etc., were used during the course of the
therapy. At first, we thought that the mockery was one feature of
a pervasive and shared manic defence. Later, we were able to see
in more detail that although mockery was part of a manic defence
against experiencing pain, it was also against being the recipient
of all interpretations which struck home. There were two separate
uses of it: it was used as a defence against acknowledging their
destructive impulses and if that defence failed the aggressive
impulses were acted out concretely; it was also used as a defence
against good experiences such as developmental impulses and good
identifications and against the two therapists when they were at
their most helpful. This use was under the sway of envy. It was in
this state of mind under the influence of envy that the sudden

relapse occurred so that the two therapists felt hopeless and were anxious lest their endeavours had been set to nought.

Caricaturing was a specialized kind of mockery. Simon used it a great deal but so also did Father. As we stated earlier, Mr Stone deskilled and patronized females. My wife suffered from these attacks more than I did from Mr Stone who would repeat her words incredulously, and then smile as if to imply: 'You are madder than I thought you were.' Caricaturing also had an element of less destructive identification about it, and especially in the case of Simon consisted of quickly seizing the identity of the other person without any discrimination or working through. It resembled the imitation of words by a parrot rather than the learning of a language by a person (see Melanie Klein, 'On Identification' (1955)).

THE LAST PHASE OF FAMILY TREATMENT

Simon had settled into a new and better job. Things seemed to be a lot better. Then we were told that Mr and Mrs Stone were going away on holiday together leaving the young people to look after the house and after themselves. But at the next family meeting it was clear that there had been disturbances. Simon had become very keen on a young woman and according to Carole had hardly been in the house, and had given her no help during the absence of the parents. She said that he had been a parasite upon her and that she had done her best to do all her own work and also act as 'mother' in the home. Simon said that Carole had been diligent and excessively fussy and demanding of his time and attention. It was stated that Carole got into a 'state' when Simon brought home his girlfriend late at night, though he had not taken her to his bed. On the return of the parents Carole had complained bitterly and they had scolded Simon who then became destructive in the old pattern of behaviour and they said that he must leave home and find a place for himself. Simon left home at once not for the first time but for the third. On this occasion however he went out and found his own place while previously his father had found a place for him. Meanwhile he had broken up the furniture at home and had ended up in a disturbing and upsetting fight with his father. It was all very alarming, and we wondered whether relapse was total, but through it all we were aware of a plea implicit in Simon's destructiveness, which ran as follows: 'As long as I remain embedded in this family I will never be able to behave responsibly and control the destructive little-boy part of myself.' We interpreted this and the parents and Carole were outraged, but Simon agreed seriously and sadly, looking very relieved. During the interval between sessions Simon had shown regret for his behaviour, and apologized and had attempted to make amends as best as he could and these seemed to be reparative activities which did not have the manic quality of former times. We both felt that something different was happening.

At the next session Carole began by saying that she had decided
not to come to any further sessions because there was nothing
wrong with her and she only came to do Simon good. Simon retal-
iated by treating her as if she were the little child, calling her
piggy which infuriated her, and patronizing her, in his former
outrageous way. Towards the end of the session, when both
therapists were wondering if there were a way of interpreting an
undercurrent of tempting but frightening incestuous sexuality
which might have determined or at least worsened the troubles
when the parents were away on holiday, the next event took place.
Carole, goaded beyond endurance, suddenly got up from her
chair - rushed across the consulting room and bashed Simon
several times about the head and shoulders. As she did this I
thought that she looked more like an outraged wife or fiancée
whose spouse or lover had been unfaithful to her, than an angry
sister. To our surprise Simon was not violent in retaliation but
instead tried to control his sister as gently as possible. He looked
awkward and embarrassed and finally picked up his sister and
half pushed her onto the consulting room couch. Before letting
her go he lingered over her in what looked more like an embrace
than an attack. I thought of Romeo and Juliet. We interpreted
along these lines, linking what had just happened in the session
with the difficulty that had arisen during the parents' holiday. We
pointed out that they had been left together to play the well-
known game of 'mummies and daddies'. This was very exciting and
very frightening, particularly to Simon who, it had been reported,
had made many sexual advances towards his sister when they
were both young children. We also pointed out how, at the beginning of family therapy, all of them had refuted our interpretation
about the incestuous undercurrent that was going on between
Simon and Carole.

Carole did not come again; but events moved rapidly with Simon
who stated that he wanted to get married soon. He told his girlfriend about his difficulties and he asked whether the therapists
would be willing to see him with her for one interview and then to
find him someone who would help him with his own problems. He
was very worried lest he should wreck what was felt by him to be
a very good relationship. We did see them together and also saw
Mr and Mrs Stone as a marital couple at a later date. Simon was
referred to a colleague for individual help.

SUMMARY

In looking back and considering what happened during four years
of fortnightly psychotherapy, there was first the phase of the
embroilment of the two co-therapists in the confusing cut and
thrust of life in the Stone family. The experience of being drawn
into an interactive situation which was verbally and sometimes
physically violent made it possible to see how convenient it was for
the most disturbed member of the family, Simon, to become the

scapegoat target for all the family projections. These included violence, arrogance and dependency in its infantile sense.

When this phase had been understood, though not brought under control for very long at a time, the violence began to move round the family from Simon to father to mother and then to Carole. Violent feelings were aroused in the two co-therapists who were thus enabled to see and feel what life in the Stone family was like. Glimpses, and sometimes longer views, of the shared parental need to keep the baby adolescents at home (in the family pond) and the collusive aspects of the exploitative young people were obtained.

In our particular method of working, the family was treated as a unit and family interpretations were made. As well as this, however, individual interpretations were made and these were intended to illuminate the behaviour of a family member who was acting on behalf of the family or rebelling against the pressure to act on their behalf. Transference interpretations were made and countertransference issues discussed fully by the therapists between sessions.

During the first stage of treatment the emphasis was on containing some of the explosiveness in the family, then a loosening and sorting out of the projections, the uncovering of the incestuous undercurrents and finally the freeing of the index patient, Simon, to ask for individual therapy, were substantial achievements. It was clear that the family by the end of family therapy was able to countenance the end of the nuclear family phase and the young people were fit and ready to move out of the enclosed, restrictive home into the wider social milieu.

9 THE AFTERMATH OF MURDER

Roger Kennedy and
Jeanne Magagna

INTRODUCTION

This paper describes the consequences of an act of murder and murderous phantasies in a family seen in weekly therapy by male and female co-therapists. We shall discuss details of sessions with the family in order to illustrate various themes, in particular, the way that a murder affected the object relations of the individual family members and thus the family dynamics; the difficulty the family experienced in coming to terms with the loss of the murdered mother; and the role that perverse sexuality seemed to have in preventing adequate mourning for the mother. The two main hypotheses suggested here are: (1) When there is a strong murderous phantasy, or an actual murder in the family, there may occur, during the phase of regret and remorse, a life-risking psychosomatic symptom which symbolizes an identification with the attacked or murdered person. (2) Perverse sexuality may be used to fend off experience of damage and loss which has occurred either in phantasy or in actual life, because experience of the damage and loss presents such a new catastrophic shock to the psychic structure of the people involved. We think that these hypotheses have consequences for understanding family dynamics, individual pathology and the predisposition to murder.

FAMILY BACKGROUND

The 'family', particularly disguised for reasons of confidentiality, consists of the presenting patient Roy, aged fourteen, his sister Jill, aged eighteen, and the uncle and aunt, who raised the children. The actual mother of the children was murdered several years before the referral. Their father has had only intermittent contact with them and he was not involved in the family therapy sessions.

Roy was referred by his school because of their concern that his preoccupation with sex could be a danger to the girls there. He was thought to be oversexed, obsessed by pornography and involved in stealing incidents while truanting. He had a somewhat supercilious, smiling and 'could not care less' attitude. He had no close friends, apart from his sister, preferring, as he described it, 'to sail his boat alone'. He was of average intelligence, had difficulty concentrating and was poor at reading.

Jill gave the impression of being fiercely independent. She had educational problems, and had a reputation at school for 'precocious sexuality'. The children had a close 'conspiratorial' relationship, and both, but particularly Jill, were often hostile to their aunt and uncle, while idealizing their father. The father had had no regular work and he appeared to have been involved in various small-time criminal activities. The uncle and aunt had been barely on speaking terms with him for several years. The uncle, a banker, was rather enigmatic. He came for only two sessions, said he disliked talking, indicating he was a stutterer as a young man, and also that he had a strict and intimidating father. His wife was strong, dominating and somewhat obsessional and rigid. She was articulate, rather abrasive and had a tough over-confident veneer. The dead mother was described by the aunt as sweet and gentle, but taken advantage of by the father, through his ventures with money and other women.

In the initial assessments, the aunt clearly showed strong ambivalent feelings towards the children. She conveyed, on the one hand, extreme bitterness and resentment about having to care for them since their early childhood and at times it seemed that she intensely wanted to be rid of them as soon as possible. On the other hand, it was evident that she was very concerned about Roy's predisposition to follow in his father's footsteps. The uncle seemed to have washed his hands of the children.

We have several versions of the murder of the mother. It seems that a waiter, the lover of the family's maid, robbed, strangled and then cut the throat of the mother while the father was away. Although Jill claimed she witnessed the murder, others reported that she found the body in a pool of blood after the murder and ran to a neighbour saying her mother was unwell. There was a suspicion, though not substantiated, that the father was somehow implicated. Pornographic material involving murder was found among his possessions.

ASSESSMENT AND TREATMENT

Roy was first seen for an individual assessment while his aunt and uncle were seen jointly by another worker. Because Roy had little motivation for getting help, individual therapy was felt to be unsuitable. It was also felt that he was in the middle of a profoundly difficult and perverse system of family relationships which required exploration before individual therapy for any of the family members would be feasible. When family therapy was suggested, the aunt and uncle reluctantly agreed to follow this recommendation.

We shall look at three phases of family therapy: an 'introductory phase' in which there was a consolidation of the relationship

between the aunt and Roy, the only family members present at
this point; a second phase, 'abandonment and horror' in which
feelings of being abandoned and the horror about what might be
revealed in the sessions predominated. The children came alone
apart from a few sessions during this phase; a third phase of
'somatization and flight' in which, although Roy's symptoms had
improved, the family members had various physical illnesses
including the aunt having a near fatal complication following minor
surgery. Subsequently, the family broke off therapy. The discussion of the various phases will be followed by a summary in
which we shall bring together the various themes in this unusual
family history.

I INTRODUCTORY PHASE

In the first session, the aunt did most of the talking, in her
rather breathless way. She made excuses for her husband, saying
that he was too busy. If nothing happened, he would not be able
to stand it. Jill was unable to get time off work. It seemed that
the aunt had brought Roy to be individually treated. She was
incensed with our suggestion that, although recognizing Roy's
difficulties, we felt the family shared some of them. Roy often
smiled superciliously in a passively aggressive manner.
  The aunt began by saying that things were not so bad, and
that they could all cope really. She continued by talking about
what she had to do for others which took up so much of her time.
For example, she had two 'geriatrics' to look after, her mother
and mother-in-law. She mentioned concern for her own capacity
to mother: 'Roy had the same bad upbringing as my children had.'
Roy did not volunteer anything. He had to be asked several times
by both therapists before he would speak. He said that he was
annoyed that, when he was in his previous boarding school at
the time his father was in an 'open-air prison', he had not received
his father's letters. His aunt pointed out that he had in fact read
them, but Roy still could not remember. The aunt mentioned what
a bad lot his father was, always in trouble, and having to be
bailed out by her and her husband.
  In the last part of the session, the aunt discussed Roy. She
hated him when he lied or was lazy. The previous day she went to
work hating him, but when she returned he had cooked dinner,
and so she forgave him everything. She seemed easily swayed by
his charm. Her anger, she said, was 'all or nothing'. We commented
on how difficult it must have been for her, being and yet not being
a mother to the children. She responded saying that what she
didn't like about Roy was that he did not bother. We commented
on how the whole family was not bothering to come together to
the sessions and we wondered whether Roy's attitude reflected
something about the whole family's attitude. This made some sense
to them. The aunt also said to Roy, 'Why don't you attack me?'
We pointed out that he seemed to be attacking her by not accepting

what she gave him and through his passivity. Near the end of the
session we were discussing Roy's educational problems. The aunt
was angry with a teacher (who had the same name as Roy). Her
last words were, 'I would like to ... her.' The unspoken word
seemed to imply some kind of violence.

In the next session, the aunt complained about how much she
had to organize and check up on Roy. We commented on how Roy
seemed to be kept in this position like a much younger boy in
relation to her. Roy described his own attitude. 'I'm conceited ...
I love myself, I do. If I do something well, I think I'm the
greatest.' We discussed how this attitude might hide his pain
about not being able to do successfully everything he attempted.
We then talked more about the relationship between Roy and his
aunt.

She found Roy's early physical maturity surprising – saying
how big he had become. She talked with some excitement about
the difficulties in coping with such a large boy. We discussed how
Roy might be a source of excitement for the family and how, by
his behaviour, he might keep things more lively at home. The aunt
said that she and her husband were so busy worrying about others
that they had no time to worry about their own problems. There
was a veiled hint that this excitement over the boy's misdemeanours
might have kept the aunt and uncle together. However, she added,
she was looking forward to the time when the children left home:
'My mothering days are over', she said.

In the next session the aunt said Roy had begun to take more
interest in school work. We also learned more about the family's
home life. There was little family discussion. The aunt did most
of the housework while the others watched television. It appeared
that she was quite obsessional about tidiness. Roy's room was
untidy. He shoved everything under his bed, but more recently
he had stuffed his belongings into a wooden crate there, a crate
which he and his sister named the 'coffin'. This naturally led on
to some discussion of the murder.

Roy had been told about it by his sister, when he was younger,
at the time when he had asked her why he did not call his aunt
his mother. At this point, when for the first time in the session
he revealed some immediate anxiety, he started to blow his nose.
(In the original individual assessment, Roy had said that he often
wondered what his mother was like. He had seen pictures of her,
which made him cry and he wondered when he looked at them,
'Is that my mother?')

We discussed Roy's wish for a mother and how it contrasted with
the aunt's original plan to have the children for a limited time. We
also looked at her current feelings of being tired of being his
'mother'. There were subtle indications that the aunt wished that
we would take over the parenting, or at least become the 'grandparent figures'.

We were able to discuss fairly openly her problem of being an
aunt and the lack of the usual incest taboo which exists between
mother and son. They revealed some sadness about some of the

closeness which had been missed in their relationship. The aunt
felt that Roy's relationship with his father spoiled the possibility
of a good one with her. When he turned to his father, she withdrew from him.

The last session of this phase, before a holiday, began with
silence and difficulty in talking which, when interpreted, led on
to fears of what might happen if the sessions went any further.
There was also a fear of showing anger, particularly towards us,
with the aunt flattering and appeasing us with gifts. What was
apparent now was a split in the couple's relation to us and the
real father, with the therapists idealized as good and the real
father as the mean parent who deserted children. The children's
split was in reverse, with the real father held as ideal and the
therapists as non-understanding and unforthcoming. In both
instances, these splits prevented the children and the couple from
experiencing their anger with us for deserting them for our
holiday.

Comments on introductory phase of therapy
The aunt and Roy's relationship was somewhat improved in these
sessions, but the family was difficult to treat, both because of
the members' shared memories of a horrific past and because of
their current 'knife-edge' balance; the family seemed to have
erected various precarious defences against intolerable anxiety
related to their knowledge of the past. No doubt any family would
have to be exceptionally united and understanding to deal with
such strong pressures from memories of actual violence.

What was clear was that this family had difficulty in talking
about tender and depressive emotions. Both in the past and in
their present relation with us, they suffered from the absence of
someone like a mother whom they could feel would bear their distress and their complaints. This was indicated in the aunt's own
remarks concerning her mothering days being over; also by her
remarks about what a bad upbringing the children had had and
her denigration of mothers, suggested by her reference to her
own mother as 'a geriatric'.

Roy, the presenting patient, seemed to be carrying the delinquent, pornographic, murderous phantasies regarding the mother
for the others, thus relieving them of the burden. The murderousness was stuffed under his bed like the contents of the wooden
crate which he called 'the coffin'. The father, with whom Roy
strongly identified, seemed to be the idealized, criminal father,
who was also carrying projections. Roy referred with pleasure to
the 'open-air prison', a contradiction in which, in Roy's view,
his father was enjoying his stay in prison rather than being
punished there. Idealizing his father seemed to occur partly
through equating breaking the law with strength. Presumably this
was done to hide the absence of a functioning father in reality.
The uncle was a weak, substitute father, while the real father was
rarely present. The need for a capable father was particularly
present in the family's intense leaning on the male doctor/therapist.

In this phase, the aunt revealed her excitement in the relationship
with Roy which was unfettered by the normal incest taboo. This
lack of an incest taboo and the absence of a strong father were
perhaps factors destructive to the building of affectionate bonds.
She fanned up Roy's conceit and his narcissism to create 'the
strong, sexual man' whom she desired but perhaps had not found
in her husband.

There were various allusions to murderous phantasies, for
example, the killed off geriatric grandparents, the killing of affection, the coffin under the bed, and the wish of the aunt to '...
the female teacher'. Also their ignoring of the female therapist's
comments was a way of killing them. The exaggerated focus on
the male therapist and their pointed disregard for the female
therapist made it seem that there was no place for a live mother
or for a couple to work together.

In the family, the father's place, and with it the symbolic
father's law was not present. As Roy put it, he had not received
his father's letters from prison. He was mystified as to where the
letters had gone. Although his aunt insisted that in reality he had
received and read them, at a symbolic level it made more sense,
for it suggested that he was unconsciously aware that he lacked
a good internalized father to whom he could relate and with whom
he could identify. The fact that he had not received letters from
a criminal father was also perhaps a sign of hope. His confused
sexual identity later illustrated this lack of an experience of a
father (his real one or his uncle) relating to the 'mother'. Thus,
although in reality Roy had received the father's letters, he had
not remembered this. His denial of the reality of a communication
from his father reflected his feeling of the lack of a father. That
is he had denied the letter of the father's law, what Lacan calls
the symbolic 'name-of-the-father'. 'It is in the name of the father
that we must recognize the support of the symbolic function which,
from the dawn of history, has identified his person with the
figure of the law' (Lacan 1977, p.67). In addition, as his father
was a criminal father, perhaps Roy's forgetting and his putting
him in phantasy into a 'holiday-camp prison' was also related to a
wish to deny his father's criminality and to absolve him from blame.
Thus, there was the conflict between the wish to identify with his
father, to receive the father's letters and to respect his father's
name, and his anger with him split off into his relationships with
his aunt and uncle 'who didn't give enough'.

II PHASE OF ABANDONMENT AND HORROR (COVERED BY CONFUSED SEXUALITY)

The first session after the break, the aunt had phoned us to say
she had flu. The two children came alone for a few sessions. Roy,
as he often did throughout the therapy, placed a newspaper with
the headlines uppermost on the table nearby. After some initial
embarrassment, Jill bombarded us with her talking, making it

difficult for us to insert a word. The family had been talking a
little about the murder. There was then, in the session, some
criticism of the children's aunt and uncle, 'Did the couple just
foster the children out of guilt, or only to stop the children being
separated, because their father could only cope with one of them?'
Jill talked about how it was she who had to look after Roy. 'Yes,
I'm the baby', he replied jokingly. She felt guilty about 'corrupt-
ing' him by her complaints against the aunt. Then, when Roy
tried to speak, Jill spoke over him. This was partly to make up
for the fact that we knew Roy well, and she wanted to tell us
about herself. But also there seemed to be a confusion between
them, between who felt what. It was clear that they needed to feel
the same and to be very close. Finally, we discussed their fears
about all of us meeting together. Jill was worried that no one
would say anything. We commented that perhaps just the opposite
was worrying them, that they feared too much would be said.

In another session, Jill said that she was relieved that the family
was not together because of her fear of what might happen, but
she was also afraid that the therapists would 'tell on them'. We
took up some of their concerns about us and the difficulty the
children had in saying what they felt about us. Then she talked
about how, at home, the aunt and uncle would send them away
when they wanted to discuss things. She added that they would
have tried to keep her from knowing about her mother, but 'I was
there.' Roy added that he was also there, in the cot.

Jill also blamed the aunt and uncle for allowing the murder to
happen. She said that her mother had telephoned them the night
of the murder saying that she was afraid and unwell, but they
never did anything. Next, she talked about how abandoned she
had felt soon after when she and Roy were sent to boarding school.
From then on she felt she had to look after herself. Roy asked
quietly why he had to go with her. We linked what they had said
to their feeling abandoned by their absent uncle and by us in the
session. Then, Roy quickly spoke in defence of his aunt, saying
that things were much better. He was 'on the right side of her
now'. He was not getting into trouble, and was working harder
at school. But Jill soon commented that Roy should ask when
taking things. Roy grinned sheepishly, saying, 'But I don't take
things, apart from your make-up.' Jill explained that this went
back to when Roy was a certain age (the time he learned of his
mother's murder). Jill had come into her room and had found Roy
'with everything on'. His nails were varnished, and he had on
lipstick and mascara. Now, whenever she loses things, she goes
to Roy complaining 'Are you the one who took my mascara?' Roy
replied jokingly, 'I only take your bubblebath.' Jill added that
he was always in her purse. Later, they said that when they
returned home from the session, their aunt and uncle would cross-
examine them, 'Did you find out anything? Who's mad then?' We
interpreted how they might feel we were like policemen coming to
investigate their private lives, to which they agreed.

Subsequently in the same session, with all the family together,

the aunt and uncle, for the first time in years, said they were
just about to go off on holiday alone. The uncle was quite jovial
and pleasant, and said he'd had a stiff whisky before coming. We
were complimented rather too much about Roy's progress. There
was a holiday atmosphere, like a going-away party. The aunt felt
that the children's seeing us did a lot of good. She added, 'They
can spit off a lot of venom.' Having acknowledged the presence
of the uncle, we wondered if he had felt left out of the sessions.
He began talking about himself, explaining that his memory was
bad, though he remembered a particular year. We wondered if
this was when they married. He said it was, and the uncle and
aunt exchanged affectionate confidences, while the children were
obviously embarrassed. Jill mentioned how little they knew of their
aunt and uncle. But she was then attacked by the aunt for not
knowing things, for her naivety and babyishness. Near the end
of the session, the aunt said that she had told various people
involved with the family to get in contact with the male therapist,
if anything went wrong with the children while they were away.

In the following session, without the aunt and uncle, Jill and
Roy seemed very tired. Jill complained about Roy, saying he would
do nothing to help her clear up. She said that she felt like her
aunt, working all the time at home. Jill accused Roy of being deaf
to what went on, and complained that he just watched television.
Roy mentioned that their aunt and uncle were glad to have a
holiday. Jill said they were probably glad to get rid of them. They
were quite taken aback when we pointed out how much they might
be missing their aunt and uncle, but they then agreed that they
were. They seemed quite depressed at this point, but soon changed
subjects by referring jokingly to sexual difficulties, with some
vague allusions to menstruation. They did not turn up for the
next couple of sessions, at first telephoning excuses, such as Roy
had hurt his eyes, and then failing to let us know.

Comments on the second phase of therapy
The children were clearly left in the therapists' care, which we
found somewhat disconcerting. We were to become the caretakers,
and to provide a place where they could, as the aunt said, 'spit
off venom', which might refer to her envy of us which was split
off into the children. It seemed that the children could be treated
as bad foreign parts which had to be got rid of from the family.
The infantile part, represented by them, was pushed around in
the family and then attacked. One can see this in the aunt's
attacking of Jill's naivety. Weakness in the children can only be
criticized by parents at this point, not understood or cared for.

Now, possibly our easing some of the difficulties between Roy
and his aunt created the possibility for her to feel more concern
for the children and, thus, guilt about her destructive attitude
towards them. Perhaps too, as she became more maternal towards
the children, she may have feared taking the place of the mother
because the mother had been murdered. Also, the aunt's own
unconscious wishes to 'take the life out of' her own mother,

indicated in her reference to her as the 'geriatric', made it
difficult to mother the children.

In the sessions with only the children, their feeling of being
abandoned was evident. It was also clear how they seemed to cope
with loss, by a conspiratorial confusion of roles, in which Jill
partly identified with her aunt, and in which sexual excitement
and perversion were also involved, as is shown in, for example,
Roy's transvestism. This latter sexualized feminine activity began
after he learned of his mother's death. This could also be indicative of identification with her, a way of keeping her alive, and
also might show his dilemma as to how to assume his sexual role.
This might help to understand his passive attitude to his aunt
and sister, in which he let himself be nagged and seduced in a
sado-masochistic relationship. Of course, some of this is specula-
tive as the therapy lasted for only a few months.

A striking element was the children's preoccupation with 'being
there' at the murder of their mother. This fixation at an early
stage of their sexual development permeated their sexual phantasies, their interest in pornography being evidence of this. It
helped divert them from mourning. Whereas normally death is an
experience to expect in the future, their lives were preoccupied
with death and destructiveness from the onset.

The family situation is somewhat reminiscent of the children in
Henry James's short story 'The Turn of the Screw'. There, the
two children, Miles and Flora, are left in the charge of their uncle
after the death of their parents. They are then put in the care of
a governess, but are haunted by the ghosts of the previous
governess and the valet, both of whom were probably in life involved in some kind of perverse and dangerous sexual game. The
governess is particularly sensitive to the children's plight, and it
is she, perhaps like the therapists, who first names the ghosts.
The ghosts exert a terrifying power over the living. They beckon
the children to come to them. Tragically, Miles succumbs, though
the little girl, who refuses to be taken over by the ghosts, is
saved. With the family, one can see the dilemma of how to deal
with a horrific past event - does one stick to it, like headline
news and be continuously excited by it, or does one try to face
the painful consequences?

III PHASE OF SOMATIZATION AND FLIGHT

The family met all together with us only twice after the aunt and
uncle returned. The uncle wanted to make the children apologize
for not coming. We pointed out that it seemed that we were to be
the caretakers, but the children didn't come. The uncle replied
jokingly that the male therapist was a lousy step-father. Taking
up this projection, we interpreted that maybe we were rejected
so that the children did not have to face their own feelings of
being rejected by their aunt and uncle. Jill said she had difficulties in their absence similar to those her aunt had with Roy,

while Roy dealt with their absence by truanting. This might be
seen as Roy's comment on the aunt and uncle's holiday. As the
aunt and uncle had packed their bags, so too he had packed his
bags and truanted.

At the end we were earnestly invited to come back home to see
how things were there and to help the family talk. In the next
session, the aunt was rather defensive when her husband, who
was busy at work, did not turn up, saying that business was,
after all, very important for them. She herself was sitting in pain
on some cushions we had offered her because of inflamed piles,
for which she was soon to have an operation. We discussed the
fact that we would be taking a holiday during the usual vacation
time. This came as a surprise to them. Soon the aunt mentioned
that Roy had once truanted this week. We commented on the
family's truanting, not all coming, and mentioned the question of
our 'truanting' at holiday time.

A little later, the aunt said that each evening after the session,
she examined her feelings, thinking of what she did right or
wrong, adding that she would like to be criticized by us. We
briefly discussed the dates of the forthcoming holidays before
Roy broke in to discuss his own plans. The aunt continued discussing how she found it difficult to understand Roy. He added
that he wished his uncle were here to 'brighten things up'. We
talked a little about Roy's sadness. The aunt mentioned Roy's
father, to whom he felt close. The children had a closer relationship to him, even though the aunt and uncle had raised them. She
said that maybe it would be better if Roy lived with his father,
a 'blood relative' who must certainly love him more.

Just before the break, the aunt began by focusing on Roy, and
what one was to do with him. She was looking very frustrated by
him. When we tried to understand the whole family, she replied
that it did not do any good trying to understand him. He did not
want to do things he was expected to do. She added that soon
the children would be growing up and leaving home. Then she
talked about her husband doing things separately. She took care
of the old ladies, while he enjoyed himself. If he did not do what
he liked, he was unpleasant. One therapist said that it sounded
like she did the work, while he got the pleasure. She replied that
they shared work. We took up that maybe they had wondered
whether we did things together in the holidays. They were
astonished. One therapist said that there seemed to be a block
on phantasies. But Jill added that she thought of us as interroga-
tors, who asked questions and gave nothing in return. The aunt
said we were like brick walls, not forthcoming. She added that
when she left the sessions, she felt like a porcupine.

We soon asked how she would feel if she discussed her coming
operation which was perhaps worrying her. She thought we would
be bored. Roy added that he had a tummy-ache and went out to
the toilet. Finally, the aunt, in his presence, said that he was now
doing well at school and he added that he now wanted to stay on
and study to be a navigator, which surprised everyone. As they

left, the aunt showed us her bloodshot eye, which we had not taken up in the session.

During the holiday, the aunt suffered a near fatal complication after rectal surgery. When she had recovered from the acute crisis, she telephoned the male therapist and in a very distressed way told him what had happened, and that she would be convalescing with her husband, though the children would come to the clinic. It turned out that the first session after this event was to be the last. It was a flat and rather dead session. We sympathized with their aunt's trouble. Jill said that now she had to be the 'mother' again. The uncle was irritable, angry and was drinking heavily. We took up Jill's mothering of Roy, and of his being the baby. We also a little later discussed some of the past – how difficult it was for them when their aunt had been in such danger in view of their having lost a mother. Jill said, in a dry, mechanical way, that she felt lost and empty because she had never found the right mother in her aunt. She added that she did not trust us, and said that her skin condition from which she occasionally suffered, was flaring up. We talked about the anxiety they must have felt with their aunt's illness, and compared it to the deadness of feelings in the session. There was then a strange feeling of embarrassment about naming these feelings. The female therapist mentioned that their sadness about being left by the aunt and uncle was not being named. The children giggled a little, in a sexually seductive way. They then talked together about Roy's attitude to food. He had once had food allergies when they were left alone, and Jill had felt in need of help. Roy only liked the food Jill made, and not the spicy food his aunt made. We interpreted their sticking together, turning away from us and not wishing to accept 'our food' which involved some pain and less excitement. Jill ended the session by criticizing our supposed lack of response.

Soon after, we received a letter from the family thanking us for our help, but saying that they felt they could not return. We encouraged them to at least have one session to discuss this, but without effect; and so we left it open for them to return in the future if they wished.

Comments on the third phase of therapy
In this phase we felt particularly that we were dealing with a precarious balance of forces, once Roy became less of a scapegoat, and the pathology was redistributed. Death was ever-present, though often unnamed. Unfortunately, the aunt became a victim. She felt we should be criticizing her, no doubt to make her feel less guilty. There also arose a strong wish to be cared for, especially on her part when she handed our phone number to friends when they went on holiday. Also, they wanted to bring us into their home. But we were criticized as being brick walls and uncaring, while the aunt felt like a porcupine after sessions. Presumably this was in part related to the problem of the breaks, and their sense of hopelessness about caring unless it was continuous over these periods. The situation reached a crisis with the aunt's illness.

Her near fatal medical complication could have been bad luck, but we feel that it had some further meaning. One could describe her anal symptoms as being related to the way in which an obsessional person might deal with loss (cf. Abraham 1924, p.426). As it were, losing became painful, irritating, produced violent pressure in her rectum, and was mixed up with blood loss. Also her symptom perhaps revealed that there was something painful being torn away, that 'needed to be operated on'. Unfortunately, we cannot describe how clearly her symptom resembled those of the dying mother for reasons of confidentiality.

The somatic symptoms seemed to have been a piece of repetition. In Freud's words:

> occasionally it is bound to happen that the untamed instincts assert themselves before there is time to put the reins of the transference on them, or that the bonds which attach the patient to the treatment are broken by him in a repetitive action (1913, p.154).

It seems that the life-risking complications indicated a psycho-somatic symptom whose aetiology related to the problem of mourning. The depressive current could not be developed in this family, because of the overwhelming persecutory guilt over the past, which involved a traumatic murder and also because of the intense hopelessness, associated with the absence of mothering re-evoked through our absences. It seems that the aunt's symptom symbolized in a concrete way, by a process of projective identification, her identification with the dead mother. Because she could not imagine the death of the mother she became, in a very concrete way, a nearly dead mother.

In short, one could say that what cannot be mourned may be identified with. Her symptoms followed on her becoming more sympathetic to the children and being more aware of depressive feelings and alive to the children's needs. It might be that there was something about this family that exposes a member, particularly the mother, who recognized and named depressive feelings, to great risks. It is possible that this was an effect of the murder trauma or was already built into the family structure before the murder, or perhaps both these viewpoints have some truth.

Maybe we could have avoided the unfortunate turn of events, but the great problem was the extreme forces with which we were dealing, recalling Book Eleven of Homer's 'Odyssey' in which Odysseus conjured up the shades of the underworld by a blood sacrifice. This was done within the context of a symbolic ritual which allowed him to withstand the horror of what he was seeing although even he, at the end, had to run away. So too, in the family therapy, various shades of the underworld were conjured up and it was with great difficulty that we and the family were able to deal with them, in view of the family's weak capacity for symbolization. They seemed to either act out the experiences which they began to have, for example, Roy and Jill dramatizing their confused sexuality, or somatize and then face severe life-risking complications.

DISCUSSION

There are many threads in the history of this family. We will try
to unravel some of them, including two main areas - the effect of
the trauma of the murder on the family and the possible light this
family sheds on what conditions predispose to murder.

We were very concerned about the family when they were referred.
It seemed important to intervene in some way. As the aunt expressed it, she was afraid that Roy would turn out like his father.
He had already begun delinquent acts. We were also afraid that
the original murdering situation could be repeated at some later
date.

From the sessions, the following family dynamics can be observed: in a sense, the family we saw was not a family, the aunt was
not the children's mother, and so on. The children showed that
they wished their aunt and uncle had been more like real parents,
and the aunt responded a little to their wish after having some
help through therapy, though the uncle did not. So, initially, the
place for real live parents of the children was vacant. This
ambiguity made it hard to work with them. The resentment over
the lack of real parents interfered with their appreciation of what
was available. Both the uncle and his brother, the real father
in name only, are enigmatic figures; perhaps they hold an important key to the understanding of the family. There were several
hints from the aunt and uncle that they wished the father dead,
that they were sorry he was not the murderer, and blamed him
for spoiling any relationship they might have with the children.
There had already been a split in the family between the brothers
- one, the good businessman, irascible and a former stutterer;
the other, the bad but rather ineffectual criminal, the family
liability. There was always bad feeling between them. All we know
of the paternal grandfather is that he was strict and intimidating,
and constantly rowed with his wife, and that the uncle was glad
when he died. Anyway, one can say that there was a certain
amount of criminality around in the family, which might be related
to the harshness of the grandparent figure and in the next
generation to the splitting of fathers so that neither can function
fully as a father. We have already mentioned the aunt's mothering
difficulties (though to be fair, and we emphasized this in the
therapy, the aunt and uncle were loath to give themselved credit
for a tough job) while the paternal grandmother and the dead
mother seemed to be rather passive, perhaps perfect victims for
their partners' aggression.

Now, it is one thing to have death wishes, another to murder.
One can only speculate whether there was something inherently
murderous in the family, but what arose from the therapy was a
clear current of latent murderous phantasies. Indeed, at times,
it seemed as if the murder had just occurred. Some of these phantasies were directed towards fathers, as in the usual oedipal
structure, but most were directed towards mothers, and they
became the victims. It seemed that the fathers kept themselves

safe by being absent, as with the father during the murder,
and the uncle during therapy. Indeed, the events in the course
of therapy were disturbingly reminiscent of the original murder
of the mother. The uncle was nearly always absent, either at
business, or enjoying himself, as the aunt put it. The therapists
were outsiders, perhaps similar to the soldier and the au-pair
girl having an affair. The aunt nearly died, leaving the children
abandoned. So, one can say that the murdering constellation had
remained around, latent in the family, and a murdering type of
situation arose once memories of the past, and with them guilt
and remorse, were revived. The family had fended off these
memories and feelings in various ways: the murderousness and
delinquency was projected into Roy (and also into the 'absent father
in name'), relieving them of the burden. It is as if there were an
encapsulated, split off and murderous part in the family (Hyatt
Williams, 1964). There was also a general difficulty in showing affection, as if it was too dangerous to handle. Roy in particular showed
an 'evacuation' of feelings (cf. Bion 1962a) e.g., in his mindless
watching of television and his inability to hold on to feelings in
the session. As well as this difficulty in expressing affection,
there was a failure to mourn the dead mother and absent father,
so that the murder remained 'unmetabolized'. Perhaps Roy's display to us of the newspaper headlines indicated that the murder
was still headline news. The murderousness was kept going
(through talking about the murder and father's criminality)
because it had not had a chance to be properly worked through.
Roy, who was an infant during the murder, that is the non-
verbal child, carried the unmetabolized projections. Roy also
carried the sexual excitement. Such excitement between the children, the aunt and Roy in their relationship, seemed to prevent an
adequate process of dealing with loss and also interfered with the
giving of care. There seemed to be a general tendency not to talk
much about what was important, but rather to act. This might
indicate a rather weak family capacity to symbolize. The aunt's
anal symptoms and collapse might be evidence for such a tendency
towards non-verbal communication.

There is another main theme - that of the murder of mother-love
and of the life-link between mother and child. As is well known,
separation from the mother, during vulnerable phases of infancy,
puts children at risk, particularly of developing a character disorder and of developing an antisocial tendency (Winnicott 1965).
The children, especially Roy, showed such features. Perhaps
this could only have been prevented if the caretaker parents had
been exceptionally good parents, and not just 'good enough'.
However, the aunt had great difficulties for reasons of her own,
in dealing with the children's understandable angry attacks on
her mothering capacity.

Jill was overtly hostile to the aunt and to the possibilities of a
new mother-child link, though she also desperately wished for
this link. Roy attacked the aunt by not accepting, in a rather
passive way, what she gave him. Also, the aunt was not helped

by the father's managing to absolve himself from blame in the
children's eyes, nor by her husband's weak fathering capacities.
The fact that he was a stutterer may indicate that he also had a
tendency to make phantasized attacks on the mother-child link,
the maternal tongue being cut-up in the stuttering. Perhaps these
attacks on the link between mother and child are related to more
general questions of attacks on linking and the ability to symbolize. Traumatic experiences may remain undigested when there is
a limited capacity for symbolization. Bion (1959) writes:

> attacks on the linking function of emotion lead to an overpro-
> minence in the psychotic part of the personality of links which
> appear to be logical ....but never emotionally reasonable. Con-
> sequently the links surviving are perverse, cruel and sterile.

Such mechanisms may account for the repeated examples of mind-
lessness, deadness and denial of care encountered in the therapy.

Now, no doubt there are murderous phantasies in every family,
as this is basic to the Oedipus Complex, but normally they are
not acted upon. Perhaps one should ask what it is that stops
people from murdering, rather than what makes them murder. The
question which this family raises is what it is which prevents
murder from recurring. Perhaps one can see in this family elements
that without intervention could possibly lead to such an act.
These elements include: (1) A great sense of grievance indicated
in the deep and mutual feeling of resentment between the children
and the aunt and uncle; (2) The absence of a named real father
to lay down the law which in the family can create a tendency
towards criminality; (3) Problems in dealing with a traumatic loss,
real or imagined: these may include: (a) problems in symbolization
due to murderous type attacks on the life-link between the primal
object and the child, on the link between the mother and the
father, accompanied by no symbolic father, and on linking functions in general, (b) the use of perverse sexual excitement to deal
with the loss, (c) intense fear that acknowledging depressive
feelings may lead to some internal catastrophe; and (4) an
economic factor, say for example, a constitutional disposition to
an excessive amount of destructiveness or envy.

Family therapy probably could not have resolved the effects of
the murder, or have completely taken the danger out of the family
situation. We consider it a necessary preliminary to individual
therapy which in this case was not initially accepted by the referred patient. In spite of being incomplete, we think it began the
process of bringing the family to a point where the murder could
be experienced as a natural, and not fantastic event, and they
could indicate initial signs of the capacity to mourn. This was
particularly true for the children who were brought slightly
nearer the depressive position. It was clear that we faced great
problems in working with them. These were: the danger of re-
enactment of the original trauma in some way; the tendency to
somatize when hitherto denied impulses are uncovered but not
recognized; and their feeling of being persecuted by us with
which we were not able to adequately help. Their own preoccupa-

tion with the gory details of murder, in lieu of viewing their emotional experience, affected us at times. Indeed, there is truth in their accusing us of being police investigators. After all, as Freud pointed out (Freud 1906) there is a parallel between the psychoanalytic search for the truth and the confessional nature of therapy, and the process of crime detection, which in a case such as this, with a real crime in the past, is difficult to avoid.

10 USE OF AN ENDING TO WORK WITH A FAMILY'S DIFFICULTY ABOUT DIFFERENTIATION

Nonie Insall

In this chapter I am going to describe the planned ending of therapy with a family where treatment had become a way of life, and where the family was unable to imagine itself existing without contact with an outside agency. By thinking with the family about the actual experience of separating from us, we hoped to work on the central dynamic that prevented them from functioning independently.

BACKGROUND

I first became involved with the Daleys when Rosanne, a young teenager, was referred for in-patient treatment to the Unit where I was working, by a psychiatrist with whom she had been in contact for several years. He described her as a severely disturbed, solitary girl who was unable to get to school, and who did not seem to have benefited from out-patient treatment. He had wondered whether her illness was a severe hysterical one, perhaps having psychotic features. She was said to be more concerned with her love-hate relationship with her mother, from whom she could not bear to be apart, than with her peer group, for whom she had little interest. She had been severely disturbed too at the time of her younger brother's birth; and recently had been in psychiatric treatment for some months, ostensibly because of her school refusal.

The psychiatrist mentioned Mrs Daley's history of chronic depression, since a breakdown following Rosanne's birth, during which time Rosanne had been looked after by her paternal grandparents while Mrs Daley had been hospitalized. Since that time, there had always been an intense hostility and rivalry between Rosanne's mother and paternal grandmother, particularly over Rosanne. Mrs Daley had been in continuous psychiatric treatment (usually out-patient) up till the time of Rosanne's referral to us. Neither John, the ten-year-old son, nor Mr Daley had had psychiatric treatment.

The apparent precipitating factor for Rosanne's referral had been a visit to the home of a French pen-friend some fifteen miles from where her family were on holiday. After a couple of days she

had had to return to her family, feeling very unwell. Later in
the summer she went to stay with the girl who had been her next-
door neighbour, but again, after three days was so ill she had
had to return home. Since then, about five months prior to this
referral, she had been sick and unable to get to school. We later
learned that during this summer Mrs Daley had been taken into
hospital for a minor operation, and the family felt that this too
had added to Rosanne's disturbance.

Mr and Mrs Daley visited Rosanne a few days after she had been
admitted to the Unit, and Rosanne told them she would not stay
on the ward any longer. Her parents were very confused about
how to handle this situation, quite unable either to be firm with
her and insist she stay, or to agree with her and remove her from
the ward. The psychiatrist in the Unit and I suggested that we
should all meet to explore the issue. After some discussion,
Rosanne said she would stay on the ward, and we agreed that we
should continue to meet all together whilst Rosanne was an in-
patient. When she was discharged four weeks later, we agreed to
carry on with these sessions at three-weekly intervals. The family
lived almost 100 miles from the Unit, but despite the effort involved in travelling there, they seemed keen to continue contact
with us, attending about five or six sessions. During this time
Mrs Daley was admitted to hospital for a further minor operation;
Rosanne appeared to cope well with this situation, being able to
remain in school despite her anxiety about her mother and also
with the added setback of knowing she was to stay down a year
at school because she had missed so much time there.

When I left the Unit to work at the Tavistock, my colleague and
I began to think about transferring the Daleys to the Tavistock.
There were various complications, one being that we would only be
able to work together with them for about four months, as my
colleague would then be starting a new job elsewhere. We had to
decide on this basis whether it was appropriate to arrange the
transfer for a relatively short time, shortened still further by a
holiday break, and if so, how best to use that time. The Daleys
were eager to transfer, though were quite understanding that
this might not be possible, and overtly were not worried when
the arrangements took longer than anticipated.

CLARIFICATION OF THE FAMILY'S PROBLEMS

We were considerably influenced by the Daleys' motivation to
transfer and continue family sessions; however, in our discussion
with new colleagues at the Tavistock, it became clearer that this
'motivation' could well be seen as part of the family's great
difficulty in separating and being independent of us. In retrospect the effort they made to come and see us after Rosanne's
discharge from the first Unit was probably part of the same thing.
We began to see that their very wish to continue therapy could
even be seen as the core of the problem. Further, it seemed that

we had been made to feel very important, indeed indispensable, and had unwittingly been drawn into the family's way of functioning. While we were important to them as objects with whom to identify, at the same time we seemed undifferentiated from each previous contact with other agencies, and as such could easily be substituted by other contacts. As long as the Daleys failed to differentiate between their objects, they would neither have to acknowledge their dependence on, nor their separateness from, a specific object. In avoiding the experience of separation, they would repeatedly avoid too the experience of being independent and self-reliant, with all its conflicts and anxieties. Their dependence on us, far from being the sort where they could use our help in aid of their growth towards separateness and independence, might be seen rather as a parasitic one where the family wanted to take over our resources, and live through us; but as long as we were required to be inseparable, this family could have no confidence in their own capacities to function as an independent unit. In clarifying our thinking about this we have found particularly helpful a paper by Rosenfeld, called 'The Psychopathology of Narcissism' (1965b), in which he writes precisely about this dynamic.

We realized that by transferring the family to the Tavistock, we were going along with their push to make each professional contact undifferentiated from the other, and that we were in danger of colluding with their difficulties in separating. However, we felt we had not worked on this crucial aspect in the previous Unit, and now we had a further opportunity of doing so. In effect, we provided a framework within which they could work on this fundamental problem.

It is also worth noting that their apparent lack of anxiety about whether they could be transferred to the Tavistock was a further part of the dynamic. They appeared to assume that they could slip from one contact into another, and denied totally any idea of anxiety about what was a most unsatisfactory situation where they did not know whether to bid me farewell or not, and whether they would ever see me again. At the same time, they expressed an intense wish to continue the sessions. As a person, I was completely unimportant, but as a figure on to which to project potency in contrast to their helplessness, I was crucial; but they gave the impression that any other worker could have been substituted.

In thinking about all this, it was no surprise in retrospect that the presenting problem had become much more serious when the first child was on the verge of adolescence when she had to face the real possibility of growing up separately. At the age of thirteen, she had become unable to leave home, either to go to school, or to stay with friends. The thought of actual separation, and all the feelings this stirred up, had become too threatening, both for her and for her family.

INITIAL PHASE

Some months after their last appointment at the previous Unit,
Mr and Mrs Daley brought Rosanne, though not John, to the
Tavistock. We suggested that we could all meet for four sessions
until the holiday break, and that during that time, we could think
together about the possibility of meeting for eight further sessions.
    On their first visit they appeared to be very preoccupied with
Rosanne's attendance at school, and whether to force her to go,
even if she were not very well; how could they know whether she
really was ill? Rosanne talked about the difficulties at school;
about how she had to be the joker, to make out to be something
she was not, 'so that people in her new class would accept me;
they wouldn't want to know what I was really like.' This led Mrs
Daley to talk about how she felt she had to hide what a failure
she felt she was; and gradually she began to tell us about her
admissions to psychiatric hospital. She became increasingly distressed as she unfolded the events: how she had been told it
would be a holiday for her, but the reality was rows of mental
people, doors with no handles. It was terrifying. She never talked
about it, but she constantly thought about it; she was so ashamed
of it. Rosanne talked about her own particular shame: her isolation, as if she too had felt locked away. In primary school, she
had been isolated because of severe eczema on her hands, and no
one would hold hands with her. Recently, someone had said her
hands were like a grandmother's, but although she had laughed,
she had been desperately upset, and could not show it.
    We were left after the session feeling flooded by this deluge of
emotions; Rosenfeld talks about how 'any disturbing feeling or
sensation can immediately be evacuated into the object without
any concern for it, the object being generally devalued'
(op.cit., p.171). The family had not been able to acknowledge
the gap in our contact, or the uncertainty about the resumption
of meetings; it seemed as if the reality of a possible separation
had been obliterated. Now by pouring out all their distress, they
were showing us how much they needed somewhere to put their
pain: they could not contain it within themselves.
    Although we had asked John, Rosanne's brother, to come to the
first session, we were told he could not be taken away from
school, but at our request they brought him to the second session.
My co-therapist, however, was ill, so unable to come. When the
issue of the long gap before transfer came up, and now the weekly
appointments, Mr Daley denied the gap had any particular significance to them: they had noticed it at the time, but now it was
over. Rosanne agreed, saying she knew at least that sometime
she'd be coming back. She had come to accept that it was part of
her life. Clearly, there was no sense of an experience of possibly
losing us. This had been avoided by minimizing the fact of the
delay and denying any feelings about it. We were like pieces of
furniture in their lives, as if we would always be around. 'When
the object is omnipotently incorporated, the self becomes so

identified with the incorporated object that all separate identity
or any boundary between self and object is denied' (ibid., p.170).

In the third session there was increasing talk about Rosanne's
sexuality; whether she could have boyfriends and go to parties.
She seemed to want to be more sociable than she had ever been
before, but her anxiety was whether she could actually make
friends. Her mother's anxiety was how Rosanne would behave,
especially with regard to the emergence of her interest in her
sexuality. There was a long interchange within the family about
how, when and whether one could let teenagers be responsible
for themselves, and the dilemma facing parents about how to cope
with this. Mr Daley said that they just had to take the risk,
whilst Mrs Daley said that Rosanne was too young. When Rosanne
was seventeen, she would let her go to parties because by then
she, mother, would not be able to do anything about it. Mrs Daley
seemed to have no idea about accepting Rosanne's need to grow
and be independent. Separation could only be an unavoidable
event or a forced ejection, and this echoed their feeling about
our ending of their contact with us.

At the fourth session Mr Daley wanted us to tell him whether
they should come for further sessions after the break, but he
said he knew we would not. Immediately there ensued a discussion
about how interfering his parents were. We linked this to us and
wondered whether they really wanted us to make the decision for
them. Rosanne said she would like to continue coming after the
break as she would miss it: she would feel empty inside without
it; and that here, the family had a chance to think more deeply
than they would at home. Mr Daley said he too would miss that.
While acknowledging these positive feelings, it was as if they could
not allow any negative feelings to be expressed. The conflicts
and fears about coming back began to emerge when the children
started to talk about their fear of their mother's anger, and Mrs
Daley herself spoke of her own dread of its potency. She feared
it could even kill her parents-in-law. She told us she would just
walk out of the room, rather than let it come out. We said we
thought this was linked to their wish to walk out of our room,
rather than face both what they felt about coming here, and their
fear of what might come out when they were here. At the end of
the session, there was a mutual decision to continue coming weekly
after the break for eight further sessions.

GRADUAL AWARENESS OF THE PROBLEM ASSOCIATED WITH
SEPARATION

After a three-week gap, the family returned. They were uncertain
why they were here. They 'had been so busy that it did not seem
like anything more than a week between sessions'; and several
times John called the previous session, 'last week'. Again they
were obliterating the experience of what it meant to do without
something. It was as if we had been there all the time. As I looked

at them I became aware of how they all seemed to be in uniform.
Rosanne and John were both in their school uniforms; father wore
a green army sweater and mother a blue naval sweater. I commented that I felt like a teacher in front of a class. Rosanne took
this up, saying that it was like reporting back to a teacher: that's
what they came for, in the hope we would be able to do something
with their reports. We said it seemed as if they were dependent
on us to do all the work in the sessions, just as they felt they
could not do anything without their grandmother's support.
Straight away they denied we were anything like the grandparents.
They said we were not important, we were too far away, and there
could be no repercussions from anything they told us. It did seem
they needed either to idealize or to denigrate our contributions:
it was difficult for them openly to acknowledge dependence on us
when they actually had no power to control whether we would be
there or not. It meant they would have to get in touch with their
feelings both about our meaning to them and the consequent fact
of losing us.

Awareness of separation would lead to feelings of dependence
on an object and therefore to anxiety. Dependence on an object
implies love for, and recognition of, the value of the object,
which leads to aggression, anxiety, and pain because of the
inevitable frustrations and their consequences (ibid., p.171).

At the start of the sixth session my co-therapist and I were
aware that whatever we said was refuted. Then John said that,
going home last week, his mother had asked him to remind her
to tell my colleague that she was frightened of being independent.
Mrs Daley said she had forgotten she had said that. Rosanne then
said that Mrs Daley had also asked her to tell us that it would be
as difficult for her to accept if her parents-in-law were to be as
positive to her as they were currently negative to her. At this
point, Mrs Daley seemed to be using John and Rosanne as her
message carriers, as her memory, in relation to the therapy, while
she herself was apparently turning her back on it. We could link
the fear of independence that they were expressing, and their
uncertainty about the paternal grandparents' attitudes with their
ambivalence about what they wanted from us. After a silence, they
said they would not really be losing us; just as, in the gaps,
they hadn't noticed they were not coming, so we would still be
in their minds and only slowly fade out and it would be au revoir,
not goodbye. Rosanne had been silent throughout this, but now
said she didn't mind leaving us. She then began to talk about her
new boyfriend, Nicholas, and said she dared not become too
involved with him because 'he will be hurt' when he left the area.
We felt she was also speaking of her own fear of getting involved
with us, and being hurt by the end of the therapy.

There was a further aspect here that was important about the
family's difficulty in acknowledging the significance of a separation. It seemed as if a glimpse of an awareness of actual separation felt to them tantamount to a total obliteration of the relationship. Maybe they had little idea of holding an object inside them

- of it being internalized - so that the physical absence of an object felt as if the relationship no longer existed, even in the mind. In order to separate adequately, a person or family needs to be able to internalize an object and have some confidence that it will remain in mind as a living relationship, and not be annihilated by that separation. If a relationship feels like 'out of sight, out of mind', it leaves such a void, that it is preferable to feel that the object is part of one, incorporated inside oneself, and so never absent.

In this session, Rosanne produced two letters from Nicholas which she wanted us to read. She made it very obvious though that she had not, and would not, allow her parents to read them. This raised two related issues. First, it felt like a flaunting of Rosanne's private relationship with us (and with Nicholas) to the exclusion of her parents. It linked with Rosanne's relationship with her grandmother, which was a frequent topic, and which sometimes had a similar quality, that of flaunting a relationship with someone other than Mrs Daley. It seemed that the possibility of a genuine, warm, caring relationship with another person - and there is no doubt that Rosanne was genuinely close to her grandmother - got distorted, so that it was used in a destructive way and felt to be very provocative.

Second, it raised the whole issue of what could be kept private in this family. Could privacy be allowed, or was it felt by its very essence to be an aggressive exclusion of another person? Privacy threatened the whole idea of fusion in a relationship, as it implied someone's commitment to separateness. There was little toleration of anyone's privacy therefore and things could only rarely be kept private. Instead there was a pseudo-openness, with no akcnowledgment of appropriate boundaries within and between relationships.

When they came to the eighth session, after missing a session, Mr Daley tried to justify their absence, denying they had made a choice about not coming. The family seemed to fear that any move away from us on their part would be met with anger and hostility, as if we too could not let them go.

Later, during this session Mrs Daley became very angry with me, saying 'you tell us we don't get angry with you - but nor do you ever get angry with us. You don't tell us what you think about us. You don't tell me you think I'm to blame, that I'm a bad mother. You don't tell us we're a pathetic family', and she continued in this vein. Mr Daley supported her, saying that they wanted to know what we thought, whether or not they had made progress. They knew they had to assess themselves and felt that some things had changed; but we must have thoughts and feelings about them, and we never told them. They were clearly persecuted by what they felt we kept private. We took this up, as not only our sending them away without answers, but also their feeling that we had all sorts of thoughts we were not prepared to share with them. They were making us into omniscient, withholding parents. We linked their fear of what we thought about them with their concern about what Mr Daley's parents thought of the family, and how hard it was to free themselves from this constantly perceived criticism, as if they had no way of thinking about themselves other than by what was felt to be an external critic.

Mrs Daley, who in particular was most sensitive about her in-laws, then told us that Rosanne had telephoned her grandmother from a telephone box in secret. Mrs Daley felt Rosanne had been disloyal, but more than that, that Mr Daley's mother was subverting Rosanne, trying to regain, or possibly keep, control of Rosanne, and she found it very hard to accept that both children wanted to keep in touch with and visit their grandparents. Mr Daley said he could not understand why it worried Mrs Daley so much, as he just ignored them. Mrs Daley appeared relieved when I pointed out that she cared enough for two, as if she had to feel his feelings for him.* It seemed that she experienced for both of them the notion of a harsh controlling mother who would never let go, and could only be got rid of by total expulsion or rejection. It is feared that the rage this object evokes can only be expressed in such a violent way that the object itself will be killed off. We were reminded of Mrs Daley's fear that her anger could kill her mother-in-law, and of their fear of our reaction should they choose to do something as a family and miss one session. We also recalled their fear of our reaction right at the beginning of our contact with them when they had wondered whether to take Rosanne home from the in-patient Unit.

There seemed to be a preoccupation throughout this session not only with what would happen to them at the end of treatment but also about why we were sending them away. Was it to do with what we thought of them? Was it because they were such a hopeless family? How did parents make decisions? It was also noticeable how powerful I felt in this session. We later thought this was to do both with their feelings of utter powerlessness in the face of being thrown out, and also with their need to have a strong controlling object. Similarly, my colleague seemed to be untypically authoritarian at the end of the session: the parents had asked if John need come to the next session because he wanted to do something else, and my colleague found himself saying unusually firmly that we would expect them all. It seemed as if temporarily we had enacted the projection of being the powerful controlling object.

During this session, Mrs Daley said with great emotion how frightening it was to change but also how she did not want to stay the same. It was as if she was beginning to have some notion that she could be different, something that she had steadfastly denied before. She had constantly told us that all the troubles were her fault, and that she could not change; therefore, nothing could change. As we finished the session, Mrs Daley looked at me

*For a discussion of the concept of 'shared objects in marital relationship', see Teruel 1966. Also Chapter 9 above.

and asked if I knew a particular women. She fired the question
at me like a bullet. She said that this woman, who she thought had
been treated here, had committed suicide two months previously.
I could only acknowledge, as the family were going out of the
door, that it felt like a dangerous place to come to, if it could
have that effect when one left.

MOVES TOWARDS DIFFERENTIATION IN THE FAMILY

They all duly came to session nine, John lurking behind a duffle
coat with which he covered himself, as he sat in the chair Rosanne
usually sat in. He told us it was next week, and not this week
that he did not want to come. He wanted to go to a disco. He
became increasingly embarrassed as he and Rosanne sparred about
boyfriends and girlfriends. This was a change in the family.
Always before, John had been very denigrating about Rosanne's
interest in boys, and had joined their parents in saying she should
not stay out late at night, should behave herself, and so on. Now
he was sitting in Rosanne's chair and having to acknowledge
openly that he too had similar interests to Rosanne's. It looked as
if he was now beginning to negotiate his own entrance into adolescent sexuality. The question in his mind was whether he would
succeed where Rosanne had had so many difficulties.
    Rosanne told us that yesterday she had done gym for the first
time and she felt very proud of herself. For a couple of years she
had refused to join in. Now she had, but she still had not been
able to have a shower in front of the others. There was some
acknowledgment that Rosanne was feeling better than a year ago,
and she agreed. Mrs Daley then recalled that John had had some
nightmares in the past week, and it now seemed that John was
being presented as the patient with problems, so that we should
not terminate treatment. I raised the issue of the patient who
committed suicide after ending treatment at the Clinic and maybe
they were very frightened of what would happen to all of them.
Mr Daley said he was not frightened. They then told us about a
family who was being thrown out of treatment, and who had
asked for the treatment not to end. 'They were thrown out for
fighting, for not co-operating; maybe they were untreatable.
The psychiatrist had said there was nothing more to be done',
we were told. As we related this to their fears about why we were
terminating our sessions, Mrs Daley became more miserable, feeling she would probably continue to be like this for life. Rosanne
talked about her own difficulty of going away (ostensibly, to stay
with friends) and I said that she seemed to be expressing the
whole family's problem: how do you go away? Mr Daley said he
could not leave his family of origin because he was still working
in the family business and had an investment in it. After interpreting this my colleague noticed that Mrs Daley was very tense
and so he asked her what she was holding on to with her closed
fists. She was just thinking, she said, 'Of what?' She began to

weep gently as she said she just wanted to keep her children
cuddled up tight and safe and let no one in. 'How do you let children grow up?' she asked with desperation. Later on though, when
talking about the children being separate, she said she thought
she was a recluse, a hermit, who did not want anyone else around.
Rosanne was very tense at this moment and I found it so unbearable that rather than take up her feelings, I cut across them and
went back to how Mrs Daley wanted to cuddle the children tightly.
Rosanne said at school she would never say she hated her mother,
like other girls; she was loyal to her. I had responded to
Rosanne's tension by action, rather than acknowledging how
Rosanne herself could not accept it when her mother talked of
separation and how she hated her at such times. It must have felt
difficult for Mrs Daley to think about letting the children go
because the hostility, in this instance from Rosanne, was so
great, and this immediately would stir up in Mrs Daley her feeling she was not the real mother of Rosanne and that Rosanne
might return to the grandmother.

They arrived at the tenth session from Somerset where they had
been for the funeral of an uncle of Mrs Daley. We were told about
two Valentine cards that the grandmother had sent Rosanne and
Mrs Daley wanted to show them to us so that we could interpret
the meaning of the words the grandmother had written inside.
However, any comments we made about what was going on were
ignored or denied. Mrs Daley then told us of a panic attack she
had had the other night; she had not had one for a long time.
This week it was she who was being presented quite explicitly as
the patient. John was sitting very close to his mother, quite
unlike the John of last week who had been big and independent;
today he looked small and vulnerable. Throughout the session,
especially when it got tense, he touched her knee or her coat.
There was much talk about Rosanne wanting to be with her grandparents, but how Mrs Daley felt she was disloyal if she went.
Mrs Daley returned to the subject of the Valentine cards, and Mr
Daley got very irritated with her. My co-therapist commented
how a lot of things seemed to be out of their control: John being
told to come for today's session: the cards being sent; the
funeral; as well as us finishing the sessions. Mr Daley denied
anxiety, saying that that was all right as long as it did not affect
other people's happiness. In contrast, Mrs Daley wondered what
would happen after death; nothingness - it was terrifying; but
also she sometimes thought she would prefer oblivion. Again this
was linked to the end of therapy, and their fears of what would
happen. It felt as if they were beginning to grapple with what
it would be like to experience an ending.

As the discussion about Rosanne going to her grandmother's
home continued, Mrs Daley got increasingly distraught. My
colleague commented that it was difficult to let someone go if you
were never sure you had them. Rosanne continued that, despite
wanting to remain in contact with her grandparents, it did not
mean that this need affect her relationship with her mother.

Suddenly Mrs Daley stood up, saying, 'I'm not going to listen
to this anymore', and stormed out of the room. Mr Daley seemed
to need help from us to be able to go after her, and the children
remained, huddled and silent. Rosanne said her mother would
not come back, that she had done it before. I felt very angry
with Mrs Daley for using such a powerful weapon to control her
children's attempts at independence and, perhaps in some
identification with the children, found it hard to think about what
she was expressing for the family. Rosanne said her mother
would not talk to her now, that her mother had always wondered
'if she loved her grandmother' - I thought Rosanne was going to
say, 'more than her' - and Rosanne did not disagree when I said
that, though she herself could not complete the sentence. Mr
Daley had been gone for about seven minutes and there were only
about three minutes left of the session when he returned with
his wife. Mrs Daley, standing by the door, said it was time to
end but she reluctantly came in and sat down. Rosanne apologized
to her mother, in a very flat way. John again huddled very close
to his mother, and Mrs Daley's hand was on the couch beside her
and seemed to want to hold John's hand. John held his hand on
his mother's coat. Rosanne and Mrs Daley were now weeping
quietly. Mrs Daley said that they were back to the beginning
again: whose child was Rosanne? This presumably was not only
a reference to the grandmother, but also to the relationship of
Rosanne to us.

At the end of this session, we noticed a difference between how
we both felt; my colleague felt more anxious about Mrs Daley than
I did. We thought this may have been because he was carrying
Mr Daley's anxiety about having to look after his wife, but maybe
too the family was beginning to see us as separated and differentiated people, so able to arouse differing reactions in us.

At the start of the eleventh session Rosanne told us that she
had been able to spend the night away from home with an aunt.
She now intended to spend a night at her best friend's house at
the end of the following week (one night after we would have had
our last session). When I said that Rosanne felt she had achieved
something, Mrs Daley said that one step was not the whole way.
We commented that they seemed to feel that although some progress had been made, they were not sure whether they could
make further steps. Mrs Daley said that, if it were not for herself, everything would be all right, but both children became
very annoyed with her. They recalled last week's session and how
furious Mr Daley had been with his wife for walking out of the
session. She said he had told her she had no right to behave like
that, but that she felt that maybe that was how she was. It felt
to us that she was asserting that she did not have to be controlled
by other people, and this was a shift from her automatic reaction
of blaming herself. Anger was felt to be less dangerous now.

At times, in this session, they seemed to feel that only we had
the capacities and they had none. They could make us very powerful but the more they did so, the more impotent they became.

They described us as a safety valve. We wondered what would
happen when we were not around. Rosanne said she thought we
would not miss them as much as they would us – we would be
seeing other people in their place and would wipe the slate clean
of them. We would have other people to talk to. For them, on the
other hand, it was more important, and they would have no one
in our place.

They seemed now to be struggling with and recognizing that
there was to be an imminent separation, as if they really had some
notion of the loss of us as specific people. The quality of this
goodbye was very different from the time they had thought they
might be saying goodbye at the previous Unit. Now they were
aware they would miss us, though were concerned that we would
not miss them, a concern which suggested that they expected us
to be unable to experience the loss of them, just as previously
they had been unable to experience any sense of loss of us. There
was still an uncertainty about whether it was possible for the
memory and significance of people to be retained – for objects to
be internalized.

They arrived a little late for the final session. Rosanne was
wearing a large badge, saying 'Join the lovable losers' and John
was carrying a small child's toy. The atmosphere was sad. Mr
Daley eventually said John would be glad not to come again; he
did not like the car journey. John initially agreed but then went
on to say that it was upsetting too. They had been coming for
ages and now it was a dead end. This attempt by Mr Daley to put
his feelings about the ending on to John was not taken up by
John: John seemed able to hold his own separate feelings. There
was some talk about the expectations they had had from coming
here, and their disappointment we had not given them prescrip-
tions for action. It was a more realistic appraisal of us; we were
neither perfect nor irrelevant. During the last two sessions there
had been confusion about which of us was leaving and now Mr
Daley tried to clarify the situation. My colleague commented that
maybe Mr Daley was wondering if they wanted to, who they would
be able to get in touch with again. He initially denied this but
then agreed. Rosanne said she would like to know if she could
come back. She often thought of things she would like to say to
the doctor and they never spoke as deeply at home as they did
here; she could not say the things she said to us, to anyone else,
or she would be told she was silly, so she wanted to stay in touch.
Her eyes were red. She seemed to feel that this was a place
where her distress and her anxieties were taken seriously, without arousing too much fear. Mr Daley cut across this and asked
his wife what she thought. I wondered why he had done that and
not heard what Rosanne was saying. Rosanne angrily said he was
the culprit, but she too was seeming to expect perfect parents
and, like all the family, found it hard to accept that even if
things were not perfect, there may be other things (about her
father in this instance) that could be valued. Mrs Daley now
began to cry, saying she was terrified. She was holding on to

John's hand and his mascot. Mr Daley said he hoped that coming here would somehow have relieved him of his responsibilities and Mrs Daley said that she now knew no one could help her, that she had to do it all herself. Rosanne said that she was intending to go to her friend Helen's home tomorrow night and would not be able to tell us how it had gone. She said that she might lose courage, knowing she would not be able to tell us. We tried to point out again how they were putting all the power for change in us, and here again Rosanne was saying she could only do this particular thing if she knew we were around. She still was not certain she had enough strength inside herself to do it alone, a remaining uncertainty about the degree to which we could be internalized. There was also a sadness in her thought that she would not be able to share the next step with us.

The family told us that there were now more rows in the family than before, so things were not all right. We acknowledged that they had expected that the ending of our sessions should prevent any disagreements and because it was not like that, they felt disappointed. However, to us the important part of this communication was the greater capacity of the family to tolerate rows, which were now no longer felt as annihilating. The family could fight and not be overwhelmed, and this seemed to us a significant shift. They could test out their mixed feelings with less fear. Mr Daley then brought up the possibility of coming back, asking if they could come back if things went disastrously wrong. We had wondered about the possibility of a follow-up and had decided to suggest it, hoping it would not be used as an avoidance of an actual ending. Now, in fact, it was Mr Daley who raised it. We said that maybe they could come back to let us know how things were going anyway, and not wait for a disaster. Mr Daley wanted exact dates. Both he and Rosanne seemed relieved they could come back, though Mrs Daley and John were rather noncommittal and acknowledged the mixed feelings.

The ending was sad and they filed out of the door, looking dejected, but we felt they had worked up to the end about the meaning of leaving us as specific people for whom substitutes could not so easily be made.

FOLLOW-UP

The follow-up was three months later. My colleague saw the family sitting in the car outside the Clinic over half an hour before our appointment was due. We fetched them from the waiting room, and they followed us sluggishly along the corridor. John went straight to the chair which Mr Daley had occupied throughout the earlier sessions, Rosanne sat in her usual chair, and for the first time, Mr and Mrs Daley were seated beside each other on the sofa. After a long silence, I said it was three months since we had met; John said it did seem a long time. Mr Daley said he didn't think it was very long, and it was just as if he had never left. Gradually, Mr and Mrs Daley began to tell us about all the ways in which Rosanne had not improved, implying they were back to the beginning again. Although Rosanne had managed to stay away from home on a few occasions, there had been a row the previous week about Rosanne going away, and Rosanne had ended up telephoning the Samaritans. Furthermore, Rosanne had taken a couple of days off school, as she was feeling unwell, and, in retrospect, the family felt that she had not been ill; there was obvious concern that she was reverting to the earlier symptoms that had led to her referral. We then heard about the local boys' school, and how the boys from it would come and see Rosanne constantly, using the house so often that Mr and Mrs Daley felt like doormats. Both parents felt exploited by Rosanne's expectations that these boys should be able to visit whenever they wished, but they denied that they felt envious of Rosanne's apparent enjoyment these days. While Mr Daley said he felt proud of her, Mrs Daley expressed concern about Rosanne's relationship with the various boys, but it was apparent that both parents were obviously very uncertain how to handle Rosanne. It was very obvious that there was a double message from the parents to Rosanne. On the one hand, they said they expected her to be able to go away from home, to stay with friends (this was what the row had been about last week), and on the other hand, they did not seem able to let her join in the activities that would give her the confidence to be able to stay away from home.

We, as therapists, were also in receipt of a double message. Initially, we had heard how badly things were going, that things were as bad as ever; now we were hearing that things were actually changing, and that Rosanne was becoming much more outward looking. This very change appeared to be the crisis the parents felt ill-equipped to face, but the one around which we had been working.

I was aware of picking up a lot of the family's anxiety about how things were going, and think I was probably tuning in to Mrs Daley's anxiety about Rosanne's obviously increasing independence. Certainly, at the end of the session, I was left feeling very unsure about how the family would get on. My co-therapist felt far less concerned than I did about them and may have been reflecting Mr Daley's greater capacity both to be able to let Rosanne grow up, and to let his wife be responsible for her own feelings. Mrs Daley, despite her considerable anxiety, appeared to be more able to think for herself, and to hold some idea that things were not necessarily catastrophic when they had to rely on their own resources.

There was an acknowledgment from Rosanne about how difficult it was sometimes to be able to talk to friends about things that mattered, and how much safer she felt when she could talk to us, as she felt we would not divulge what she had told us. We wondered if she was asking for more treatment in her own right, and made it clear that if, in the future, she felt she wanted something for herself, we would be able to see her to discuss this possibility.

She was very tearful at the end and seemed to be the one who felt most difficulty about leaving.

Despite all the anxieties, however, it was obvious to both of us that the family had made considerable moves towards independence. Rosanne's social life and school life seemed to have improved considerably; certainly in our sessions she had been much more able to stand up for herself. John was continuing his interest in an adolescent social life; and Mr Daley seemed to feel less responsible for his wife. She herself seemed freer from the persecuting, controlling object, and although she felt rather abandoned by us, and at a loss to know how to cope with Rosanne's increasing sexuality, yet it was as if she had some idea that she did not need us around all the time; she said to us, as if suddenly realizing she might change, 'if no one else will change, you have to yourself.' This beginning acknowledgment of some possibility of change on her part, though grudging and somewhat defiant, was a new element and gave us some hope that there really had been a significant shift for them. Similarly the fact that she was also far less preoccupied with world disasters, a theme that had arisen frequently, seemed to corroborate our feeling that she had made the corresponding psychic shift so that her internal world did not feel in imminent danger of catastrophe.

DISCUSSION

In thinking about this family, we were aware at the beginning of the very strong pressure on us to provide a supportive, caring environment, where there need be no conflict because there was no separateness. We were felt to be omniscient but withholding parents who could have given them all the answers if only we had wanted to. They put pressure on us to fall in with this picture – we were supposed to sustain the phantasy that there was someone who could enable them to be a harmonious family where there was no pain; at times early on, we acceded to their pressure, unaware of what they were requiring of us. We were made to feel very powerful and helpful, and colluded with the myth of there being such an all-powerful, all-providing object. It flattered us that they came so far to see us, and wanted to continue seeing us despite various obstacles. The other side of this type of dependent relationship became clear when we questioned or challenged it. We were then seen as persecuting, controlling people who were critical of all aspects of the family. They felt that were we really to say what we thought, we would be telling them what failures they were, and confirming their experience of themselves as devoid of all capacities. At such moments, they would again deny our significance, make us useless, obliterate any gaps there had been between sessions, deny any feeling about my colleague being absent, and so on.

We realized that we would need to try to understand with them how they saw us, and the difficulty they felt in functioning apart

from us. With their increasing awareness of this process, we would
need to provide space and containment for their reactions; and
our interpretations brought with them aggression, anxiety and
pain as they began to recognize their separateness from us. No
longer could boundaries between us be blurred or denied. We were
separate people with lives of our own, and they were not in control of our comings and goings. This awareness brought with it
feelings that were hard to bear.

As they began to realize they too could lead a separate life, so
there was a presentation of different patients towards the end, as
if attempting to remain attached to us. Once Rosanne had begun
to look outwards from the family, John was presented as of concern because of his nightmares, and significantly this was in the
session when he had begun to display his own adolescent interests.
Then Mrs Daley presented herself, and her renewed panic attacks,
perhaps as she realized she too might be able to be separate. She
wasn't sure she wanted to be, or could deal with it; nor was she
at all sure how to let the children negotiate their own increasing
separateness. Each member of the family, in their double messages,
repeatedly showed their ambivalence about going it alone, both
wanting it and terrified of it. Rosanne was both pleased with
and scared by the progress she made; John at times identified
with controlling parents, disapproving of Rosanne's activities,
and at other times identified with the more outward-looking
Rosanne. Both parents found it hard to know how to let Rosanne
become independent gradually, and found themselves either pushing her out too quickly to stay with friends before she was ready,
or stopping her going to parties and other activities appropriate
to her age. In the countertransference, we as co-therapists, felt
the same ambivalence: were we pushing them out too soon, towards
disaster, or if we continued to see them, were we holding them
too tightly and never wanting to allow them to grow away?

The idea of working in the way we did, using the external
reality as a boundary, grew from a clearer understanding of how
this family functioned, using the ending to work on the particular
kind of difficulty the Daleys had in achieving separateness. In
our work with them, we hoped to provide them with a space
where each member of this family could have an experience of
ending, could have the accompanying conflicts and anxieties
acknowledged openly, so that they could then allow themselves
to separate, an experience that previously had been abandoned
constantly because of a terror of catastrophe. At the end of the
therapy, and later on in the review, it was obvious that both
children were beginning to negotiate adolescence with some confidence, and they neither looked so young nor felt so infantile.
Both parents were more in touch with their own anxieties, and had
less need to project these into the external world. There was more
notion of sharing both the responsibilities and pleasures of being
a couple and of being parents.

Through the work we did on the family's relationship with us,
there was a shift in their notion of dependence from that of a

parasitic one where any attempts at separation aroused fantasies of expulsion, rejection and death, and was therefore denied by a total lack of differentiation between any external people, to that of a positive task-orientated dependence where there could be an overt acknowledgment of our importance to them, without this being experienced as a subservient abandonment of their own capacities. Rather, there could be an idea of us having something to give and of them being able to receive. We could all work together towards an ending, where they felt that they could use their capacities to function as an independent unit, albeit with the pains, anger and anxiety this aroused, but also with the sharing and co-operation that could give each member the know-ledge that he or she could function both separately and as part of a family.

11 CHANGE IN FAMILIES

Some concluding thoughts

Sally Box

On thinking about this concluding chapter of the book, my mind
is beset by a variety of competing concerns which seem to need
acknowledging or addressing in some way. I am aware, for instance,
of a number of relevant issues which we scarcely touched upon,
and of others that raise new paradoxes and new problems. But
many of them, I think, are related to a central preoccupation
about the nature of change - or perhaps I should say, of different
kinds of change since it is clear that the notion implies so many
different dimensions and there are so many unspoken assumptions
about it. Does one mean, for example, a change in behaviour,
change in attitude, in a state of mind, or something else?
    In her discussion of the paper by Madanes and Haley, Sue
Zawada highlights some of the contrasting approaches - for
instance, between the interest in behavioural or 'symptomatic'
change, on the one hand, and on 'the growth and development of
the whole family' on the other. Such contrasts are clearly important and involve corresponding differences in method. At the
same time, some of the polarities that develop around them may
be misleading and the significant differences not necessarily the
most obvious ones. Perhaps the most interesting questions arise
from considerations of the relationship between these different
sorts of change.
    For instance, when a mother successfully learns 'techniques'
from the therapist for handling her child, does she in the process
have an experience of being held and understood, and does this,
however minimally, increase her own capacity to provide such an
experience for her child? Alternatively, as the pattern of behaviour in a family changes, when is there an accompanying shift in
the members' perception of each other, a greater capacity, for
example, to appreciate each other's point of view and be more
responsive to each other's distress, and when, in contrast, does
the change seem to represent simply a more competent way of
exporting the tensions and conflicts out of the family?
    These sorts of issues cut across traditional differences of method-
ology and sometimes involve factors which are very difficult to
define. Who can measure the therapist's state of mind, for example,
and his available resources for being himself contained. Yet these
must be relevant whatever the proposed approach. Other important

issues are, for instance, the relationship between changes in one or two individuals and changes in the culture as a whole. When is one person's change another one's burden? Or when is it such that a more positive cycle is set in train?

It is clear that the problems we have struggled with and attempted to discuss in relation to families can be seen to some extent in every institutional group or community. What are the irrational processes that prevent good ideas and agreed plans from getting implemented there? What is the role of the outsider (like therapist or consultant) in relation to the change process? Over and over again one sees an apparently enlightened idea founder for lack of interest or support, and the line between a healthy scepticism and an apparently obdurate refusal or incapacity to entertain something new is very often difficult to draw. The tendency of living organisms to move in established pathways and to revert to them has been variously referred to at different times and in different contexts; and from the point of view of stability and steady continuity of individual and cultural life the biological principle of 'conservatism' (or 'homoeostasis', as similar processes have been named) is absolutely functional; the phenomenon of resistance, or at least discrimination, is a natural and even necessary one. Gregory Bateson, in his most recent book 'Mind and Nature' (1979), identifies the paradox in terms of the apparently contradictory needs for stability and innovation.

Britton, discussing it in chapter 4 in terms of the 'constancy' principle, draws on Freud to suggest what it is about man which conflicts with this tendency to revert back to a 'dynamic equilibrium' and provides the impetus to let go of old patterns in favour of something relatively new and unknown – of new life, in fact. He shows how an apparently new initiative may actually be serving the purpose of restoring the status quo and avoiding substantial change; and he draws the important distinction between change as an 'alternative to realization' on the one hand, and as a consequence of it, on the other. The examples demonstrate that without such 'realization', it is all too easy to become involved in re-enacting old patterns in the name of something new. It is clear that the term 'realization' in itself implies here a complicated process including again the capacity to manage the anxiety and pressures towards enactment sufficiently to recognize them and reflect upon the situation relatively independently of them. It is also possible that an individual's capacity for such realization expands without him being very specifically conscious of it, for instance, as his capacity to contain anxiety develops.

Most of the chapters of the book have been oriented toward discussing the more technical problems involved in getting to grips with the emotional obstacles to this sort of realization so that family members have more freedom to make independent choices. It is clear that the kind of change being valued throughout is of a radical kind, however tiny, a change from the roots that implies some involvement of the whole being and integration into its system. But it is also clear that this is not wholly or

necessarily a function of the length of the therapeutic encounter.
There are some families, like the Langs described by Margot
Waddell who can, in just a few sessions, reach some new awareness which enables them to develop more fruitful patterns on their
own; and others, like the Browns in Beta Copley's chapter who,
rigidly ensconced as they were, still seemed able to gain a little
flexibility and new perspective from their brief experience with
her.

I think by this stage of the book a fairly clear idea will have
been gained of the kind of criterion that we have used and found
relevant for evaluating where different families are in these terms
and for gauging different levels of functioning. For instance, the
value attached to the capacity to suffer experience and learn from
it as a measure of healthy functioning is quite explicit; and the
effect of the level of persecutory feelings prevailing in the family
is frequently referred to. Linked with this, a number of contributors have demonstrated the relevance of the particular ways
that each family uses the processes of projective identification
and the importance of the therapist's countertransference experience as a clue to this. One might add the specific suggestion
that a major criterion of difference between the families is their
way of dealing, individually and collectively, with the demands of
containment that are made upon them - not only by the direct
thoughts and feelings of each other but also by those which find
expression in indirect ways such as projective identification and
by the therapist's interpretations during the sessions. Again his
experience of their response may provide an important clue to this.

For instance, in some families, such as the Johnson family described by Gianna Henry in Chapter 7 or the Dun family in Chapter
5, there is considerable sensitivity to each other's feelings, but
the more painful aspects of these are felt to be so intolerable that
great efforts are made to dispel them. They stay to some extent
within the family, increasingly located in one member - perhaps
the one most open to them or most prone, certainly most vulnerable at the time - and tend to become more and more exaggerated
there, taking on the characteristics that Henry describes as
'pathological depression' and evoking ever more frantic moves to
counteract them. The struggle to contain anxiety in these particular families took the reciprocal form of a sort of sponge-like
response in the identified patient and a rather unporous barrier
of efforts to cheer up, advise and generally 'engender hope' on
the part of the other members of the family - both representing
faulty, though somewhat complementary forms of containment.
But the roles did not seem to be too rigidly fixed and could be
seen to change in each family during their treatment so that there
was already some sense of space despite the continuing tendency
for persecutory feelings to take over at times of stress.

In other families by contrast, such as the Stones (Williams,
Chapter 8), the Garcias (Halton and Magagna, Chapter 6), or the
Browns (Copley, Chapter 3), thoughts and feelings have relatively
little currency and seem to have become quite divorced from

awareness. The focus is much more on behaviour and what people
do to each other. There are suggestions, in the more extreme
cases, of causing concrete physical damage, such as ulcers,
heart failure and even death. Distressing feelings not only find
no place but are liable to be forcibly returned with interest, as
it were; projective identification is rampant and, in some of the
families such as those described by Williams and Kennedy and
Magagna, is manifested in quite primitive expressions of sexuality
or violence.

With these families there tends to be far less space anywhere,
including in the therapist's mind, for reflection: and the problems
of containment are relatively obvious compared to the more subtle
forces at work where enactment takes more intricate verbal forms.
In fact, in many of these cases, it may be more accurate to speak
of containment of non-anxiety since it is the difficulty these
families have in entertaining their anxiety at all that makes it so
hard to work with them. They incidentially exemplify – in rather
an extreme form – the kind of vicious circle that ensues when
excessive feelings can find no container, tending in consequence
to become ever more excessive and to provoke a correspondingly
negative response. But the phenomenon is present to some extent
in all these families and can be seen to threaten especially when
the containment provided by the treatment is interrupted.

Relating this sort of situation to the model of mother and baby,
Bion says:

> If the mother cannot tolerate these projections the infant is
> reduced to continued projective identification carried out with
> increasing force and frequency. The increased force seems to
> denude the projection of its penumbra of meaning (1962a).

A much less obviously uncomfortable pattern of projective identification (from the therapist's point of view) is found in another
group of families where the ubiquitous problems associated with
separation are dealt with by unconscious phantasies of fusion.
These families, like Nonie Insall's Daley family or the Manners
described by Copley, often seem unusually eager initially to engage
together in the therapy and take its continuation for granted.
But they apparently differentiate very little between one therapist
and another and movements towards differentiation, on anyone's
part, tend to be met by more or less violent reactions. This kind
of pattern and the gradually increasing capacity to allow differentiation between each other and between the therapists can be
traced in the treatment of those two families; and again there are
signs of some shift in the particular roles or aspects of the family
dynamics represented by its different members.

These three examples of different patterns found in different
groups of families are not, of course, intended to be conclusive
or exclusive. They are ways that may be useful and at best may
stimulate others to modify or add to them. As with the rest of
the book, if it serves in any way to take other people's thinking
further and provoke new ideas, it will have served a useful
purpose.

The emphasis throughout is clearly on change in the internal dynamic of the family rather than in the externally observable structure, but perhaps the notion of role serves to bridge the two to some extent. There has been discussion of the shared internal object and one can see how a shared internal relationship may also be enacted in the family with different members playing the complementary roles in it. In the Dun family I discussed in my chapter the reciprocal aspects of the unsatisfactory feeding relationship were played out in different ways; similarly, in the Johnson family, were the feelings of being the one left outside the door in contrast to the relatively comfortable and self-satisfied 'insider' feelings. These internally determined relationships are often re-enacted by the family as a group in relation to the therapists – hopefully with a different response – and the process constitutes, of course, the nub of the therapeutic activity. Eventually the whole pattern may be modified, but often a significant step on the way seems to be marked by a change in the reciprocal roles, so that someone else in the family begins to represent the problems originally carried by a presenting patient, as when young John Daley began to demonstrate similar fears as those he had previously scorned in his sister (Chapter 10). In these instances, steps towards integration seem to go along with little increases in the repertoire of roles available. But is is obviously not easy to tell if they are going together.

In the family sessions described in the book, the therapists were as questioning about attitudes of glib acceptance to what they had to offer, as about those of adamant refusal; and perhaps an important quality that links with the kind of change that occurs as a 'consequence of realization' is that of discrimination, in contrast to a relatively unthought of reaction of submission or resistance. It implies sufficient internal freedom to make an evaluation and a decision about the relative values of alternative possibilities. An important aspect of the therapist's task seems to be to embody the possibility of such discrimination without somehow trying to impose his views of the implications of it. It brings us back to the question of values and raises another apparent paradox. For notwithstanding all these signs of change that we may recognize and welcome, as well as our obvious values in terms of growth and development, we have also indicated the efforts made to eschew the entertainment of specific wishes or goals for the family being treated and to emphasize rather the struggle to provide the opportunity for its members to establish their own directions. The paradox in the juxtaposition of these two stances is evident and may lead to charges of inconsistency and even hypocrisy. 'How can you pretend you don't have goals and aims?', etc.

Bion (1970) has reminded us how, in work with individual patients, even the wish for signs of progress and the pleasure in it have to be disciplined. And this, I believe, holds true of our work with families and represents one of its most taxing requirements. It also has a quite practical value as well as its significance

as a principle in itself. If the underlying attitudes in a family contain elements of human perversity, the therapist may find that
even his unexpressed wishes become food for their resistance to
feed on. The preoccupation with specific symptoms and specific
goals for the family may pre-empt in a quite practical sense the
space for them to think for themselves. In view of its relevance
to current debates about technical problems it may be worth
dwelling on this matter a little further.

Presumably everyone in the field of human relations, whether
with individuals, families or other institutions, has to struggle
with the phenomenon of negativism and perversity, in themselves
as well as their clients – the tendency, for example, to do the
very opposite of what the voice of authority, from inside or out,
suggests would be for the best; or the readiness to deify objects
or qualities that are essentially anti-growth or anti-life.

It is this phenomenon, I surmise, which leads to the use of
techniques such as the 'paradoxical injunction' which are designed
to beat the perverse characteristic at its own game so to speak
and get the members of the family to change their behaviour in
spite of themselves.

In terms of the book, these tendencies are examples of the kind
of emotional obstacles referred to earlier that must be understood
and dealt with if people are to be freed from the pressure simply
to react.

From our experience with families we can see especially clearly
the link that such tendencies have with the fear of experiencing
a position of unwanted dependence on another human being,
particularly one who is in a parental role and whose physical and
emotional presence is in any way unpredictable or felt to be outside their control. If, in such cases, the object representing the
much needed source of supply is unable to tolerate the powerful
feelings engendered by its absence, or is otherwise unable to
help with them, then the dependency situation must become more
or less insufferable, and awareness of it to be resisted at all costs.
There is what must feel to the child a fearful conflict provoked
by his utter dependence on an object whose frustrating quality
is not matched by the kind of opportunities for relief and satisfaction which usually serve to mitigate it. To express his hatred and
frustration or terror openly may in such cases imply the danger
of losing even what source of supply there is or being even more
erratically treated by it.

In this sense a so-called perverse reaction can be seen as one
form of resistance to powerful forces that cannot be confronted
directly. Whatever its precise aetiology, our work suggests that
any possibility of its modification depends upon the way that the
hidden attitudes and internal relationships involved can emerge
and be engaged with through the medium of other relationships.
Moreover, in the relationship of the therapy it seems particularly
important that every effort is made to avoid any exploitation of
the dependent situation involved to impose specific goals and
intentions of our own. So there is a sense in which the effort to

free the mind of such intentions – at least during the sessions –
is a crucial part of the therapist's task.

Waddell comments on the way 'the most relevant concepts in
thinking about these processes and in actually working with
families turn out to be strikingly similar to those prevailing in
early infancy', and she reminds us of Bion's emphasis on the
relevance of these same processes in the way that groups function.
Again we can see how the family, as the place where the group
becomes also the institution, can provide a valuable focus for
observing and experiencing in detail the enormous influence of
these primitive processes in the life of the institution and the
community in general, and we can also attempt to study there what
enables them to be harnessed and worked with sufficiently to allow
for new qualities of concern, thoughtfulness and creative action
to emerge of the kind that in the book have been associated with
shifts towards the depressive position and the capacity to tolerate
frustration, conflict and ambivalence.

Bateson talks about the 'profound differences' between a change
in the 'characterological state of an organism' and changes in that
organism's particular actions. The latter is a 'relatively easy one',
he says, the former 'profoundly difficult' (1979).

The path to change is not always at all obvious or direct; and
progress, like the pilgrim's, is fraught with unexpected blocks
and pitfalls. We, as therapists, cannot chart it or predict it. We
can only try to provide the space for the emerging conflicts to be
lived out in the sessions and thought about.

GLOSSARY

A DISCUSSION AND
APPLICATION OF TERMS

Errica Moustaki

[The following pages describe relevant key concepts within a theoretical framework used in psychoanalytic work with individual patients and groups. The work with families discussed in the book draws on this framework, while at the same time providing the opportunity to explore and test out its specific applicability and relevance to family work.

The terms are organized alphabetically, each presented in a separate section. These begin with a description of the meaning of the term, usually followed by reference to relevant historical and theoretical factors. Finally, the application of the term to family work is presented. Each section includes a brief bibliography of relevant literature.]

CONTAINMENT
This concept originates in Bion's (1962) model of container (♀) / contained (♂) and draws on Klein's (1946) description of the mechanism of projective identification. It is based on the model of the mother as a container for the infant's projected feelings, needs and unwanted parts. This function is provided by means of a capacity which Bion has called reverie. It implies a particular state of mind in which the mother is open and ready to take in and reflect upon what the baby projects, and convey back to him the sense that his anxieties and communications are bearable and have meaning.

It is the internalization of this process and the identification with mother's containing function that is regarded as enabling the emergence of the individual's capacity to be open to the emotional impact of new experience without being disrupted by it. This, it is suggested, depends on allowing the experience to exist in his mind sufficiently for it to be understood and integrated into his view of himself and the world. That is, the individual can retain his knowledge and experience and yet be prepared to reconstrue past experiences in a manner that enables him to be receptive to a new idea.

Relating 'containment' to our work with families
The therapist in the transference has to be able to tolerate the family's frustrations as well as his own, and to help the family

160

'modify' rather than 'evade'. In order for containment to occur, the therapist needs to retain his own sense of 'goodness' or effectiveness, despite the family's projection of the opposite into him; he needs to tolerate the doubt that is being created, and like the mother with her baby, to hold the unwanted feelings until they can be relayed back to the family in a form which may be assimilable. This provides the basis for the family's growth and learning from experience through which the emergence of an internal container is hopefully achieved. While the containing function of the work with the family is essentially the same as with individuals, it is further complicated by the concurrent variety and power of the conflicting projections and identifications of family members. In co-therapy, the co-therapists need to provide some containment for each other's countertransference and frustrations, both in the sessions and in discussion between the sessions.

References
Bion, W.R. (1962), 'Learning from Experience', London, Heinemann.
Grinberg, L., Sor, D. and Tabak De Bianchedi, E. (1975), 'Introduction to the Work of Bion', trans. from the Spanish by Alberto Hahn, Perthshire, Clunie Press for the Roland Harris Educational Trust.
Steiner, J. (1979), Psychotic and Non-Psychotic Aspects of Borderline States, unpublished paper, Tavistock Library.
Klein, M. (1946), Notes on some Schizoid Mechanisms, in 'Developments in Psychoanalysis', (1952), London, Hogarth Press and Institute of Psychoanalysis.

COUNTERTRANSFERENCE
The whole of the analyst's/therapist's feelings and unconscious reactions experienced in relation to his patient, especially to his patient's transference (Racker 1974).

There are three different views regarding countertransference. In the first the therapist's reactions are regarded as part of his own pathology and therefore as something to be overcome. This view originated in the early days of psychoanalysis and still exists to some degree today. Countertransference was seen as a neurotic disturbance in the analyst, preventing him from getting a clear and objective view of the patient. It was seen as a source of danger and an unconscious interference with his work; 'the analyst's unsublimated, regressive instinctual strivings', 'transference in reverse' (Ruesch 1961).

According to the second view, it is not inappropriate for the therapist to be stirred up by his patients and have feelings in response to them since that is an inevitable phenomenon in any contact between two people. In these cases, the therapist is, in fact, encouraged to share his reactions with the patient, without necessarily trying to understand their meaning in the transference (e.g., Ferenczi 1919).

In the third view, countertransference is seen not only as an inevitable process, but also as an integral part of the therapy, which

if understood, processed and utilized properly can provide a
source of valuable information about the patient's unconscious.
This is the view described and drawn on in this book.

Although Freud in his earlier writings maintained the notion of
'The analyst's continuous efforts to achieve a benevolent neutrality',
as early as 1913 he gives some cues about the value of exploiting
the countertransference manifestations in a controlled fashion for
the purposes of the analytic task. Freud's remark was that 'everyone possesses in his own unconscious an instrument with which he
can interpret the utterances of the unconscious in other people'
(1913, p.445).

Paula Heimann (1950), in her classic paper on the subject, carried
further the notion that not only is countertransference useful, but
that it also represents one of the most important tools for the
analyst's work and involves a particular kind of relationship between
two people. She maintained, in contrast to earlier views, that the
aim of the analysis is not for the analyst to share his feelings as
such or to produce interpretations on the basis of intellectual
procedure, but to sustain the feelings stirred in himself by the
patient in order to subordinate them to the analytic task as opposed
to discharging them.

Hanna Segal (1977) further elaborated on the distinction between
the analytic relationship and other relationships, stressing that
while the analyst is opening his mind freely to his impressions, he
has also to maintain distance from his own feelings and reactions
to the patient, so that he can observe them and draw conclusions
from them, but not be swayed by them. She draws our attention
to the notion that the patient is in a constant non-verbal interaction
with the therapist in which he acts on the therapist's mind, and thus
the therapist is seen not as a mirror on to which the patient projects,
but rather as a container. Segal also stresses that the therapist's
capacity to contain instead of discharging the feelings aroused in
him by the patient, is his means of 'processing' the patient's
projections into him, so that he can return them to the patient in
a more acceptable 'digestible' form. (This is further elaborated
under 'containment'.)

Being aware of the countertransference highlights the power of
the projections to which the analyst is exposed. The more disturbed
the patient, the more pressure there may be on the analyst to
identify with the patient's projections and be pulled into action,
losing his capacity for containment. In this context, projective
counter-identification is the term used by Grinberg to describe
the analytic experience of being in the 'grip of something' (Grinberg
1962). There is of course the danger that the countertransference
concept, as Segal (1977) points out, can be abused if it is resorted
to as a justification for failure to understand.

Relating 'countertransference' to our work with families
A link may exist between the nature of the infantile feelings and
phantasies, that the paternal couple find difficult to bear in themselves, and the problems in the family. Other members of the

family may have been assigned the role of carrying some of these for the whole family, and projections that they have carried hitherto may now be experienced by the therapist in the countertransference and made available for understanding. Countertransference is, in fact, the tool with which one knows what is to be contained.

The use of the countertransference is particularly important in this approach to work with families. In co-therapy, each therapist may react differently to the countertransference experience in relation to the different family members and to the co-therapist. This experience can provide internal evidence to be used, together with external evidence, for understanding conflicts in the family. The therapeutic pair need to sustain and bear the differences and work on them both within and between themselves, so that they can communicate to the family their understanding of the underlying anxieties. Understanding the projections experienced in the countertransference takes place partially during the sessions but it also requires thinking and discussions outside them. Thus, in this kind of family work, containment takes place in the field created through the therapist pair's relationship.

In the case of the single therapist, the functions fulfilled by the pair vis-à-vis the projections are now to be carried by some sort of internalized couple within the single therapist. He must look at his own reactions in order to provide the family with an experience analogous to that with a 'therapy/parental couple'.

References

Freud, S. (1913), The Disposition to Obsessional Neurosis, 'Standard Edition', V: 445.
Grinberg, L. (1962), On a Specific Aspect of Countertransference due to the Patient's Projective Identification, in 'International Journal of Psychoanalysis', 42: 436-40.

Heimann, P. (1950), On Countertransference, in 'International Journal of Psychoanalysis', 31: 81-4.
Laplanche, H. and Pontalis, J.-B. (1973), 'The Language of Psychoanalysis', London, Hogarth Press.
Money-Kyrle, R.E. (1956), Normal Countertransference and some of its Deviations, in 'International Journal of Psychoanalysis', 37: 360-6.
Racker, H. (1968), 'Transference and Countertransference', London, Hogarth Press and Institute of Psychoanalysis.
Segal, H. (1977), Countertransference, 'International Journal of Psychoanalytic Psychotherapy', 6: 31-7.
Singer, E. (1965), 'Key Concepts in Psychotherapy', New York, Random House.

DEPRESSIVE POSITION (SEE UNDER PARANOID-SCHIZOID/ DEPRESSIVE)

IDENTIFICATION (PROJECTIVE IDENTIFICATION - INTROJECTIVE IDENTIFICATION)

(1) PROJECTIVE IDENTIFICATION

This term refers to the phantasy of entering the object with the whole or part of the self which may lead to an altered perception of the identity of the self and object in relation to each other. It was first described by Klein (1946) in her work on the emotional development in the first months of life, and is seen as being active from the beginning of life. Its usage has been further enlarged, clarified and developed by such writers as Bion (1959; 1962), Segal (1964), Rosenfeld (1965; 1969), and Meltzer (1967).

This term may well be confusing as it is used to describe a whole range of purposes such as for primitive communication, to keep good parts of the self safe from internal harm, as well as to get rid of bad parts; to control, attack or destroy the object, and to avoid the experience of separation.

In 'Attacks on Linking', Bion (1959) supposes there is a 'normal degree of projective identification', which, associated with intro-jective identification, is the 'foundation on which normal development rests'. He emphasizes the normal function of projective identification, when in conjunction with a containing object that modifies the intolerable projections, constitutes a stepping stone in human development, one of the main factors in symbol formation and thus in communication.

Segal (1964) draws attention to it as 'the earliest form of empathy' and points out that the capacity to 'put oneself in another person's shoes' develops through processes of projective identification.

For projective identification to take place, the projector must experience some temporary differentiation between self and object. However, the process of projective identification leads to a loss in the sense of self, hence a blurring of the boundary between the self and the other. It interferes with the experience of loss if the object is absent and consequently prevents the formation of a symbolic representation of the lost object. In excessive use of projective identification, phantasy and reality become confused and the patient's capacities for verbal and abstract thinking are crippled.

Segal (1964) describes the two most important anxieties liable to follow projective identification as:

the fear that the attacked object will retaliate equally by projec-tion; and the anxiety of having parts of the self imprisoned and controlled by the object into which they have been projected.

This last anxiety is particularly strong when good parts of the self have been projected.

Projective identification in clinical work

Work in the transference may relieve the projections of their unbearable quality and make it possible for the patient to reintroject them. Three of the different forms of projective identification which are highlighted by Rosenfeld (1969) in his paper 'The Importance of Projective Identification in the Ego Structure and the Object Relations of the Psychotic Patient', are graphically illustrated.

(1) Projective Identification as 'Communication'. This he relates

to Bion's work on the container/contained model. He writes about how a patient unconsciously projects impulses and parts of himself into the analyst so that the analyst may feel and understand those experiences and be able to contain them enabling them to lose their unbearable quality. If the analyst is able to interpret this experience, the patient may then learn to own and tolerate his own impulses and start experiencing feelings which were previously experienced as meaningless or too frightening to assimilate.

Bion (1962) had suggested earlier that the degree of readiness of the receiver to contain the projections will finally determine whether projective identification could take the form of communication. By readiness is meant that the receiver is open to taking in the projection, capable of surviving their impact including any aggressive elements, and therefore able to provide an opportunity for the patient to differentiate phantasy from reality. If the intended receiver does not offer himself as a container in this way then there is a kind of boomerang effect in which the projected element may be returned to the sender in the form of 'nameless dread'.

(2) Projective identification 'as a defence' to get rid of unwanted parts. Here the mechanism is used for the denial of psychic reality. The patient splits and projects unbearable anxieties into the analyst in order to evacuate disturbing mental content. For instance, it can be used to defend against aggressive impulses which are sometimes an expression of anger related to separation anxiety, but can also have a distinctly envious character. When in the grip of this form of projective identification, the patient primarily wants the analyst to condone the evacuation and denial of his problems; he experiences interpretations as critical and reacts to them with resentment

(3) A third use of projective identification is 'as a means of control'. This is shown when the patient attempts to control the analyst's body and mind, and seems to be based on a very early infantile type of object relationship. The patient believes that he has omnipotently forced himself into the analyst and, as with the infant and mother, he is fused and confused with him, preventing the experience of separation, but at the expense of being tortured by anxieties relating to the loss of the self.

Any of these three forms of projective identification can occur singly or together in one patient and their distinction has important clinical implications both in terms of treatment technique and prognostic evaluation. In general, the more that either of the latter two predominate, i.e., as a means of defence or as a means of control, the greater is likely to be the degree of disturbance.

Relating projective identification to our work with families
Box (1978) suggests that the
concept of projective identification provides the major link between concepts such as role and unconscious process, between individual and group and between individual and family; and it is this concept

which is most central in the approach to families being developed
(p.119).

In much of this work we attempt to understand how unconsciously
shared elements which cannot be tolerated by one or more of the
family members are reallocated inside or outside the family in an
attempt to avoid the experience of internal conflict. Often such
families insist that the disturbance is all located in the index patient
who may have unconsciously colluded with the family system which
has 'chosen' him to become a receptor. In a similar way that disturbance is projected, other facets, say being the 'good child', may be
located in one member to the detriment of his fuller life and general
development. All the projections lead to a depletion of family
members' individuality.

The therapists in their interaction with the family by means of
their countertransference experience attempt to take the projective
identifications into themselves, find space for and try to understand
the nature of the elements disowned by the family and thereby provide
some containment. They also need to remember that this may be a
communication that the family does not know how to make in any
other way. Where the projective identification is for the purposes
of evacuation or control, the attempt at understanding may be so
hated that there is great risk that the therapy may be broken off.

The attempt at unravelling this process can hopefully lift some of
the burden that a particular family member or members may carry
for the rest, and may therefore free family members to express parts
of themselves that were locked and obscured by having carried
particular roles for the family.

References
Bion, W.R. (1959), Attacks on Linking, in 'Second Thoughts'
    (1967), London, Heinemann.
Bion, W.R. (1962), A Theory in Thinking, in 'Second Thoughts'
    (1967), London, Heinemann.
Box, S. (1978), An Analytic Approach to Work with Families,
    'Journal of Adolescence', 1: 119-33.
Klein, M. (1946), Notes on some schizoid mechanisms, in 'Develop-
    ments in Psychoanalysis' (1952), London, Hogarth Press.
Meltzer, D. (1967), 'The Psychoanalytic Process', London, Heinemann.
Rosenfeld, H. (1965), 'Psychotic States: a Psychoanalytic Approach',
    London, Hogarth Press.
— (1969), Contribution to the Psychopathology of Psychotic States:
    The Importance of Projective Identification in the Ego Structure
    and the Object Relations of the Psychotic Patient, in 'Problems
    of Psychosis' vol.I, ed. P. Dauret and C. Laurin, Amsterdam,
    Excerpta Medica.
Segal, H. (1964), 'Introduction to the Work of Melanie Klein',
    London, Heinemann.

(2) INTROJECTIVE IDENTIFICATION
This concept describes a process of taking in aspects, qualities
or skills of the object in such a way that they are gradually

identified with and inform the character of an individual. Meltzer has drawn attention to the significance of the acknowledgment of separateness and the freedom to come and go as necessary preconditions for this process to occur.

Relating 'introjective identification' to our work with families
There is some evidence of introjective identification having occurred when the family shows that it can metabolize and process experience and anxiety in the absence of the therapists with a clear sense of their separateness from them and acknowledgment of where the skill they have acquired has originated. Rather than mere instant imitation of the therapists' ways of functioning, painstaking, and therefore more lasting, internalization must take place for healthy development to continue.

This differs from the defensive type of projective identification in which characteristics of the object are surreptitiously taken over without a struggle with feelings of envy and competitiveness. Introjective identification not only involves allowing the therapists their freedom, but also involves admiration and respect for their qualities, in the work of the sessions. Such admiration should be distinguished from indiscriminate idealization. In contrast to projective identification, introjective identification implies the emergence of the capacity for reality testing, and differentiating what belongs to the self and what does not. Hence, the case may occur where 'bad' qualities of the object are introjected but are recognized as separate to the self.

References
Heimann, P. (1952), Certain functions of introjection and projection in early infancy, in M. Klein et al., 'Developments in Psychoanalysis', London, Hogarth.
Meltzer, D. (1967), 'The Psychoanalytic Process', London, Heinemann.

INNER WORLD
The world of figures formed on the pattern of the persons first loved and hated in life, which also contains aspects of oneself; these inner figures exist in phantasy, engaged in apparently independent activities 'as real' or 'even more real and actual to the person in his unconscious feeling than external events' (Rivière, 1955). When the phrase 'inner world' is used as a specific term, internal objects do not denote exact replicas of the external world, but 'are always coloured by the infant's phantasy and projections' (Segal 1979, p.64).

As Rivière (1955) points out, 'the inner world' is exclusively one of 'personal relations'. Everything happening in it refers to the self, to the individual's own urges and desires towards other people and of his reactions to them as the objects of his desires. Our relation to our inner world has its own development from the inception of life onwards, just as that to the external world has.

Relating 'inner world' to work with families
The crucial part of work with families is to provide an opportunity

for changes to take place in their inner worlds. What we attempt to do is to examine, in various ways, which predominant internal conflicts and relationships are shared by members of the family and played out between them. Our notion is that the experiences in each person's inner world provide the impetus for re-enactment both in the external world and within the therapeutic setting.

The family therapy described is aimed at working with the shared inner world of the family through working with what is transferred to the therapists (see transference, glossary). At any particular time in the work, although communications may come from individuals and be regarded as such, they are also seen as linked to the family's unconsciously shared phantasies.

References
Rivière, J. (1965), The Unconscious Phantasy of an Inner World Reflected in Examples from Literature, in M. Klein et al., 'New Directions in Psychoanalysis', London, Tavistock Publications.

PARANOID-SCHIZOID/DEPRESSIVE POSITION
These terms, introduced by Melanie Klein, refer to different levels of mental development. The first is characterized by primitive mechanisms of defence such as splitting, idealization and denial. The second is indicative of greater integration. It involves the capacity to bring together the feelings of love and hate in relation to a whole object of person rather than splitting them between separate parts. It is this capacity that enables the individual to experience concern for the object and survive its absence so that it can become symbolically represented in the mind and allowed a separate existence.

In practice, especially following the work of Bion, these two positions are seen to describe different states of mind which may fluctuate from moment to moment and are both more or less present for everyone at different times so that it is unlikely for anyone to be free of experiences associated with the paranoid/schizoid position. The capacity to bear and contain the conflict this fluctuation implies is an essential feature of the depressive position.

These two positions can be described in more detail from a developmental point of view:

(1) *Paranoid-schizoid position*
In the first few months of life the infant has relatively undeveloped perceptual powers and only very limited capacities to conceptualize; the mother or the person who looks after him is perceived not as a whole person, but in parts, such as eyes, breasts, hands, which are relatively unrelated to each other. At this stage also, a feature of normal development is the sorting out of experiences and objects into pleasurable experiences stemming from gratifying, idealized sources on the one hand and painful, frustrating experiences felt to be derived from bad, denigrated part-objects, on the other. The frustration and deprivation due to the absence of a 'good' object are often experienced as if they were caused by the presence

of a 'bad' object. This phase is thus characterized by a prevalence
of splitting of good and bad in the ego and in the object.

(2) *The depressive position*
Gradually during early infancy, the capacity both to perceive the
mother as a whole person and to sustain conflictual feelings towards
her. While this state of mind prevails, the polarization between good
and bad is bridged. The infant may, therefore, recognize that his
hostile feelings and phantasies have harmed or destroyed the gratifying loved one, not just the depriving one. As a result of this
integration, he begins to experience feelings of concern for the
mother lest his hostile feelings should predominate over his loving
ones. Some capacity to hold on to the painful anxieties at this
phase, that is, some negotiation of the depressive position, is
important for future growth and maturation. Without such negotiation the infant remains dominated by the more primitive persecutory
anxiety, based upon a feeling of being got at and threatened, which
may lead to an abiding sense of grievance. With some success in
dealing with the depressive position, depressive anxiety, which is
to do with anxiety over harm done by the self predominantly to
one's good object, is able to be felt and sustained. The tolerance
of this kind of anxiety promotes feelings of responsibility, attempts
at reparation for harm done and the development of creativity.
   The working through of the depressive position during the first
year of life is never complete. There are various defences employed
to avoid such painful feelings, for instance, a lapse into a schizo-
paranoid state of mind or a flight into a manic one. Re-negotiation
of the anxieties and relationships to do with the depressive position is necessary again and again, particularly at times of personal
crisis and developmental change such as adolescence, the meno-
pause, the mid-life crisis in the thirties described by Professor
Elliott Jaques, etc. 'Successful re-negotiation of the depressive
position may be followed by a further efflorescence of creativity'
(A. Hyatt Williams 1975).
   In our work with families we attempt to provide initially an external
containment of conflict which might help members develop an internal
capacity to contain a depressive feeling. This in turn diminishes
the pressure to project into others unwanted parts of the self or
persecutory objects throught the use of Projective Identification.

PHANTASY (The Kleinian development of the term)
This concept refers to the primary content of unconscious mental
processes and does not refer simply to a repressed fantasy.
   Phantasy is (in the first instance) the mental corollary, the
psychic representative of instinct. There is no impulse, no
instinctual urge or response which is not experienced as unconscious phantasy... The first mental processes, the psychic
representatives of libidinal and destructive instincts, are to be
regarded as the earliest beginning of phantasies... All impulses,
all feelings, all modes of defence are experienced in phantasies
which give them mental life and show their direction and purpose

(Susan Isaacs 1952, p.83).

Hanna Segal highlights the important implications of this view for psychoanalytic thought about the development of the ego:

Phantasy-forming is a function of the ego. The view of phantasy as a mental expression of instincts through the medium of the ego assumed a higher degree of ego-organization than is postulated by Freud. It assumes that the ego from birth is capable of forming, and indeed is driven by instincts and anxiety to form primitive object relationships in phantasy and reality (Segal 1964, pp.2-3).

Phantasies are always inferred, not directly communicated as such. They are present and actively influential in every individual throughout life. They are not restricted to pathological processes, and what determines the distinction between 'normal' and 'pathological' is the nature and degree of the desire or anxiety associated with them, and the way they interact with each other and with external reality. There is evidence that disturbances in the capacity to symbolize in phantasy are accompanied by corresponding problems in development, talking, playing and working.

Unconscious phantasy is in a constant interplay with external reality, both influencing and altering the perception or interpretation of it and also being influenced by it. It is to be distinguished from the popular concept of conscious fantasy used to describe a means of escaping from external reality, as in daydreaming, for example.

Although not necessarily defensive, phantasies may have a defensive aspect, e.g. phantasying gratification, or fulfilment of instinctual drives to deal with the external reality of deprivation; and/or phantasying as a defence against other phantasies, as when a manic phantasy serves to counteract the painful effect of a depressive one.

Relating 'phantasy' to work with families

The significance attached to phantasy relates directly to our emphasis on the use of transference in work with families. To the extent that current and perennial difficulties in relationships are a function of these primitive object relationships in phantasy, it is the manifestations in the transference of those internal relationships which form the core of the material to be worked on in the sessions.

Bion has shown how group processes tend to mobilize primitive levels of mental life and basic human phantasies which are shared at an unconscious level. In institutionalized groups such as the family, these phantasies become crystallized into forms that are specific to that group and its particular life - aided presumably by the constant interaction of projection and introjection between the members. They have been termed 'shared phantasies' and explored by Dicks (1967) in relation to marriages. It is this notion that forms the basis and rationale for the emphasis on interpretations made to the group rather than to particular individuals within it: the interpretations are intended to illuminate the current shared phantasies underlying the communication from the family.

References
Bion, W.R. (1961), 'Experiences in Groups', London, Tavistock
   Publications.
Dicks, H. (1967), 'Marital Tensions', London, Routledge & Kegan
   Paul.
Isaacs, S. (1952), The Nature and Function of Phantasy, in
   'Developments in Psychoanalysis' (chapter III), London, Hogarth
   Press.
Segal, H. (1973), 'Introduction to the Work of Melanie Klein',
   London, Hogarth Press.

TRANSFERENCE
Transference, in the context of therapy, refers to all that is projected into/on to, and experienced in relation to the therapist,
and the treatment setting via the unconscious phantasies accompanying the patient/therapist experience.
   The clearest early description of transference was made by Freud
in the case history of Dora:
   What are transferences? They are new editions or facsimiles of
   the impulses and phantasies which are aroused and made conscious
   during the progress of the analysis; but they have this peculiarity,
   which is characteristic for their species, that they replace some
   earlier person by the person of the physician. To put it another
   way: a whole series of psychological experiences are revived, not
   as belonging to the past, but as applying to the person of the
   physician at the present moment. Some of these transferences
   have a content which differs from that of their model in no respect
   whatever except for the substitution. These then - to keep the
   same metaphor - are merely new impressions or reprints. Others
   are more ingeniously constructed; their content has been subjected
   to a moderating influence - to sublimation, as I call it - and they
   may even become conscious, by cleverly taking advantage of
   some real peculiarity in the physician's person or circumstances
   and attaching themselves to that. These, then, will no longer be
   new impressions, but revised editions (Standard Edition V and
   VII, p.116).
   The Kleinian view emphasizes the importance of experiencing 'the
revised editions' in the 'here and now' in the therapeutic setting.
Transference does not only refer to the unravelling of repressed
feelings and traumata, but also to the whole set of internalized
object relationships. Thus, the therapist comes to stand for the
internal figures; and all that the patient brings contains elements
of the transference even from the moment he enters the therapeutic
situation. The 'here and now' in the therapeutic setting is the
meeting point of the past and the unconscious phantasy accompanying it as it expresses itself in the present.
   The latter way of thinking and use of the 'here and now' may have
a direct link with the function of transference in the task of containment. By the therapist's spelling out the content of the different

projections or phantasies as they refer to himself, the patient
may not only understand but may also have an experience of containment conducive to a modification of his inner world. This takes
place by virtue of the therapist's recognizing and offering a con-
textual space including the clearly defined boundaries of the setting
which enables the work in the transference to take place.

Hanna Segal (1973) says that:

A full transference interpretation should include the current
external relationship in the patient's life, the patient's relationship to the analyst, and the relation between these and the parents
in the past. It should also aim at establishing a link between the
internal figures and the external ones...

(She modifies this view by saying that in actual practice an interpretation is hardly ever 'full' nor can the therapist be in an active
preoccupation as to how to achieve it.) As H. Rey says, transference
involves looking at 'what, in what state, does what, with what
motive, to what object, in what state, with what consequences?'
(Steiner 1979).

Relating 'transference' to our work with families
Although it is the 'pathology' of the individual patient with which
we are presented, we feel that the individuals comprising the family
have a meeting ground which is their shared inner world, implying
the existence of shared anxieties. Thinking in this way, we therefore
regard every 'communication' as being linked to their common underlying anxiety. When we say we are working in the transference with
families, we mean that in relation to the separate communications of
different members, we concentrate on trying to understand what is
the common transference, seeing each as part of a whole system,
engaged in an unconsciously joined interaction not only with each
other, but also with the therapists. This relationship between
individuals in the session springs from the relationships of their
inner objects. Understanding this with the family provides the
opportunity for each family member to recognize its specific
relevance to himself as a separate individual and to allow an internal
process of modification to develop. Our attempt is to understand not
only the content of the communications, but also how a particular
communication is expressed.

References
Freud, S. (1905), 'Fragment of an Analysis of a Case of Hysteria',
    Standard Edition, VII, 1917 Introductory Lectures on Psycho-
    analysis, 27th and 28th Lectures, Standard Edition, XVI.
Laplanche, J. and Pontalis, J.-B. (1973), 'The Language of
    Psychoanalysis', London, Hogarth Press.
Segal, H. (1973), 'Introduction to the Work of Melanie Klein',
    London, Hogarth Press.
Steiner, J. (1979), Psychotic and Non-Psychotic Aspects of Border-
    line States, unpublished paper, Tavistock Library.

BIBLIOGRAPHY

Abraham, K. (1924), Development of the Libido, 'Selected Papers of Karl Abraham', London, Hogarth Press.

Ackerman, N. (1966), 'Treating the Troubled Family', New York, Basic Books.

Ackoff, R.L. and Emery, F.E. (1972), 'On Purposeful Systems', London, Tavistock Publications.

Bartlett. F.H. (1976), Illusions and Reality, R.D. Laing, 'Family Process', 15: 51-64.

Bateson, G. (1979), 'Mind and Nature', London, Wildwood House.

Bateson, G. et al. (1956), Towards a Theory of Schizophrenia, 'Behavioural Sciences', 1: 251-64.

Beels, C.C. and Ferber, A. (1969), Family Therapy: A View, 'Family Process', 8:280-318.

Bentovim, A. (1979), Family Interaction and Techniques of Intervention, 'Journal of Family Therapy', 1: 321-43.

Bertalanffy, L. von, General System Theory - a critical review, Buckley, W. ed (1968), 'Modern systems research for the behavioural scientist', Chicago, Aldine, pp.11-30.

Bion, W.R. (1953), Notes on the Theory of Schizophrenia, Bion (1967), pp.23-35.

— (1956), Development of Schizophrenic Thought, Bion (1967), pp, 36-42.

— (1959), Attacks on Linking, 'International Journal of Psychoanalysis', 40, and in Bion (1967).

— (1961), 'Experiences in Groups', London, Tavistock Publications.

— (1962a), 'Learning from Experience', London, Heinemann.

— (1962b), A Theory of Thinking, Bion (1967), pp.110-19.

— (1963), 'Elements of Psychoanalysis', London, Heinemann.

— (1965), Transformations, 'Change from Learning to Growth', London, Heinemann.

— (1967), 'Second Thoughts', London, Heinemann.

— (1970), 'Attention and Interpretation', London, Tavistock Publications.

— (1974), Bion's Brazilian Lectures I, Rio de Janeiro, Imago Editora.

Boszormenyi-Nagy, I. and Spark, G.M. (1973), 'Invisible Loyalties', New York, Harper & Row.

Bowers, M. (1961), Family Psychotherapy, 'American Journal of Orthopsychiatry', 31:40-60.

Bowlby, J. (1949), The Study and Reduction of Group Tensions in the Family, 'Human Relations', 2: 123-8.

Box, S. (1977), 'Problems of Parents with Difficult or Disturbed Children', London, Tavistock, Document no. NT1719.

Box, S. (1978), An Analytic Approach to Work with Families, 'Journal of Adolescence', 1: 119-33.

Byng-Hall, J. (1973), Family Myths used as a Defence in Conjoint Family Therapy, 'British Journal of Medical Psychology', 46: 239-50.

Deutsch, H. (1942), 'Psychoanalysis of Neurosis', London, Hogarth Press.

Dicks, H.V. (1963), Object Relations Theory and Marital Studies, 'British Journal of Medical Psychology', 36: 126-9.

— (1967), 'Marital Tensions', London, Routledge & Kegan Paul.

Fairbairn, W.R.D. (1952), 'Psychoanalytic Studies of the Personality', London, Routledge & Kegan Paul.

Fechner, G.T. (1873), 'Einige Ideen zur Schöpfungs - und Ertwicklungsgeschichte der Organismen', Leipzig.

Flugel, J.C. (1921), 'The Psychoanalytic Study of the Family', London, Hogarth Press.

Freud, S. (1905), Fragment of an Analysis of a Case of Hysteria, 'Standard Edition VII', London, Hogarth Press and Institute of Psychoanalysis (1953).

— (1906), Psychoanalysis and the Establishment of the Facts in Legal Proceedings, 'Standard Edition IX', London, Hogarth Press and Institute of Psychoanalysis (1950), pp.99-114.

— (1909), Analysis of a Phobia in a Five Year Old Boy, 'Standard Edition X', London, Hogarth Press and Institute of Psychoanalysis (1955).

— (1913), The Disposition to Obsessional Neurosis, 'Standard Edition XII', London, Hogarth Press and Institute of Psychoanalysis (1958).
— (1914), Remembering, Repeating and Working Through, 'Standard Edition XII', London, Hogarth Press and Institute of Psychoanalysis (1958), pp.147, 156.
Freud, S. (1917), 1917 Introductory Lectures on Psychoanalysis, 27th and 28th Lectures, 'Standard Edition XVI', London, Hogarth Press and Institute of Psychoanalysis (1963).
— (1918/14), From the History of an Infantile Neurosis, 'Standard Edition XVII', London, Hogarth Press and Institute of Psychoanalysis (1955).
— (1920), Beyond the Pleasure Principle, 'Standard Edition VIII', London, Hogarth Press and Institute of Psychoanalysis (1961).
— (1930/29), Civilization and its Discontents, 'Standard Edition XXI', London, Hogarth Press and Institute of Psychoanalysis (1961).
Frude, N. (1980), Methodological Problems in the Evaluation of Family, 'Journal of Family Therapy', 2: 29-45.
Gibran, K. (1926), 'The Prophet', London, Heinemann.
Goffman, E. (1961), 'Asylums: Essays on the Social Situation of Mental Patients and Other Inmates', New York, Doubleday.
Grinberg, L. (1962), On a Specific Aspect of Countertransference Due to the Patient's Identification, 'International Journal of Psychoanalysis', 42: 436-40.
Grotjhan, A. (1929), 'Arzte als Patienten Subjektive Krankengeschicten in ärztlichen selbstschilderungen', Leipzig, Georg Thieme.
Gurman, A.S. and Kniskern, D.P. (1978), Technolatry, Methodolatry and the Results of Family Therapy, 'Family Process', 17: 275-82.
— (1979), Research on Marital and Family Therapy Progress, Perspective and Prospect, S.L. Garfield and A.S. Bergin (eds), 'Handbook of Psychotherapy and Behavioural Change', 2nd ed., New York, Wiley.
Haley, J. (1977), 'Problem Solving Therapy', California, Jossey-Bass.
Heimann, P. (1950), On Countertransference, 'International Journal of Psychoanalysis', V: 31, 81-4.
— (1952), Certain Functions of Introjection and Projection in Early Infancy, M. Klein et al., 'Developments in Psychoanalysis', London, Hogarth Press.
Henderson, R.E. and Williams, A.H., An Essay in Transference, London, Tavistock, Document no. NT1729.
Isaacs, S. (1952), The Nature and Function of Phantasy, 'Developments in Psychoanalysis', London, Hogarth Press, Chapter III.
Jackson, D.D. (ed.) (1968), 'Therapy, Communication and Change', Palo Alto, Science and Behaviour Books.
Jaques, E. (1955), Social Systems as a Defence against Persecutory and Depressive Anxiety, M. Klein et al. (eds), 'New Directions in Psychoanalysis', London, Tavistock Publications.
Jones, M. (1952), 'Social Psychiatry: A study of therapeutic communities', London, Tavistock Publications.
Joseph, B. (1975), The Patient who is Difficult to Reach, 'Tactics and Techniques in Psychoanalytic Therapy', 2.
— (1978), Different Types of Anxiety and their Handling in the Analytic Situation, 'International Journal of Psychoanalysis', 59.
Klein, M. (1932), 'The Psychoanalysis of Children', London, Hogarth Press and Institute of Psychoanalysis.
— (1935), A Contribution to the Psychogenesis of Manic-Depressive States, M. Klein, 'Contributions to Psychoanalysis', London, Hogarth Press and Institute of Psychoanalysis (1948), pp.282-310.
— (1940), Mourning and Its Relation to Manic-Depressive States, M. Klein, 'Love, Guilt and Reparation', London, Hogarth Press and Institute of Psychoanalysis (1975).
— (1945), The Oedipus Complex in the Light of Early Anxieties, 'International Journal of Psychoanalysis', 26: 11-33; and M. Klein, 'Contributions to Psychoanalysis', Hogarth Press and Institute of Psychoanalysis (1950), pp.339-90.
— (1946), Notes on Some Schizoid Mechanisms, M. Klein, 'Developments in Psychoanalysis', London, Hogarth Press and Institute of Psychoanalysis (1952), pp.292-320.
— (1955), On Identification, M. Klein et al. (eds), 'New Directions in Psychoanalysis', London, Tavistock Publications.
— (1957), 'Envy and Gratitude', London, Tavistock Publications.
— (1975), 'Envy and Gratitude and Other Works, 1946-63', London, Hogarth Press and Institute of Psychoanalysis.
Lacan, J. (1977), 'Ecrits', London, Tavistock Publications.
Laforgue. R. (1936), La Nervose familiale, 'Revue Française de Psychoanalyse', IX: 327-55.

Lagache, D. (1964), La Méthode psychoanalytique, L. Michaux et al., 'Psychiatrie', Paris.
Laing, R.D. and Esterson, D. (1964), 'Sanity, Madness and the Family', London, Tavistock Publications.
Laplanche, J. and Pontalis, J.B. (1973), 'The Language of Psychoanalysis', London, Hogarth Press.
Madanes, C. and Haley, J. (1977), Dimensions of Family Therapy, 'Journal of Mental and Nervous Diseases', 165: 88-98.
Magee, B. (1978), 'Men of Ideas. Some Creators of Contemporary Philosophy', British Broadcasting Corporation.
Martin, F.E. (1977), Some Implications from the Theory and Practice of Family Therapy for Individual Therapy (and vice versa), 'British Journal of Medical Psychology', 50: 53-64.
Medawar, P. (1969), 'Induction and Intuition in Scientific Thought', London, Methuen.
Meltzer, D. (1967), 'The Psychoanalytic Process', London, Heinemann.
— (1978), 'The Kleinian Development, Part III', Perthshire, Clunie Press.
Menzies, I.E.P. (1970), A Cast Study in the Functioning of Social Systems as a Defence against Anxiety, London, Tavistock Institute of Human Relations.
Minuchin, S. (1967), 'Families in the Slums', New York, Basic Books.
Money-Kyrle, R.E. (1956), Normal Countertransference and Some of its Deviations, 'International Journal of Psychoanalysis', 37: 360-6; and 'Collected Papers of Roger Money-Kyrle', Perthshire, Clunie Press, pp.330-42.
Palazzoli, M.S. (1978), 'Self Starvation: From Individual to Family Therapy in the Treatment of Anorexia Nervosa', New York, Aronson.
Palazzoli, M.S. et al. (1978), 'Paradox and Counter-Paradox', New York, Aronson.
Parsons, Talcott (1967), in W.C. Mitchell, 'Sociological Analysis and Politics: The Theories of Talcott Parsons', London & New Jersey, Prentice Hall.
Racker, H. (1968), 'Transference and Countertransference', London, Hogarth Press.
Rice, A.K. (1975), Selections from Systems of Organization, Arthur D. Coleman and H.W. Bexton (eds), 'Group Relations Reader', California, Grex, esp. pp.52-68.
Rivière, J. (1955), The Unconscious Phantasy of an Inner World Reflected in Examples from Literature, M. Klein et al., 'New Directions in Psychoanalysis', London, Tavistock Publications.
Rosenbluth, D. (1965), The Kleinian Theory of Depression, 'Journal of Child Psychotherapy', 1 (3).
Rosenfeld, H. (1965a), 'Psychotic States: A Psychoanalytical Approach', London, Hogarth Press, chapter X.
— (1965b), The Psychopathology of Narcissism, 'Psychotic States: A Psychoanalytical Approach', London, Hogarth Press.
— (1969), Contribution to the Psychopathology of Psychotic States: The Importance of Projective Identification in the Ego Structure and the Object Relations of the Psychotic Patient, 'Problems of Psychosis' vol.I (ed.) P. Dauret and C. Laurin, Amsterdam, Excerpta Medica.
Rosenbleuth, A. and Wierner, N. (1961), Purposeful and Non Purposeful Behaviour, W. Buckley (ed.), 'Modern Systems Research for the Behavioural Scientist', Chicago, Aldine, pp.232-7.
Satir, V. (1967), 'Conjoint Family Therapy', revised edition, Palo Alto, Science and Behaviour Books.
Schank, R.L. (1954), 'The Permanent Revolution in Science', New York, Philosophical Library.
Scott, R.D. and Ashworth, P.L. (1969), The Shadow of the Ancestor. An Historical Factor in the Transmission of Schizophrenia, 'British Journal of Medical Psychology', 42: 13-32.
Segal, H. (1964), 'Introduction to the Work of Melanie Klein', London, Heinemann
— (1973), 'Introduction to the Work of Melanie Klein', London, Hogarth Press.
— (1975), Countertransference, 'International Journal of Psychoanalytic Psychotherapy' (1977), 6: 31-7.
— (1979), 'Klein', London, Fontana.
Shapiro, R.L. (1967), The Origin of Adolescent Disturbances in the Family: Some Considerations in Theory and Implications for Therapy, G.H. Zuki and I. Boszormenyi-Nagy (eds), 'Family Therapy and Disturbed Families', Palo Alto, Science and Behaviour Books.
Singer, E. (1965), 'Key Concepts in Psychotherapy', New York, Random House.
Slipp, S. and Kressel, K. (1978), Difficulties in Family Therapy Evaluation: i. A comparison of insight vs problem solving approaches. ii. Design critique and recommendation, 'Family Process', 17: 409-22.
Skinner, B.F. (1953), 'Science and Human Behaviour', New York, Macmillan.
Skynner, A.C.R. (1969), Indications and Contraindications for Conjoint Family Therapy,

'International Journal of Social Psychiatry', 15: 245-9.
— (1976), 'One Flesh: Separate Persons', London, Constable.
Steiner, J. (1977), The Borderline between the Paranoid Schizoid and the Depressive Position in the Borderline Patient, 'British Journal of Medical Psychology', 52.
Steiner, J. (1979), Psychotic and Non-Psychotic Parts of the Personality, in 'Borderline States', Tavistock Clinic, Document no. LT3245.
Stierlin, H. (1977), 'Psychoanalysis and Family Therapy', New York, Aronson.
Strachey, J. (1934), The Nature of the Therapeutic Action of Psychoanalysis, 'International Journal of Psychoanalysis', 15: 127-59.
Teruel, G. (1966), Considerations for a Diagnosis in Marital Psychotherapy, 'British Journal of Medical Psychology', 39: 231.
Turquet, Pierre (1974), Leadership. The Individual and the Group, Graham S. Gibbard et al. (eds), 'Analysis of Groups: Contributions to Theory, Research and Practice', San Francisco and London, Jossey-Bass, pp.349-71.
Walrond-Skinner, S. (1976), 'Family Therapy: The Treatment of Natural Systems', London, Routledge & Kegan Paul.
— (1979), 'Family and Marital Psychotherapy: A Critical Approach', London, Routledge & Kegan Paul.
Watzlawick, P. et al. (1969), 'Pragmatics of Human Communication', New York, Norton.
— (1974), 'Change: Principles of Problem Formation and Problem Resolution', New York, Norton.
Wiener, H., Cybernetics in History, in W. Buckley (ed.) (1968), 'Modern Systems Research for the Behavioural Scientist', Chicago, Aldine, pp.31-6.
Williams, A.H. (1964), 'The Psychopathology and Treatment of Sexual Murderers in the Pathology and Treatment of Sexual Deviation', ed I. Rosen.
Winnicott, D.W. (1965), 'Maturational Processes and the Facilitating Environment', London, Hogarth Press and Institute of Psychoanalysis.
Wynne, L.C. (1968), Pseudo-Mutuality in the Family Relations of Schizophrenics, G. Handel (ed.), 'The Psychosocial Interior of the Family', London, Allen & Unwin.
Zinner, J. and Shapiro, R. (1972), Projective Identification as a Mode of Perception in Families of Adolescents, 'International Journal of Psychoanalysis', 53: 523-30.
Zuk, G.H. (1971), 'Family Therapy: A Triadic Based Approach', New York, Behavioural Publications.

INDEX

Abraham, K., 131
Ackerman, N., 27
Ackoff, R.L., 56
acting in the countertransference, 70
acting out, 3, 14, 52, 73
adolescence, adolescents, 5-6, 61, 94, 105, 109, 111, 119, 138, 144, 151
adult/infantile confusion, 41
adult, 'pseudo', 40, 41-2, 64-5
agency function, 39, 43, 45
ambivalence, 71, 76, 79, 121, 141, 151
analytic theory, 7
analytic work, 21, 23
anorexic, 3, 34
anxiety, 11, 12, 15, 16, 18, 19, 23, 51, 55, 61, 62, 68, 77, 78, 81, 82-3, 84, 86, 88, 90-1, 101, 102, 103-4, 110, 124, 130, 138, 140, 145, 149, 151
'as if' personality, 87
assessment, 76-8, 79, 121-2

baby-battering, 11
bad objects, 15, 52, 55, 62, 103
Bartlett, F.H., 28
Bateson, Gregory, 27, 154, 159
Beels, 28-30, 31
behaviourist models, 7
Bentovim, A., 31
Bion, W.R., 2, 4, 6, 11, 12, 23, 25, 42, 45, 50, 52, 53, 55, 60, 61, 90, 133, 134, 156, 157, 159, 160, 164, 165, 168
boundaries, 142, 151
Bowlby, J., 27
Box, Sally, 21, 155, 157, 165
brief intervention, 37, 39, 46-7
Britton, Ronald, 6, 154

Child Guidance Clinics, 5, 48-9
'child in the parent', 84, 88, 89-92
co-therapy, 5, 13, 38, 44, 93, 106-7, 111, 161, 163
Complementary Acting Out, 51-2
Complementary Action, 51-2
'conductors', 28-9, 30
constancy principle, 6, 154
container/contained, 4, 60, 160
containment, 11-12, 21-3, 26, 42, 60-1, 73, 84, 151, 155, 156, 160-1, 162, 169
Copley, Beta, 5, 78, 155, 156
countertransference, 4, 7, 21, 23, 26, 30, 35, 42, 43-4, 45-6, 50, 51, 64, 80, 81, 84, 85, 86, 88, 90, 91, 92, 94, 101, 102, 119, 151, 155, 161-2
Cybernetics, 56

death instinct, 57
delinquency, 27, 132, 133
denial, 12, 23, 50, 74, 87, 125
denigration, 17, 23, 124, 141, 144
dependence, 63, 70, 71, 141; parasitic, 138; task-oriented, 152
depression, 64, 66, 72, 80, 88-9, 93-4, 98, 101-4, 136
depressive anxiety, 93, 97, 99, 101, 110
depressive position, 6, 7, 53, 57-8, 115, 134, 169
Deutsch, Helene, 87
Dicks, H.V., 28, 170
differentiation, 138, 139-40, 144-8, 156
double bind, 27
dynamic equilibrium, 6, 56

Emery, F.E., 56
enactment, 6, 54, 63, 70, 71-2, 143, 156
endings, 93, 136, 147, 148, 152

family: aspects of, 2-3; dynamics, 3-4, 5-6, 9-24, 35, 45, 46, 62, 64, 101, 120, 132, 156-7; ecology of, 108-9; as 'group', 15-16; as institution, 10
Ferber, 28-30, 31
Flugel, J.C., 25
Freud, Sigmund, 2, 4, 6, 23, 25, 26, 49, 51, 52, 55, 57, 131, 135, 154, 162, 171
Frude, N., 31
frustration, 2, 12, 49, 50, 66, 72
functionalism, structural, 56
fusion, 45, 46, 142, 156

General Systems Theory, 6, 31, 56
Gibran, Khalil, 104
Goffman, E., 26
'good' child, 14, 36, 37
good objects, 15, 55, 103
Grinberg, L., 161, 162
Grotjhan, A., 25
group, family as, 15-16
guilt, 22, 76, 77, 82, 84, 85, 92, 113
Gurman, A.S., 32

Haley, J., 32, 33
Halton, Anna, 5, 155
Heimann, Paula, 162
Henry, Gianna, 7, 155
'here and now', 30, 43, 44, 99, 171
'hidden agenda', 15, 16
hierarchies, 31, 32, 56
homeostasis, 28, 108, 154
homosexual fears, 18-20

Hyatt Williams, Arthur, 5, 155, 156, 169

idealization, 6, 12, 17, 23, 86, 88, 103, 104,
    107, 121, 124, 141
identification, projective, see projective
    identification
individual work, 75, 78-80, 121
infantile/adult confusion, 41
infantile development, 10-11
Insall, Nonie, 7, 156
internal objects, 44, 83, 92
internalisation, 8, 10-11, 83, 142, 147,
    148, 160
interpersonal contexts, 49
intrapsychic object systems, 31
intrapsychic situations, 49
introjective identification, 166
Isaacs, Susan, 55
isomorphism, structural, 56

Joseph, Betty, 50-1, 64, 65, 83
Jaques, Elliott, 2, 55, 169
jealousy, 76, 79, 80, 90, 91, 92, 100, 116

Kennedy, Roger, 6, 156
Klein, Melanie, 2, 6, 10, 12, 16, 26, 49, 50,
    53, 55, 57, 75, 76, 84, 103, 112, 117, 160,
    164, 168
Kniskern, D.P., 32
Kressel, K. 32

Lacan, J., 125
Laforgue, R., 25
Lagache, D., 50
Laing, R.D., 28
Laplanche, J., 50
learning 'from experience', 1, 2
loss, 73, 86, 91, 92, 97, 98, 100, 103, 128,
    131, 133, 134, 147

Magagna, Jeanne, 5, 6, 155, 156
Magee, Brian, 59
manic defence, 86-9, 92, 102-3, 116-17
manic-depressive, 64
Martin, Frieda, 5, 30, 34, 46
Medawar, P., 31
Meltzer, D., 83, 101, 164, 167
mental growth, 2
micro-environment, 108-9
Minuchin, S., 3, 30, 34
Money-Kyrle, Roger, 55
mother/child relationship, 133-4
mother/infant relationship, 10, 11
mourning, 7, 34, 74, 87, 97, 100, 102, 103,
    120, 128, 134
Moustaki, Errica, 7, 42, 44
murderous phantasies, 120, 124, 125, 132,
    134

narcissism, 4, 57, 125
negativism, 3
non-differentiation, 45, 46, 138, 139-40

object-formation, 12
object-relations, 2, 7, 16, 26, 41, 54, 58,
    88, 120
obsession, 20-1, 123, 131
oedipal situations, 20, 96, 103, 132

Oedipus Complex, 55, 134
omnipotence, 11, 12, 57, 86, 89, 107

pairing, 13
Palazzoli, M.S., 3-4, 30, 34
paranoid-schizoid position, 6, 7, 12, 41,
    47, 53, 110, 168
parent, 'super', 86, 87, 89
parental authority, 36
parenthood, 10
parenting, 11, 76, 87
Parsons, Talcott, 56
persecutory feelings, 62, 86, 87, 99-100,
    102, 103-4, 109, 113, 131, 134, 142, 150,
    155
perverse relationships, 4
phantasy, 2, 4, 5, 10, 14, 49-50, 52, 53,
    55, 81, 89, 91, 103, 107, 120, 125, 128,
    129, 150, 156, 169
pleasure principle, 53, 57
polarization, 41, 63, 67, 68, 107
Pontalis, J.B., 50
pre-transference phenomena, 43, 45
'primal scene', 55
projective identification, 4, 7, 16-23, 26,
    42, 49-50, 53, 54, 84, 87, 92, 103, 111,
    112, 131, 155, 156, 160, 164-5, 166
pseudo-adult, 40, 41-2, 64-5
psychic damage, 7, 93, 104
psychic pain, 7, 93, 97, 101, 102, 104,
    115
psychoanalysis, 4, 25, 26, 43
psychopathology, 41, 42, 49, 103

'reactor/analysts', 29, 30
'reactor/system purists', 29-30
reality, internal/external, 53, 89
reality principle, 53
realization, 54, 154, 157
reassurance, 77, 78
repetition compulsion, 6, 49, 51, 54, 57
'resonance', psychic, 54-5
Rice, A.K., 2
Rosenbluth, D., 101
Rosenfeld, H., 50, 62, 138, 139, 164

scape-goating, 16, 34, 46, 53, 103, 113,
    119, 130
Schanck, R.L., 56
schizophrenia, 27, 28
schizophrenic thought, 6
Segal, Hannah, 16, 53, 162, 164, 167, 170
sexual identity, 19, 20, 125
sexual rivalry, 91
sexuality, incestuous, 111, 118, 119, 123,
    125
sexuality, perverse, 6, 120, 128, 134
Shapiro, R.L., 16
shared objects, 10, 88, 90, 143
Skinner, B.F., 26
Skynner, A.C.R., 34
Slipp, S., 32
splitting, 6, 12, 15, 16, 23, 46, 124
Steiner, J., 62
stereotyping, 112-13
Strachey, J., 82
structural functionalism, 56
structural isomorphism, 56

'super parent', 86, 87, 89
systems approach, 56

therapeutic alliance, 64-5
therapist couple, 65, 89-90, 99, 103
thinking, 'space for', 1, 101
transference, 4, 7, 23, 26, 30, 35, 42,
   43, 44, 45-6, 47, 62, 66, 73, 82-3, 85,
   95, 100, 102, 119, 171-2
Turquet, P.M., 2

von Bertalanffy, Ludwig, 56

Waddell, Margot, 4, 42, 44, 155, 159
Walrond-Skinner, S., 26, 28, 30-1,
   46
Winnicott, D.W., 87, 133
Wynne, L.C., 34

Zawada, Sue, 4, 153
Zinner, J., 16